A Whim Set in Concrete

To

all Cardiff Residents Against the Barrage

and

Norman Robson

who inspired them

A Whim Set in Concrete

The Campaign to Stop the Cardiff Bay Barrage

Sian Best

seren

Seren is the book imprint of
Poetry Wales Press Ltd
Nolton Street, Bridgend, Wales
www.seren-books.com

ISBN 1-85411-345-3

The publisher works with the financial assistance
of the Welsh Books Council.

Cover photograph: Cardiff Bay Barrage © www.urban75.com

Printed by CPD (Wales), Ebbw Vale

Contents

Introduction

I had anticipated that objections [to the Cardiff Bay Barrage]
would be raised by those concerned with bird life on the mudflats,
but I did not envisage the steeplechase that both CBDC and my
successors would have to run. That is another story and one day I
hope it may be told.

Nicholas Crickhowell, *Westminster, Wales and Water*
(University of Wales Press, 1999) p. 48.

The Cardiff Bay Barrage was one of the costliest civil engineering
schemes undertaken on the British coastline in the twentieth century.
This book intends to show how it came into being as a purely political
project, with no substantial economic or environmental justification. By
the time the scheme could be scrutinised objectively, too many
national and local politicians had identified themselves with its future
for it to be changed or abandoned.

During six years of campaigning, 1000 hours of parliamentary
debate, seven separate bills costing £3 million[1] and much local opposition, the Barrage's supporters attempted to cobble together a
justification for the project, with little success. The scheme was not
driven by any benefit it might bring to the people of Cardiff, but by
the sheer will of particular politicians from both major parties.

The economic case for a barrage across the mouth of Cardiff Bay
was put together after the project was announced, and could never be
properly substantiated; the environmental case was effectively
destroyed before the second Barrage Bill was debated in Parliament.
Local residents, with the support of a committed and energetic MP,
and a small group of brave councillors, fought a sustained, complex
campaign against the scheme for fifteen years – the longest such campaign in the UK. They fought because of the risks it posed to their
homes, the damage it would do to local ecology and its massive,
unjustified expense to the public purse.

Anti-barrage campaigners have shown the arguments for the scheme
were not only based on irrelevant premises, but also riddled with
flaws. In spite of the millions spent on the project, the residents' case
against it has never been effectively answered; whatever happened, the
political weight behind the Barrage meant its construction was
inevitable.

A report from the Auditor General for Wales, in July 2001, set its current annual running costs at £21.4 million: the capital cost, on completion in 2000, was admitted to be more than £200 million. The benefits actually derived from it have so far resisted quantification. Those running costs now have to be met from the modest disposable budget of the Welsh Assembly Government. It is a tragic irony that many senior members of the Assembly's cabinet opposed the Barrage, at some risk to their own political careers.

It is only to be expected that professional politicians should dream of large, imaginative projects, which they believe will enhance their reputations and be a lasting record of their achievements for generations to come, such as the Cardiff Bay Barrage. However, it should not automatically follow that these dreams are realised without rigorous scrutiny. There should be procedures and mechanisms to test the assumptions and consequences of political whims.

Let us assume that a cabinet minister devises a project to achieve a given purpose, such as improving the environment of south Cardiff and making it more attractive to investors. Initial costings reveal that the minimum set up costs will be £x million, and annual running costs are likely to be at least £x/10 million; the sources of this funding are unclear, but it looks as if a large, as yet undefined, proportion of it will come from the public purse. Surely, if public funds are to be seen to be managed responsibly, at some point in the progress from dream to reality, the questions, 'Could we achieve the same result for less?', 'Could this money be better spent elsewhere?' ought to be asked, and the project's sponsor should have to answer them.

If, instead of announcing plans to build a barrage across Cardiff Bay, at a Welsh Development Agency (WDA) seminar on urban renewal in December, 1986, Nicholas Edwards. Secretary of State for Wales had simply said that several million pounds had been allocated by the Welsh Office (WO) for the redevelopment of south Cardiff, and invited suggestions for an attractive focal point for the project from the residents of Butetown, Adamsdown and Grangetown, we can be confident that a barrage would not have been very high on their 'to do' lists. Public involvement at an early stage would probably have been the death of the Barrage.

The presentation of the Barrage as part and parcel of the proposal for the Cardiff Bay Development Corporation (CBDC) guaranteed support from the most influential local councillors. A few brave elected members stuck their heads above the parapet, for the sake of their anxious electors, and spent lonely months in No Man's Land as a result. So no close scrutiny or chance of rejection there.

The Barrage Bill was delivered to parliament as a cross party measure, devised by a Conservative minister and sponsored by a

Labour council. Nominally an unwhipped Private Bill, the payroll vote, in Ron Davies' words, of Parliamentary Private Secretaries. Ministers and front bench spokesmen flocked into the Aye lobby to support it, even though the arguments against had been resoundingly won in debates, which very few of those voting had even attended. In spite of this, enough awkward questions were asked in Select Committees (SCs) for the Bill to be delayed and it was eventually talked out in the Commons. It was immediately resurrected as a Hybrid Bill, rather than a Private one – a significant distinction, as members of SCs on Private Bills are chosen by lot; members of SCs on Hybrid Bills are chosen by the party Whips. So there were no more awkward questions from those handpicked Honourable Members in Committee, debates were guillotined and the Bill sped onto the statute book.

The political processes to which the Barrage Bill was subject were completely inadequate for assessing the value of the project and deciding whether it was worth the vast resources it would consume. In retrospect, there seems to have been no point at which anyone, individual or group, could say 'These plans are unsoundly based; they will not deliver the benefits they are intended to provide – scrap them.' The major burden of assessment and scrutiny had to be borne by the Barrage's lay opponents – the little boys who pointed out the Emperor's nakedness, and were told by the grown-ups they must trust their betters, who knew good tailoring when they saw it.

Norman Robson was the lynchpin of the whole anti-barrage movement. Cardiff Flood Action Committee (CFAC), with Norman as its Chair, had been formed to achieve justice for the victims of the south Cardiff floods of 1979. In 1987, it reinvented itself as an anti-barrage group, when CBDC was established, with the Barrage as an essential part of its programme. As Mr Edwards' project would completely destroy the mudflats of Cardiff Bay, the feeding grounds of several protected species of wading birds, the local campaigners enjoyed the vigorous support of many environmental groups, from Cardiff Naturalists' Society to the Royal Society for the Protection of Birds.

In the end, the opponents of the Barrage won the argument and lost their case; this account will, I hope, honour their courage, honesty and ingenuity. Their story, as Nicholas Edwards (now Lord Crickhowell) wished, should be told, although not perhaps in a way that His Lordship might approve.

1. To Begin at the Beginning...

... if you want the story, then remember that a story does not unwind. It weaves. Events that start in different places and different times all bear down on that one... point...

Supposing an emperor was persuaded to wear a new suit of clothes whose material was so fine that, to the common eye, the clothes weren't there. And suppose a little boy pointed out this fact in a loud clear voice....

Then you have The Story of the Emperor Who Had No Clothes.

But if you knew a bit more, it would be The Story of the Boy Who Got a Well-Deserved Thrashing from His Dad for Being Rude to Royalty...

Terry Pratchett, *Thief of Time*, (Doubleday, 2001), pp. 6-7

The story of the Cardiff Bay Barrage, and the resourceful and sustained campaign to prevent it, could begin at many different points.

Perhaps it starts in 1766, with the marriage of Lord Mountstuart, son of the 3rd Earl of Bute, to Charlotte, daughter of the late Herbert, Lord Windsor: Charlotte had inherited the small market town of Cardiff and its insignificant port on the Taff estuary from her mother's family. From his own mother, Lord Mountstuart had inherited the vast estates of the Wortley Montagues. Much of their combined wealth was to be invested in the rapid industrialization of south Wales. From such a beginning, the Barrage becomes the flowering of an entrepreneurial capitalism with its roots in the rich agrarian aristocracy of eighteenth century England.

Or perhaps it should start in 1837, with the young Isambard Brunel's engagement to build a railway to carry the coal of the Rhondda, Cynon and Merthyr valleys down to the Marquis's new Cardiff docks. From this point, it's the story of a massive civil engineering feat in the great Victorian tradition, a well-crafted tribute to its begetters' confidence and skill.

Or perhaps, as Lord Crickhowell (then plain Mr Nicholas Edwards) would have us believe, in his autobiographical essays, *Wales, Water and Westminster*, it should really begin with his visit as Secretary of State at the Welsh Office (SoS), to those same docks, then long derelict, in July, 1985. It was on this visit, in an unfortunately familiar phrase, that he and his fellow ministers at the WO, conceived the notion 'that something must be done' to revive the area[1]: as subsequent events would show, the 'something' turned out to be the Cardiff

Bay Barrage. If it does start here, the Barrage is the outcome of a secretive and ill-informed sequence of political decisions of uncertain purpose, a scheme which now, and for the foreseeable future, leeches money from the Welsh economy, without any discernible public benefit and with much potential for public harm.

But wherever the Barrage story starts, the city of Cardiff has to be its setting and its justification. So how had problems dire enough to need such a complex and expensive solution, arisen?

In 1830, the 2nd Marquess of Bute, having inherited the area's freehold through his mother, had funded the creation of the Bute West Dock. Until then, ships bound for Cardiff had to moor alongside the jetties and quays on the banks of the Taff, half a mile from the entrance to the Bristol Channel. If industrial south Wales was to generate maximum wealth for its mine owners and iron founders, bigger and better port facilities would be needed, and Cardiff was ideally placed to satisfy that need.

After the completion of Brunel's Taff Vale Railway, in the 1840s, more docks were excavated to cope with the increasing output of the mining valleys to the north: Bute East Dock, Roath Basin and Penarth Dock followed in quick succession. As well as coal, Cardiff was handling thousands of tons of iron from local furnaces, like Guest Keen's, by the 1890s. In 1907, the Queen Alexandra Dock, which is still used, opened. By 1913, the port's busiest year, coal exports had reached ten million tons: it has been estimated that between 1890 and 1914, more than half the fuel for the boilers and furnaces of a steam powered world passed through Cardiff docks.

Cardiff's population grew exponentially, from 5000 in 1800, to over 50,000 in 1850. But much of the town was still cramped within the boundaries of the old medieval walls, where its citizens lived in conditions which were crowded and squalid, even by the standards of Victorian Britain. In an attempt to persuade the town corporation to implement national legislation on the provision of drainage and clean water supplies, the Board of Health commissioned a report from Thomas Webster Rammell, a civil engineer like his contemporary Edward Chadwick, with an interest in public health and sanitation. Like Chadwick's analyses of the problems of English industrial cities, Rammell's report still makes grim reading. He describes the area between St Mary Street (now part of the main shopping precinct) and the Glamorgan Canal as crammed with 45 'courts' of back-to-back slum houses, where it was common for two or three families to share a room about ten foot square. Landore Court was apparently quite typical;

At the bottom of the court is a place, open and without covering, which is used as a public privy, and also for the depositing of every kind of filth, the contents of other privies and of cesspools being occasionally emptied into it. There are two ashpits. There is no pump or water in the Court, and the inhabitants fetch all the water they use from a pump in St Mary St. [2]

As a result of Rammell's analysis, Cardiff Corporation began to build drains and sewers, and Cardiff started to spread beyond what remained of the old town walls, north and west to the village of Canton, east towards Roath and south to the dockyards.

Cardiff's prosperous middle classes could set up home in the spacious, graceful stone terraces of Cathedral Road or Newport Road, while their clerks and workmen rented miniature versions in the solidly built '2-up-2-down' brick terraces of Adamsdown and Grangetown. Working men had, of course, to live near their work, low pay and long hours didn't permit much travelling. In Victorian Cardiff, work was in the docks and factories to the south of the town, along the river estuary and the seashore, where the land was low-lying and marshy, quite unsuitable for building homes. However, the Marquises of Bute and the Earls of Plymouth, who between them owned most of that land, were shrewd men of business, who employed even shrewder men. They also excavated docks, owned coalmines, quarries, gas works and blast furnaces, all of which produced rubble in large quantities. Year by year, decade by decade, this rubble was tipped onto the marshland of the Taff estuary, until it was solid enough to build on, and the workers of Cardiff made their homes there.

From about 1865 until his death in 1881, William Burges, a leader of the Gothic revival, designed and rebuilt Cardiff's Norman castle as a suitably luxurious residence for the Bute family. The castle had been abandoned by the Herberts in favour of their Wilton estate since the seventeenth century. The town became the commercial and cultural centre of south Wales. Coal was not only shipped out of Cardiff, it was traded there; the docks area included banks, international shipping companies and one of the world's largest Coal Exchanges.

All this wealth nourished a lively cultural life – theatres, concert halls, libraries and some of the most imposing chapels in the country. Money made in the mining valleys and steel towns of Glamorgan was spent in Cardiff. The saying 'Rhondda coal, Cardiff gold' gives an eloquent hint of the relationship between the Valleys and the capital; Rhondda men sweat to cut the coal, and stay poor, Cardiff men have the soft job of selling it, and get rich. The hinterland has always looked to Cardiff with a mixture of envy and contempt, feelings that the building of the Barrage was to intensify.

In Cathays Park, a new civic centre, one of the most elegant and graceful in Europe, was opened in the early 1900s. It included the City Hall, law courts, museum and art gallery, and the University College, all blending in a remarkable tribute to the confidence and affluence of the new city. Another much admired feature of Edwardian Cardiff were the beautiful parks open to the townspeople, a consequence of the city's geology; much of the central area is very low-lying, with a high water table, so pieces of land too wet to support foundations, were laid out as public gardens.

Around the docks, a large and cosmopolitan community grew up as dockers and seamen set up home there, from Norway and Somalia, Bengal and the Yemen, China and Cyprus. Officially called Butetown, after the Marquisate that owned its freehold, the area was known to the rest of Cardiff, and the wider world, as Tiger Bay. The Bristol Channel's strong tides apparently lead Portuguese sailors to describe the port as 'a bay of tigers'.

Peter Finch describes south Cardiff in its industrial heyday,

> ... the place stank permanently of coal, fume and ash. The vast East Moors steelworks at its centre turned the air dark... Cardiff was a place of smog and dark sunrises.[3]

However, this part of the city was most vulnerable to the changing fortunes of heavy industry after the Second World War. The slow decay of the docks followed the decline of the Welsh mining industry they served, during the 1950s: as the pits closed, so did the Docks. The development of container ports in the 1960s took much of what trade remained, so the West Bute Dock was filled in during 1964 and the East Bute Dock was closed to shipping in 1970.

The picture became even bleaker with the closure of the neighbouring East Moors steelworks in 1978, when 3200 men lost their jobs, with similar losses in dependent companies in the area. There had been iron or steel production on the banks of the Taff since the late eighteenth century, and the plant had been a major employer in south Cardiff since the 1930s.

The East Moors site was cleared, and joined the former docks in an area of wasteland covering nearly 2700 acres. The 6000 residents of Butetown were marooned in a sea of industrial dereliction, which mirrored the docklands of London and Merseyside, their situation thrown into dramatic relief by the increasing prosperity of other parts of the city. Cardiff had become the Welsh capital in 1958. With the setting up of the Welsh Office in 1964, it became the administrative

centre of the Principality. Home to the largest of the constituent col-
leges of the University of Wales, it was also the regional headquarters
of BBC Wales and HTV. Those who worked in academia or the Welsh
media made their homes in the attractive and expanding northern
suburbs of Whitchurch, Rhiwbina and Cyncoed.

However, it would be inaccurate to describe south Cardiff as an
area of great social deprivation or poverty; in comparison to the former mining valleys, unemployment was not high, and much of
Butetown had been rebuilt in the early 60s. Local residents had
escaped with only a modicum of tower blocks, most people living in
human-scale social housing or the lovingly maintained Victorian and
Edwardian bay-fronted terraces overlooking the estuary.

The fact that south Cardiff was in urgent need of investment and
improvement had been a recurring theme in local political debate for
over twenty years. The most dramatic period of Tiger Bay's decline
had coincided with a major restructuring of local government in
England and Wales. As a result of this reorganization, the area was
included in the remit of two local authorities, South Glamorgan
County Council (SGCC) and Cardiff City Council (CCC). South
Glamorgan, with the greater geographical area, had the larger income
and senior status. Throughout most of its existence, the County
Council was Labour-dominated; in the City Council, there was a finer
balance, with power alternating between the major parties. Both
councils were keen to enhance the status of the city so it could be presented as a thriving prosperous capital; the 2700 empty acres of south
Cardiff were a constant reproach.

Of course, many other British cities had similar post-industrial
needs, so central government was under pressure to make funds available to support improvement and job creation. There were a number
of obstacles in the way of any revitalising project. No local authority
in the UK had access to the sort of finance necessary to redevelop
such a large area; no private development company could co-ordinate
the necessary infrastructure of new roads, drainage and power supplies that would be needed; few public or private bodies were capable
of mustering the varied professional and managerial skills that would
be needed.

So, with no overall national design or planning, a confusing pletho-
ra of schemes, projects and grants characterized urban redevelopment
in the 1970s. Local authorities had to apply to for funding, or sponsor
private developers' applications, to a bewildering array of sources. The
situation was further complicated, after the 1979 election, by the
Conservative government's unwillingness to offer direct funding to the
local councils they despised and distrusted.

But, in spite of all these obstacles, by 1983 a number of major projects for south Cardiff were ready for the Secretary of State's approval. They had been submitted by a number of developers with plenty of experience – the Heron Properties Corporation, Sir Robert McAlpine and Sons, Project Management Wales and the Tarmac Group.

The Tarmac scheme included a joint venture with the County Council for a development on the former East Bute Dock, which included, as evidence of the Council's commitment to the area, a new County Hall.

It is interesting that at this stage in the development of south Cardiff, the mudflats were still apparent, in all their ambivalent glory, but none of these companies, most of whom had considerable experience of urban redevelopment projects, were repelled by their presence.

All these projects were outlined in the County's 1985 Structure Plan, submitted to the Welsh Secretary for approval in June that year. In his introduction, the County's Chief Executive, W.P. Davey stated, with a frankness most unusual in a public servant, the impossibility of achieving the plans' aims 'against a backdrop of pressure on local government spending and cutbacks in public expenditure generally'. He further noted the large number of public bodies involved in such projects 'each with its own budget' – the SGCC, Cardiff City Council (CCC), the Welsh Development Agency (WDA), the Land Authority for Wales (LAW), the Welsh Water Authority (WWA).[4] In other words, the County's commitment to restructure and develop was strong, the resources to do so were stretched and scattered.

For redevelopment to succeed, the County had to draw together resources from central government and the European Regional Fund, for which complex applications had to be submitted, while negotiating the details of all plans with the WO and its junior partner, the City Council, and, at the same time, attracting sufficient private investment to make the whole project viable – a complex task for which neither councillors nor appointed officers were equipped.

The structure plan, coupled with the proposals for the SGCC/Tarmac development, gave a picture of an area desperately in need of major large-scale regeneration, drawing together crumbs of funding to do the job piecemeal. On 14th November 1984, Nicholas Edwards, as Welsh Secretary, addressed the Council of Europe Urban Policies Seminar. The minutes of the meeting of SGCC's Policy (Industrial Development) Sub Committee, on 12th December, record that Mr Edwards' 'speech included encouraging and supportive references to the South Cardiff Redevelopment Scheme…' It must have come as a terrible shock to all concerned when the SoS

actually made the arduous two mile trip from Cathays Park to south
Cardiff eighteen months later, and noticed that the presence of unreconstructed mudflats could undermine the success of the whole
scheme, unless something was done...

A major condition for the success of all these proposals was the
improvement of the road links between the Docklands and the M4; in
1981, a peripheral distributor road (PDR) had been scheduled, to pass
through Butetown, over the Taff, to join the motorway running west
and north of the city. There were a number of possible means of taking
the road over the river, a bridge, a viaduct and, most popular with the
leaders of SGCC, a combination of bridge and small barrage.

A barrage, it was felt, would have the additional virtue of partly
impounding the Taff, covering some of the mudflats which were such
a prominent feature of the estuary. These mudflats had been created
by sediment washed down the Taff from the narrow, steep mining valleys through which it flowed on its way to the sea. They also contained
human and industrial waste from official and unofficial outfalls along
the riverbanks. Combined with a considerable area of salt marsh, the
result was a nutrient-rich littoral, irresistibly attractive to flocks of
wading birds, largely from northern Europe, who over-wintered
there. The presence of the birds had lead to the designation of the Taff
Estuary as a Site of Special Scientific Interest (SSSI), entitled to protection from damage or destruction.

In 1981, the County's Director of Planning, Ewart Parkinson, happened to meet Dr Peter Ferns, a lecturer in Zoology at University
College Cardiff, and a Council member of the Royal Society for the
Protection of Birds. They discussed the consequences of a barrage for
the SSSI; as a result, Dr Ferns was commissioned to write a report for
the Council on the 'wildlife aspects of the Barrage option.'

His report, 'The Butetown link and its implications for the shore birds
of the Taff estuary', was eventually submitted in 1983, and concluded

> Levels of disturbance in an enclosed and industrial estuary like the
> Taff are inevitably high and will increase with the construction of
> the Butetown link. So far, the birds have managed to cope, and
> maintain their numbers, but a little help would secure their future
> and that of this small but important SSSI. The creation of a Taff
> Estuary Local Nature Reserve with carefully situated hides and
> screened access would leave the birds undisturbed and provide a
> very valuable local amenity. The area is already well visited by bird
> watchers and would amply repay all efforts made to conserve it.

Dr Ferns' recommendations were to echo ironically down the
years. They embodied a philosophy of valuing what one has and

nurturing it, appreciating the fragile and the unique, taking responsibility for a complex and irreplaceable environment. These ideas were to be recklessly shouted down in the hectoring bluster that passed for argument, when an even more expensive and damaging barrage project was discussed.

The County Council carried out a survey of local opinion on the desirability of a barrage/road crossing. The crossing was very clearly important for the commercial improvement of the area and, as such, was welcomed by the people of Butetown. But there was much concern over the PDR's proposed route: it would bisect the Butetown community, bringing heavy traffic and pollution to residential areas and, most worrying of all, pass within yards of the local primary school.

Local people, not only in Butetown, but also in the neighbouring areas of Grangetown and Riverside, were worried about the likely effects of the Barrage on groundwater in such a low-lying area. The Marquis of Bute and the Earl of Plymouth had built south Cardiff around two river estuaries on made ground; the water table was both close to the surface and easily raised at high tide and during periods of heavy rainfall. South Cardiff was subject to frequent flooding as it was; if the Taff estuary was impounded, the flow of water underground would be blocked, or even reversed, and the risk of flooding would worsen.

There was also some local anxiety about the loss of the wading birds' feeding grounds, not only from the RSPB and local naturalists' groups, but also from those who saw the dunlin and redshank as one of their neighbourhood's few natural attractions, and one they did not wish to loose. The RSPB also made its concerns known – as a result of Peter Ferns' report into the consequences of the scheme for the Bay's bird life, the Council had suggested a number of palliative measures, but no major naturalists' group found them acceptable.

If the road was to cross the Taff, it meant a substantial alteration to a navigable waterway and for this a private Parliamentary bill was needed. Private bills are very different animals to public ones. Public bills are usually introduced as part of a government legislative programme; the whips of all parties ensure that MPs vote on them as party policy dictates. Private bills, like the South Glamorgan (Taff Crossing) Bill, as it was known, usually deal with a particular area, promoted by local authorities or other statutory bodies; until procedures were changed in 1992 they were often used to get Parliamentary approval for large scale construction projects. There is usually a free vote on a Private Bill.

In November 1985, the South Glamorgan (Taff Crossing) Bill had its first reading in the House of Commons. The Bill was presented to the Commons, by the former Prime Minister James Callaghan MP for Cardiff South and Penarth, which included the docks area.

The structure suggested in this Bill was much smaller than the Barrage which now impounds Cardiff Bay. It would have reached from Windsor Esplanade in Butetown, to the top of Ferry Road, less than 120 metres, and would have dammed a modest stretch of water in the Taff estuary, leaving most of Cardiff Bay open to the sea and still tidal. The present barrage is three miles long, impounds a lake of 400 acres, completely closes Cardiff Bay off from the Bristol Channel, blocking the Ely river, as well as the Taff.

The promoters assumed that after its First Reading was heard without demur, the Bill would pass to the Unopposed Bills Committee, for brief examination, before a brisk passage through Parliament to the Royal Assent, with minimal scrutiny and debate. But, in the summer of 1985, Mr Edwards had been to Tiger Bay to see things there for himself. It must be emphasised that he had been appointed SoS Wales by Margaret Thatcher, in 1979. The Bay is less than two miles from the then Welsh Secretary's office in Cathays Park, so an apparent delay of more than six years in assessing the economic and social needs of the area, is somewhat surprising, particularly in view of his stated enthusiasm for the project.

As he describes his Damascene revelation, 'I recognized for *the first time* the huge potential of the waterside for development. [My italics] Back at the Welsh Office, we [he and his Parliamentary Secretary, Michael Roberts] immediately asked our officials to come up with ideas to exploit the possibilities that undoubtedly existed. A few weeks later, two of them, Freddy Watson and Geoff Hoad, came into my room with an idea: they wondered if a barrage might be the key to the transformation of the waterside'.[5] Mr Edwards' enthusiasm for the project was immediate and infectious. Two appraisals were commissioned by the WO, one on its technical feasibility, the other on its investment potential. Before either was published, discussions with the senior members of the County and City Councils were under way, and on 20th November 1985, plans for a barrage across the mouth of Cardiff Bay were made public[6] with leading councillors expressing enthusiastic support. According to the *South Wales Echo*, Cardiff's local paper, discussions between the Welsh Secretary and both Councils had been going on for some time, with elected members 'sworn to secrecy'. The surprise announcement came within days of the First Reading of the Taff Crossing Bill; so, two different barrage projects for Cardiff Bay were being assessed simultaneously, one in the Welsh Office, the other in Parliament. A cursory glance at a map of Cardiff Bay would have shown that it would be impossible for both schemes to go ahead, as councillors, the SoS and his civil servants must have been aware. One of them would have to fall – but which?

Considerable effort and expense had been lavished by the County Council on the Taff Crossing Bill; the project was a very public one and Labour councillors would not initially have relished seeing their plans take a back seat to a rival scheme from the Welsh Office, no matter how cordial their working relationship with Cathays Park might be. But, much of the £40 million the Taff Crossing would cost would have to be approved as a grant in aid by the Welsh Secretary; ultimately, the choice was his. As the barrage-as-road-bridge option was such an important part of the Bill, it would be impossible to exclude it from the relevant clauses, without substantial redrafting, which would seriously delay its progress onto the statute book. Such a postponement of the start on the PDR would have serious repercussions for the redevelopment of the area, for which good road links were essential.

By the most fortunate and timely of coincidences, Mr Gwilym Jones, the Conservative MP for Cardiff North, intervened in the Bill's progress at this point, by lodging an objection to it and subscribing to a blocking motion, within days of the announcement of the plans for the bigger barrage project.

This meant that the Bill would have to be considered in detail by a Select Committee of four MPs unconnected with the area most affected by it. Most important of all, individuals and groups who believed their interests were threatened by clauses in the Bill could ask to petition the Select Committee and put their case for changes to its provisions. Mr Jones' objection was predictably unpopular with some of the Bill's supporters, for the next day six petitions against it were lodged at the Private Bills Office, chiefly from naturalists' groups. Members of Select Committees are chosen (or were, in 1986) by lot, by the office of the Chairman of Ways and Means; four MPs were duly chosen; the colourful Tony Banks, Labour MP for New Ham Northwest, as Chair, with one Labour and two Conservative colleagues. They were to consider the Bill in June.

Effectively, Mr Jones' intervention meant that the progress of the Taff Crossing Bill would be delayed for several months, thus giving the Welsh Office and other supporters of the newer barrage scheme time to prepare and present their case. On Michael Roberts' death, Gwilym Jones had succeeded him as MP for North Cardiff, and after the 1987 election, was swiftly promoted to succeed him as Under Secretary of State in Cathays Park.

In the *South Wales Echo*, 31st January, 1986, Mr Jones was quoted as opposing the Bill 'because of the potential damage to wildlife from a barrage and he wanted to ensure proper safeguards were taken.'[7] It is remarkable that after his elevation to ministerial office, Mr Jones did a brisk 180 degree turn, becoming quite vociferous in his support for later, much more environmentally damaging, barrage bills. Speaking in a Commons debate on 14th November, 1989, his concern about wildlife damage was muted, to say the least. 'My great regret is that no one can guarantee how effective the compensatory measures [for the loss of the wading birds' feeding grounds] will be. I greatly regret the likely loss of birds and the fact we have to choose between the present and an uncertain future.'

Meanwhile, the Second Reading debate on the Taff Crossing Bill began on 1st May 1986, in the Commons. In his speech opening the debate, Mr Callaghan made the real purpose of the Bill clear. He emphasised the cosmetic possibilities of a barrage, and, in some obscure rhetorical flourishes, its potential for wealth creation, by exaggerating the poverty of his constituency. He elaborated the arguments against it in a way that was to become familiar to anti-barrage protesters in the next ten years.

'This area comprises very old, poor housing [much of Butetown had been rebuilt in the 1960s]... an area with the fewest amenities in the city of Cardiff [the vague 'amenities' disguised the fact that there were newer, larger areas of Cardiff that were just as deprived economically]. It is an area outside the entrance to the docks that has been a great handicap in the past... The area has been an eyesore for as long as I have represented this part of Cardiff. It is unpleasant for the residents and offputting for industry and commerce.' The implication that drowning the mudflats would enhance south Cardiff's commercial appeal would also be repeated *ad nauseam* during later arguments about the Barrage, but Mr Callaghan did not attempt to give this argument more substance; the proponents of subsequent barrage bills would also have difficulty in doing so.

Another device employed by the former Prime Minister was to be more finely honed by his pro-barrage successors; the assertion that the naturalists' case against the Barrage was at odds with the plans for improving the area and the welfare of its residents. South Cardiff could have wading birds or it could have prosperity, never both, the argument ran. '... If the choice is between 1500 redshanks [*sic*] and 5000 constituents who live in the worst possible conditions in south Cardiff, we must achieve a balance, and I know where that balance is to be struck.' He was also less than accurate in his assessment of the RSPB's willingness to discuss the proposals with the County Council, implying that the naturalists' groups had actually refused invitations to meet with local politicians. Only under pressure from Alex Carlile, Liberal MP for Montgomery, whose constituency included the RSPB's Welsh HQ, did he admit that, in fact, a number of such meetings had taken place.

It also fell to Mr Carlile to point out the vagueness of the economic arguments which underpinned the ex-PM's case; as he said, 'Information on the relative costs has not been made available, as it might have been... the estimated cost of building the Barrage, which the right hon. Member for Cardiff rightly gave as being just over £40 million, is very much not a fixed estimate.'

The aesthetic argument against the Barrage scheme, including the 'mini-barrage' of the Taff Crossing Bill, and its larger successor, was well put by Kenneth Carlisle, MP for Lincoln; it would, he said 'put something which is neat and dull in place of something which is or could be perhaps wild and intriguing.'

The Bill, as an opposed Private Bill, was duly considered by the Select Committee of four MPs. During their deliberations, the Committee could hear statements from those individuals or groups who felt their interests were prejudiced by the terms of the Bill, that is, those who had presented petitions against it.

The procedure for Private Bills assumes that a bill affecting a particular area will be presented by a local MP, who would be obliged to take good care of constituents' interests. The presumption is that if their well-being was seriously threatened, the Bill would not be before Parliament. The controversy over the Barrage Bills would demonstrate how wrong this assumption was. Petitioning against such a bill is not a right, it is a privilege, granted or withheld by the Crown through its officers: if the privilege is not granted, there is no appeal against the decision. By the same principle, if a Select Committee decides to set aside cogent and well-proven evidence or arguments offered by a petitioner, and does not include them in its report to the Commons on the Bill, there is nothing the petitioner can do about it. Brendan Behan suggested that British citizens are objects, rather than subjects, of the Crown; this is particularly true of petitioners against a Private Parliamentary Bill.

The conduct of a Select Committee on a Private Bill is a little like that of a court of law: petitioners may present their case in person, with supporting evidence, and witnesses, if they wish. In turn, petitioners and their witnesses may be cross-examined by counsel for the promoters of the Bill, who were, in this case, South Glamorgan County Council. Petitioners could also retain counsel, or parliamentary agents specialising in such work, to cross-examine the promoter's witnesses.

When appearing before the Committee on the Taff Crossing Bill,

Peter Ferns was in a difficult predicament. His report on the Crossing's consequences for the Bay's bird population recommended certain protection measures which the county council appeared to have accepted, so he appeared before the Committee as a witness for the promoters. However, he was also very closely connected to two of the groups petitioning against the Bill, the Cardiff Naturalists' Society, of which he was a member and former President, and the RSPB, as a member of its national Council. It was clear from his responses to questions from Kevin Standring, the RSPB's agent, that Dr Ferns was less than happy with many aspects of the Council's plans for the estuary and their impact on the wading birds, a disenchantment which was apparently shared by the members of the Select Committee.

The proceedings were further complicated because all concerned were aware of the research commissioned by the Welsh Office into the Secretary of State's own barrage project – the much larger one across the mouth of the Bay itself, first proposed nearly a year before. The implications of this project were touched on occasionally during the Committee's deliberations, though only briefly, as no official details were then available.

The Committee's findings were announced a few days after the hearings ended. They did not believe the unproven economic advantages of a barrage crossing for the Butetown link road justified the environmental harm it would do. The Committee also concluded that the cost of a barrage, compared to a bridge, was prohibitive, and therefore recommended that any references to a barrage be dropped from the Bill. The recommendations were eventually accepted and in November 1987, the South Glamorgan (Taff Crossing) Bill, minus barrage, received the royal assent.

As Peter Ferns wrote to Tony Banks, after the announcement,

> The remarks you made when announcing the committee's findings will undoubtedly prove valuable in trying to persuade Nicholas Edwards not to destroy the whole of the Taff Estuary. The only people who are likely to benefit from his scheme are the property development companies and certainly not the people who live in the area or the birds. I shall be doing my best to try and convince people that the docks area of Cardiff can be developed in a way which is environmentally responsible, sensitive to the needs of the local people and respectful of the maritime traditions of the city.[8]

As he sat in Cathays Park, contemplating the problems of south Cardiff, Mr Edwards was at an interesting point in his own public career. Aged 52, he had been Welsh Secretary for six years; he was to serve for two years more, nearly twice as long as any other incumbent in Cathays Park, before or since. Had the Prime Minister seen him as a potential holder of one of the great offices of state, he would have been moved in that direction long ago.

The powers of a Welsh Secretary were more wide-ranging than most other cabinet posts, as it included responsibility for agriculture, education, social services, health and the environment, but they are exercised over a rather more confined area; there is little scope for the grand gestures so dear to career politicians. Moreover, the Welsh do not, as a general rule, vote Conservative with any enthusiasm or commitment, and, in the mid-eighties, certainly did not warm to Thatcherite policies or those called upon to implement them.

The Welsh Office was not a place where a Tory aspiring to higher things might gather round him/her a loyal coterie of admirers, likely to support the ambitious in any future career. A longserving Secretary of State for Wales carried little more cachet in national political circles than the treacherous Solicitor General in Robert Bolt's *A Man for all Seasons*, 'Indeed, a man may lose his own soul and gain the whole world... But for Wales, Sir Richard?'

To appreciate the distinguishing characteristics of the Welsh Office's *modus operandi*, pre-devolution, comparisons with their colleagues in Edinburgh may be illuminating. The two departments differed in a number of respects – chiefly, the Welsh Office was reactive, waiting to see what Whitehall wanted, and then doing it as expeditiously as possible: the Scottish Office, on the other hand, worked out what would be good for Scotland, and then tried to do as much of it as they could whether Whitehall approved or not. The Scottish Office was more than three times the size of its Cardiff counterpart, with much greater scope for independent action – there was room for an elite, where the word 'mandarin' had real meaning. In Cathays Park, the culture was more that of a local authority, and not a particularly large or powerful one. As Rhodri Morgan put it in a lecture to the Institute of Welsh Affairs in 2000,

> It was very clear to me as a civil servant in the Welsh Office... you promoted staff in the Scottish Office on the basis that they had put one over Whitehall. You promoted staff in the Welsh Office on the basis that they had kept their noses clean with Whitehall.[9]

The decision that Mr Edwards would leave the Commons after the next General Election might not have been made yet, but he must have been aware that, if he was to make a significant mark on the national consciousness, he had better start soon. Finding a profitable solution to the problems of south Cardiff might have seemed a good beginning – south Cardiff needed money for redevelopment, local government could handle the necessary projects and their implementation, but didn't have access to the funds. Mr Edwards' solution was an Urban Development Corporation (UDC).

Freddie Watson, the civil servant whom Nicholas Edwards credited with first suggesting the Barrage, later described how 'he... at the behest of Nicholas Edwards had first started the Cardiff docklands regeneration going [*sic*]. Indeed it was he who eventually put together the objectives of the Cardiff Bay Development Corporation'.[10]

Among those objectives was the construction of a barrage across the mouth of Cardiff Bay, keeping out the waters of the Bristol Channel and creating a 400-acre freshwater lake. The Barrage would dam the double estuary of the rivers Taff and Ely and the lake would cover the tidal mudflats, which were a significant feature of this part of south Cardiff. Mr Watson was clear about his reasons for including this particular proposal in CBDC's brief. In his role as head of the Urban Affairs Division, when 'he was showing potential developers around the sea front.... It became apparent... in the process of making the outside world aware of what we were trying to do... that the Cardiff waterfront at high tide was seen to be a potentially superb environment, and at low tide not so much.'[11]

It was after the SoS's visit to the Bay in 1985, that Mr Watson was able to get political backing for his vision. We don't know exactly why the SoS made that momentous visit to Cardiff Docks in 1985: a sceptic might assume his interest was aroused by the contents of the Taff Crossing Bill, which would have been drafted during the summer or early autumn of that year, and which, as the WO would be a major source of funding for the project, he, and possibly, Freddie Watson, would have seen.

Or, perhaps, it was the 1985 version of the South Glamorgan Structure Plan, which as we have noted earlier, would have been dispatched to Cathays Park for Mr Edwards' approval in July – a document setting out clearly the County Council's difficulties in co-ordinating the complicated process of getting the development of south Cardiff going. Perhaps it was a combination of both – the Bill suggested a barrage, which might 'tidy up' an area perceived as commercially unattractive, while the plan pleaded for co-ordinated development of that area. A barrage could be promoted as just the scheme to give south Cardiff a fresh start, or at least a fresh image.

Certainly, Mr Edwards never mentioned the Taff Crossing Bill's barrage, in public at least, nor SGCC's enthusiasm for the earlier project, nor the successful arguments against it which had so impressed the Select Committee.

Nicholas Edwards must have noted the success of the economic and environmental arguments against the County Council's mini-barrage. However, he did not allow himself to be deterred; the Barrage he wanted was apparently a different creature altogether, and he intended to deploy resources beyond the dreams of the most ambitious local council, in order to achieve it.

During the 1970s, central government grants for large urban regeneration projects by local authorities were increasingly constrained by a growing recession. In addition, the Conservative government elected in 1979 was not sympathetic to the idea of local authorities controlling capital funding for large-scale projects, or even wielding any significant power of their own. Yet the riots in Toxteth, Brixton and the St Paul's area of Bristol during the early eighties raised the national profile of inner city decay and the poverty caused by deindustrialization. Injections of large amounts of public money were obviously needed; how could this be achieved without granting it to the despised local tribunes of the people?

The then Secretary for the Environment, Michael Heseltine, was able to respond with an appropriately capital-friendly scheme – the Urban Development Corporations. The first UDCs were set up under the 1980 Local Government and Planning Act: they were to apply the powers of the New Town Development Corporations (NTDCs) to the problems of derelict inner city areas.

However, there were important differences between the UDCs and their New Town predecessors, which were to have great significance for their implementation in Cardiff. Their application in Wales would be, of course, the responsibility of the Welsh Secretary. It was intended that UDCs would have a life of not more than ten years, which meant that the designation process had to be as quick as possible, and speed is the enemy of democracy and certainly of public consultation. Their spheres of operation, known as Urban Development Areas, were designated by Statutory Instrument – i.e. a written or verbal statement made by a minister of the Crown to either House of Parliament. Any opponents of designation could only make their views known by appealing to a parliamentary select committee – an extremely constrained and laborious means of public participation in decision making.

Unlike the New Town Development Corporations, UDCs were given extraordinary powers of land acquisition: they could acquire any land in their area by Compulsory Purchase Order. They also received generous funding to implement their powers: in 1990-1, at their peak, they spent £720 million, 61% of the government's expenditure on inner cities.[12] Also, unlike NTDCs, they usurped local authorities' planning functions and controls. They were run by boards of directors, recruited from private companies, not necessarily local. These boards were directly responsible to the Secretary of State for the Environment. Their brief was 'to seek out marketing opportunities and private investment. Broader strategic planning was to play a limited role in UDCs.'[13] This investment, however, needed considerable inducement to make its home in ravaged inner city areas.

In 1984-5, the Conservative government's urban programme, channelled through local authorities, accounted for about 75 per cent of spending on the inner cities, but in 1992-3, it was less than 50 per cent of the spending by UDCs alone.[14] In other words, by the early 1990s, the bulk of public investment in urban development was passing through unelected hands to private companies, with minimal public accountability. To a limited extent, UDCs could adapt operations to suit local circumstances, but the first generation, set up in 1981, in London Docklands and Merseyside, had very difficult relationships with their respective local authorities. They were naturally perceived as usurpers, parachuted in to do a job local government was incapable of doing, and given resources and powers beyond the reach of even the most co-operative of Conservative councils. One Cardiff councillor, when told about the resources available to the Merseyside Development Corporation, was heard to exclaim, 'I want that sort of cash for Cardiff, even if I end up shovelling it into the Taff myself!' As things turned out, much of the cash that came to Cardiff did end-up shovelled into the Taff, or at least under the Barrage.

It appears that Mr Edwards envisaged a UDC for south Cardiff would offer a chance for a striking, dramatic programme of urban renewal, in which large amounts of public money could be allocated to guaranteeing the investments of private developers, with minimal input and scrutiny by local representatives.

However, there were significant differences between the corporation proposed for Cardiff, and its predecessors: the Tory government was aware that the animosity aroused among local councillors by the setting up of similar bodies in English cities had been counterproductive and some effort would have to be made to get them on-side. To this end, the SoS persuaded County and City Councils to play a proactive role in setting up of the Corporation. This concession was made easier by the remarkable relationship Welsh councils took pride in achieving with their central government colleagues, a relationship strikingly described by Patrick Hannan:

> ... there has perhaps been as much significance in the way the Welsh Office runs things as in what it runs. It has to do with the size of Wales and the fact that practically everyone in political and

public life knows practically everyone else. That doesn't necessarily mean they like each other... but they often have a common
purpose and a common interest in getting things done. This
emerges clearly in relationships between the Welsh Office and local
government, especially when you remember that Labour councillors, who run most of the authorities, are frequently people who
think a deal well negotiated is at least as important as some distant
socialist goal, even assuming such a thing would be permitted
these days. This has meant, for example, that the sour atmosphere
which often characterises relations between English local authorities and the Department of the Environment has been largely
absent from Wales.[15]

Mr Edwards himself shared this view; as he later reflected,

> The Secretary of State for Wales in those days... had the great
> advantage that his department and the country it administered
> [*sic*] was small and there was, therefore, an intimacy about Welsh
> affairs that was conducive to good government. Everyone involved
> in public affairs in Wales knows practically everyone else. They
> meet frequently, they discuss each other's problems, there is a
> sense of common purpose, so that even political differences do not
> keep people apart.[16]

Whether 'good government' was delivered by these cosy alliances
is open to debate; collusion and secrecy certainly were. When accom-
modations are made, deals struck and schemes planned over friendly
lunches between councillors and ministers, party officials and trade
union leaders, the scope for scrutiny and public discussion becomes
limited and constrained. If a project, like the Barrage, has the full consent of all relevant powerbrokers before the public even hear about it,
then debate is a sham and public accountability a myth. The tailors
have already dressed the Emperor in his invisible suit, the parade is
underway and there's little time for honest small boys with clear vision
to ask awkward questions.

Mr Edwards chose a seminar on urban renewal organized by the
WDA on 5th December, 1986, in Swansea, to unveil further details of
his aspirations for south Cardiff and the Barrage. He emphasized how
different the Cardiff UDC would be from its English predecessors.

> The consultation has also enabled us to proceed stage by stage
> with the agreement and enthusiastic support of the principal
> authorities...That is very important and is a situation quite differ-
> ent from that experienced in the London Docks and in other
> places where Government has had to impose an organization on
> unwilling local authorities.[17]

It must have taken a little more than the mutual self-interest of the

WO and the local councils to achieve this consensus, in so short a time. We must also remember that as recently as 1983, Mr Edwards was endorsing the local authorities' plans for single-handed regeneration of the same area. Constructive and viable schemes had been prepared, all that was needed, as the SGCC Chief Executive had pointed out, was a less complex and demanding way of financing them. Mr Edwards obviously believed a UDC was an ideal way of tackling this problem, a body set up specifically to draw together the necessary money.

But the Cardiff Bay Development Corporation was to be very different from its English predecessors. For instance, it would not be known as a UDC, as it was felt that the description would not fit 'the actual and desired image of Cardiff'.[18] Also, representatives of the private sector dominated the boards of earlier UDCs, appointed by the Department of the Environment: of the thirteen members of the Cardiff board, eight would be from local authorities (four from SGCC, three from CCC, one from the Vale of Glamorgan) with one from the LAW with four appointed by the Welsh Secretary, from the private sector and, of course a chair. Elected councillors would dominate the new body, as well-paid members of a private Corporation, which could only enhance its attractiveness in their eyes. The Deputy Chair of CBDC, Councillor Lord Brooks, was to receive over £6000 a year, while other members of the board, including local councillors, received over £3000.

Even more unusually, the new UDC was to be identified from the beginning with one specific, major public project – the Cardiff Bay Barrage. It was clearly stated in the Council's proposals for a UDC that, 'The County Council promotes a private bill... for the construction of a Cardiff Harbour Mouth Barrage'[19]. From SGCC's inception in 1974, to date, no mention had ever been made of the need for such a scheme. As Mr Watson emphasized, the only purpose of the Barrage would be the creation of a lake to destroy the mudflats of the Taff and Ely estuaries, which the SGCC had earmarked for conservation in its Structure Plan, less than two years before. The WO alone was convinced of the need to weave this imperial suit.

From 1983, when Mr Watson was given the brief of attracting new enterprises to Cardiff Bay, to the present day, this has been the main argument of the supporters of the Barrage – developers would come in significant numbers only if the mudflats disappeared permanently, even though, as a feeding ground of a wide variety of wading birds and wildfowl, the mudflats had been designated a Site of Special Scientific Interest. Substantial subsidies were not enough: the buccaneering spirits of the free market would need the soothing appeal of open water to overcome their qualms about relocating to the Welsh capital. Fortunately, these qualms did not afflict the proprietors and staff of the many and varied businesses already operating successfully in the area.

Those residents of Cardiff who later doubted the Barrage's fabled ability to attract capital, tried to find out which prospective developers had so firmly rejected a barrage-less Cardiff Bay, and those who had found a concrete dam and a stagnant lake of dubious quality to be significantly attractive. Given the vast expense of the Barrage, estimated at over £113 million by consultants KPMG in 1989, and the environmental problems it would create, reassurance that they could be justified by job and wealth creation, should have been crucial to the debate. The CBDC and the WO correctly insisted that commercial confidentiality prevented them naming the former, but even the number of those who found the mudflats wanting was apparently unavailable, although one might have supposed such arithmetic would have been vital to any calculations Mr Watson would have made (one is tempted to assume he failed to make any.) On the other side, when representatives of companies who have set up business in the Bay post-Barrage, are asked by journalists or researchers what brought them to the area, the Barrage and its freshwater lake are never, ever, mentioned, at least in any published material to date.

There is no indication that the suggested Barrage was ever submitted to objective scrutiny within the Welsh Office, before it emerged into the public arena. Mr Watson's assumption that it would be essential for overcoming difficulties in attracting investment to the area appears to have assumed the status of a proven hypothesis, without even being tested: it certainly formed the basis for all subsequent official action by local and central government on the issue. Following the constructive pondering of Messrs Hoad and Watson, the Secretary of State commissioned a report from the property experts, Jones Lang Wootton. This report was commissioned to justify and support the case for the building of the Barrage, not to test its assumptions.

In 1988, the newly formed CBDC published a 29-page booklet setting out its plans for the Bay, including the Barrage. Two pages were allocated to the case against the Barrage, set out by Peter Ferns, in his role as chair of the Severnside Conservation Group. He wrote,

> Of greatest importance, to some people, is the 'unsightliness' of the mudflats. Who would want to live, work or play in an area overlooking them? Well, mudflats don't seem to bother the residents of the myriad of exclusive apartments in London docks, overlooking the River Thames. In fact, flats overlooking the river are in greater demand than those overlooking the permanent high water in the docks. Mudflats don't seem to bother residents of Hayling Island in Hampshire, and dozens of other places in Britain, where holi-

day homes overlook them. Some places designated as Areas of
Outstanding Natural Beauty, such as the Solway Firth, consist
mostly of mudflats.

So what makes Cardiff Bay so unattractive at the moment? The
answer is the piles of refuse tipped around its shores and the old
cars, prams and supermarket trolleys that lie half-buried in the
mud. Clear those up and we will be left with an environment of
considerable natural beauty. Not a fixed and monotonous pond,
but an ever changing vista of glistening mudflats, grey water and
green saltmarsh, enriched by the presence of wading birds and
wildfowl.

His article was followed by a brief rebuttal entitled 'NO, say the
promoters of the [Cardiff Bay Barrage] Bill', which failed to mention,
let alone answer, the argument quoted above, simply referring to
CBDC's plans to compensate for the loss of the estuary as a Site of
Special Scientific Interest. Unlike the other 20 brief articles in the
booklet, none of which questioned the need for the Barrage, the
response was anonymous.

So why were local and central government so enthusiastic about
the setting up of an UDC, which wasn't really an UDC, and the planning of a barrage, which wasn't really planned?

Given the constraints placed by the Conservative government on
the financial activities of local authorities, only the WO could procure
the vast funding needed to bring life back to the 2700 derelict acres
of south Cardiff. The Welsh Secretary was a man near the end of an
unspectacular, political career; a large-scale scheme (like an UDC for
Cardiff) with a flamboyant, attention-grabbing centrepiece (like the
Barrage) would make a gratifying monument to leave behind him. Mr
Edwards' role in the grand debacle of the Cardiff Bay Opera House
reveals his love of theatre and the dramatic, in more then one sense.

Any reservations the leaders of local councils might have about the
scheme were accommodated by modifications to the UDC concept,
including their own influential places in it. Any reservations about the
Barrage in particular, would be answered by Mr Edwards' view of it as
a *sine qua non* – no Barrage, then no UDC; no UDC, no money; no
money, and south Cardiff stays as it is... So they agreed to promote a
Private Bill, in 1987, to allow the building of a barrage, to create a
'freshwater lake' from the waters of two of Britain's most polluted
rivers, the Taff and the Ely. Redevelopment would create a lot of jobs:
a barrage would create even more, was to be the mantra of the WO and
CBDC when they were required to put together a justification for the
project. Time and logic would reveal not only that this 'economic' justification of the Barrage was not really a justification, but also that it was
based on a deeply flawed assessment of its power to attract investment.

It is interesting to note that the development of Cardiff Bay, like all such developments, could not fail to increase the market value of the land in the area, if only because of the large sums of public money made available for the new roads, lighting schemes, drainage systems, and so on, which private investment required. When Mr Edwards made his momentous visit in 1985, the largest landowner in the Bay was Associated British Ports (ABP), with 180 of the area's 2700 acres. Not only were their holdings substantial – they included most of the prime sites along the waterfront, well placed to gain maximum benefit from the activities of CBDC.

ABP had been formed in 1983, following the privatisation of the former British Transport Docks Board. ABP's first share issues, like those of so many newly privatised companies in the 1980s, were heavily oversubscribed; some reliable estimates suggested, by as much as 35 times. There were the familiar comments in the financial press that the price had been set far too low – the family silver was being handed over to a rag-and-bone man for a song. The rag-and-bone man was quick to realise his windfall assets – in September 1986, ABP's profits for the financial year to date were over £11 million.

This happy state was not a reflection of the profitable activities of Britain's ports, alas, but rather of ABP's success in maximising the value of its extensive waterside land and property holdings. Coupled with the spread of marinas and, very briefly, several plans for barrages, land values in former ports and dockyards soared, and ABP reaped the benefits. In November 1986, the company made a successful bid of £14.9 million for the Grosvenor Square Properties Group plc, another owner of swathes of land ripe for development. By March 1987, ABP's profits had more than doubled to £26 million.[20]

It is interesting to note that if the Cardiff Bay Development Corporation had chosen to exert its statutory powers of compulsory purchase, it could have absorbed all of ABP's potentially profitable acres. However, following negotiations with the Corporation and the County Council, as promoters of the Barrage Bill, in 1989, it was announced that ABP's holdings in the Bay would be exempt from compulsory purchase; although they could take full advantage of the millions to be invested from public funds, under a profit-sharing arrangement with CBDC.

On his retirement from the Welsh Office and the House of Commons, after the 1987 General Election, Mr Edwards, then Lord Crickhowell, became a director of ABP. In 1989, Mr Freddie Watson, chief midwife to the Barrage, left the Welsh Office to become Chief Executive of Grosvenor Waterside, ABP's major property subsidiary.

2. Working Democracy

'Democracy, don't forget, is about numbers, about arithmetic'.
Lord Brooks of Tremorfa, quoted in Mike Ungersma, *Cardiff:*
Celebration for a City (Hackman Printers, 2000) p.121.

Soon after his decision that a barrage across Cardiff Bay would be a Good Thing, the Secretary of State for Wales sought to persuade local councillors, especially the leaders of the County Council, that his vision was essential to the future prosperity of the city.

The Leader of South Glamorgan County Council at the time, was Councillor Lord Brooks. Jack Brooks was Cardiff born and bred, a former plasterer, and an amateur boxer of fearsome reputation in his youth. He had been on the local Council for over 30 years, representing the Tremorfa ward, to the south of the city, including much of the site of the derelict East Moors Steelworks. During his rise to the top of Labour party politics in Cardiff, he had acquired a reputation as a formidable and efficient fixer, relying 'on a kind of politics that would have been familiar to "Boss" Daley in Chicago and other "wheeling and dealing' American cities".[1]

Many of the councillor's opponents inside the local Labour party could have put a name to that kind of politics, and it would not have been 'democracy'.

Brooks was invited to Cathays Park to discuss the SoS's plans,

> He [Edwards] sat back in his chair, stared at the ceiling and went off to enjoy a soliloquy. 'I don't like the sound of this,' I said to myself. I interrupted him, and you're not supposed to do that, you know. 'Secretary of State,' I said, 'if you are leading me to accept a London Docklands type of set-up in Cardiff, sorry, but you'll get no co-operation from me.' His face went as black as thunder and he stood up and said, 'Very well, let me have your thoughts on paper.' I told him he would have them in two days.[2]

He demanded, and got, two things, 'no powers must be taken from any local authority and the local political leaders must be represented on any board set up'.[3]

Jack Brooks had acted as election agent for one of the city's longest serving MPs – James Callaghan, Prime Minister from 1977 to 1979, and proposer of the Taff Crossing Bill. As Chair of the Welsh Labour Party in 1978-9 the Council Leader's influence had spread far beyond the capital.

It would difficult to imagine a politician more remote from the prickly Nicholas Edwards, with his service as an officer in the Royal Welch Regiment, his love of fly-fishing and opera. But, despite history and appearances, both men shared an aspiration that was as personal as it was political – to leave an indelible mark on the city of Cardiff. Lord Brooks (he had been ennobled in Callaghan's last honours list as Prime Minister) was one of the first local council leaders to be persuaded of the advantages the Cardiff Bay Barrage would bring to the city and, possibly, its politicians, when introduced to the idea by Mr Edwards, in 1985.

Although the Select Committee on the Taff Crossing Bill had dismissed the Barrage option, both the Secretary of State and the Leader of County Council were apparently convinced that the drowning of the mudflats was essential for the redevelopment; both had made a public commitment to the concept of a 'freshwater' lake as part of that redevelopment, no towels could be thrown in, no strategic withdrawals carried out. So, the Barrage would have to have a bill of its own, this time unencumbered by any mention of possible alternatives, especially cheaper alternatives, and with a full emphasis on the cosmetic virtues of the structure and its perceived role as a bait for investors in the area.

Consequently, no sooner had the Select Committee on the Taff Crossing Bill reported that they could not recommend a barrage as an appropriate part of the road scheme, than the South Glamorgan County Council presented their proposals for an Urban Development Corporation, for the regeneration of south Cardiff, to the SoS Wales, in September 1986. It may seem surprising that it was the County Council which formally proposed the UDC to the Welsh Secretary; given their relative roles in the affair, shouldn't it have been the other way round? It is too easy to underestimate the extent of the negotiations between Cathays Park and the County. The details of such discussions are not in the public domain; one has to assume their substance from the conclusions reached, the ambitions and power bases of the participants. It seemed that to get what *he* wanted, Nicholas Edwards adapted the UDC principle so that senior South Glamorgan councillors could get what *they* wanted. Their application to him for a UDC was the outcome of an elegant pavane for which Mr Edwards wrote the music and the council leaders did the choreography.

As well as the leaders of the County Council, Mr Edwards had to involve members of the City Council in the launch of the new barrage project. The two tier structure of Welsh local government often led to interesting tensions between different local authorities responsible for the same geographical area. After the restructuring of local government in 1974, different local responsibilities were assigned to each tier, education and social services to the County, environmental health to the City, for instance. But for other services, such as planning and highways, the division was blurred. In Cardiff, this was to be further complicated by the existence of the Development Corporation, with its major planning role.

In the mid-eighties, Cardiff City was a hung council, with the Liberals holding the balance of power. The County Council was very much the senior partner of the two authorities: it covered a larger area and had a larger budget. The nature of its powers brought its elected officers and appointed members into closer, more frequent contact with their opposite numbers in the Welsh Office. Also, the City could not boast an equivalent of South Glamorgan's Jack Brooks, with the reins of the Council gripped firmly and exclusively in his hands. However, it is the Tory Leader of the City Council, Ron Watkiss, who is credited with ensuring that planning controls for CBDC's sphere of influence would remain in the hands of the local councils, in name at least. In spite of this apparent coup, other City councillors, especially in the Labour group, would be rather freer than their County colleagues to indulge in the luxury of independent thinking about the Barrage in particular and the activities of CBDC in general. As relations with the Development Corporation deteriorated, in 1988, they were to set up a liaison committee specifically to keep a watching brief on CBDC's dealings with the council. Like their County colleagues, the Chair of the City Council and two senior councillors accepted seats on the Development Corporation Board, as representatives of their authority.

The two councils would also have been concerned about one particular aspect of south Cardiff's plight, its declining population. Several leading Labour members of both councils, including Lord Brooks and Councillor Kitson, Chair of the County's Planning Committee, represented wards in the area. If the electorate there continued to decline at the current rate, fewer wards could be justified, and many serving councillors would have to look for seats elsewhere, or, worse, face deselection. Redevelopment on the scale Nicholas Edwards and CBDC planned would bring more voters into their wards – whether they would vote Labour or not could be dealt with later.

But, before announcing the Barrage project publicly, Mr Edwards had had to win over a potential opponent even more combative than Jack Brooks – Margaret Thatcher:

> On only one occasion do I recall serious prime ministerial resistance to our activities and that was when I came forward with my proposals to construct a barrage at Cardiff [*sic*] and to set up the

Cardiff Bay Development Corporation. The Prime Minister's reaction was almost certainly stimulated by Treasury hostility and the fear that once again the Welsh Office was about to set off down a route that might involve greater public expenditure than the Treasury thought appropriate...

At that [Cabinet] committee, the Prime Minister pursued the Treasury arguments relentlessly, and I had to be equally persistent to make any progress at all. Towards the end of the exchange I made it unmistakably clear that I would contemplate resignation and an early departure from the Welsh Office if I did not get support. I had already announced my intention of leaving Parliament at the coming general election, but the threat was not empty, a resignation was the last thing that colleagues wanted six or nine months before that election...

Mr Edwards also refers to his attempts to address the Treasury's concerns about the project's economic feasibility,

The initial sums were modest and we planned to fund them from within the Welsh Office block grant, without making any fresh demand for resources.[4]

In view of the cost of the Barrage alone, (in 1988, estimated to be £90 million) without considering CBDC's other charges on public funds, Mr Edwards seems to have chanced on some new definition of 'modest' in relation to financial commitment, or else one must conclude he was less than fully briefed by his advisers on this point.

He also had to work hard to sell the Barrage idea to the Treasury, because

They were, of course, well aware that once the project had been approved in principle it would be extremely difficult to block it subsequently.[5]

Events were to prove the Treasury perfectly correct.

CBDC was set up in April 1987, one of five UDCs established that year. With four more (Central Manchester, Leeds, Sheffield and Bristol) to follow in 1988, competition to attract companies with the necessary cash and experience would be tough. It was felt that a dramatic centrepiece for any development was needed, as a focus for the inevitable marketing hype – Teeside and Cardiff had both chosen a barrage as their distinguishing feature.

CBDC's Chair was Geoffrey Inkin, a stalwart member of the Conservative Party in Wales, an unsuccessful candidate for Ebbw Vale in the 1979 General Election (where he stood against the Labour Leader, Michael Foot), Chairman of the Cwmbran Development

Corporation, Chair of the Land Authority for Wales, a former Lieutenant-Colonel in the Royal Welch Fusiliers, a perfect fit for the profile of the Great and Good of the Welsh Tory establishment.

Such an appointment, in the personal gift of the SoS Wales, was a sign of the role the Chair was expected to play in the regeneration project. Sir Geoffrey was to be a reassuring presence, a guarantee that developers involved in the Cardiff Bay project could be confident their investment was in safe hands.

The attempt to establish an economic justification for the Barrage began with a Welsh Office commission for the property consultants Jones Lang Wootton (JLW), in December, 1985, to 'appraise development potential, land and investment values in defined areas of the South Cardiff'.[6] Honor Chapman of JLW had already been appointed to the WO as a personal adviser to Nicholas Edwards, and served on the Development Corporation board from April 1987 until February 1994. She caused much innocent merriment in the city by remarking, when asked what benefits the lake impounded by the Barrage would bring to the socially deprived and excluded of Butetown, that they would be able to go sailing on it... The JLW report concluded that 'the effect of the Barrage in increased land values and inward investment in construction would be between £145 million and £195 million...'[7] This was exactly what the WO wanted to hear at this point in the project's life; a ringing endorsement of the potential which only a barrage could unleash in the area, without any assessment of alternatives.

However, it became clear that not all developers agreed with the assumption that drowning the mudflats was essential for south Cardiff's regeneration. Soon after CBDC was born, Sam Pickstock, Chief Executive of the Housing Division of Tarmac Homes, and Lord Brooks met Professor Chris Baines, landscape architect and environmentalist, early in 1987. The professor was a widely respected advocate of environmentally sympathetic development, and had grave concerns about the destruction of Cardiff's SSSI.

Tarmac Homes had played a major role in the County Council's regeneration of south Cardiff so far: they were building the prestigious new County Hall at Atlantic Wharf and the housing development around it. Their involvement had begun long before the Cardiff UDC and its barrage were even thought of. Professor Baines tried to persuade both men to oppose the Barrage, and work for redevelopment which would capitalise on the Bay's unique assets – the greatest tide range in Europe and flocks of wading birds. Lord Brooks remained sceptical, but Sam Pickstock was much taken with the idea. After careful consideration, he was certain the SSSI itself could be

made into a unique, attractive centrepiece for a commercially successful development. He and his company were prepared to throw
their substantial weight behind the case that there was no justification
for a barrage.

Unfortunately, JLW had not had the advantage of Professor
Baines' advice, and their conclusions in favour of the scheme served
only to buttress existing WO attitudes, as such reports so often do; like
Count Almaviva, they went dancing, whilst Figaro in Cathays Park
played the tune.

At the same time as the report on the investment potential of the
Barrage was commissioned, the Welsh Office invited engineering consultants Wallace Evans Partners (WEP) to study its technical
feasibility. Early in 1986, they duly reported that there would be problems with siltation, drainage (especially leaching from the Ferry Road
tip on the Ely estuary), rising groundwater, poor water quality in the
rivers and the impounded lake, fish migration up the Taff would be
blocked and the SSSI would be destroyed.

> The rate of siltation in the entrance channel will increase...
>
> A number of [storm and foul water outfalls] will require diver-
> sion...
>
> ... groundwater levels in the Grangetown and Central Cardiff area
> could rise by up to 2.5m...
>
> ... the levels of coliforms and B.O.D. (Biochemical Oxygen
> Demand) entering the study area is [*sic*] still a matter of concern.[8]

However, WEP were confident that all these problems could be
solved, although further detailed studies would be required. This report
also set a pattern for the Barrage debate; the scheme would cause problems, but there was no question that the expense of solving them would
in any way outweigh the so called advantages, a relentless optimism
that would become a way of life for the Development Corporation's
staff and consultants.

Like JLW, Wallace Evans were to enjoy a long and profitable relationship with the plans for the Barrage, as its complexities demanded
further research, extra reports and 'more detailed studies'. While these
reports were being prepared, CBDC and the Barrage had become
significant issues in the run up to the June 1987 General Election. The
new MPs elected for two Cardiff constituencies were to make them
controversial as well as significant.

Until 1987, Stefan Terlezki had been an unlikely MP for Cardiff
West. The area was dominated by one of the largest council estates in

Britain, in Ely, with a significant portion nearer the city centre, Canton, rapidly being colonised by the new Welsh tellygentsia – neither of them natural Tory constituencies.

From 1945, Cardiff West's MP had been George Thomas, Methodist lay preacher, loyal supporter of the right wing of the Labour party and Speaker of the House of Commons. In 1979, his majority had been a very comfortable 7000 – he had been personally and politically popular in the constituency. There is a parliamentary convention that candidates from the major parties do not stand against the Speaker at General Elections; the Speaker is returned virtually unopposed. George Thomas had held the office for six years, and when he retired his constituency party had understandably got out of the habit of fighting elections. In 1982, Labour's candidate lost heavily.

The successful candidate, Mr Terlezki, was Ukrainian by birth. He had arrived in Cardiff at the end of the World War II, as a refugee. With considerable determination, he had built a prosperous catering business in the city. A keen member of the Conservative Party and a loyal supporter of Margaret Thatcher, no one was more surprised than Mr Terlezki by his election for Cardiff West – largely due to the apathy of his over-confident opponents and the national surge of support for the Conservative government, post-Falklands.

Meanwhile, Labour party members in Cardiff West were doing some rigorous soul searching. Their horror at the ease and thoroughness of their defeat inspired a commitment to a more positive local agenda and a very effective membership drive. As a result, several ward parties were re-animated by new blood – including trades union activists, outraged by Thatcherite job cuts, and middle class professionals, angered by the destruction of communities and the intellectual poverty of the Conservative government. They also selected a particularly strong and attractive candidate for the 1987 General Election – Rhodri Morgan. The son of the vice-chancellor of University College Swansea, a graduate of Oxford and Harvard, a former representative of the EC in Wales, a fluent and witty speaker in English and Welsh as well as Cardiff born, he had successfully avoided too close an identification with either the soft centre or the hard left in their current battle for his party's soul. Rhodri Morgan's chief asset was Rhodri Morgan – he already had a reputation for being as abrasive and open-minded as was consistent with intelligent loyalty to Labour's current agenda. He had been actively involved in Cardiff politics since the late sixties, but without acquiring the debts to local movers and shakers which a weaker personality or a less substantial intellect would have had to run up. With so little ideological

baggage, and owing so little to the power of the formidable appa-
ratchiks on the Welsh National Executive, it was felt that he would
make an excellent constituency MP.

In June 1987, Rhodri Morgan was returned as MP for Cardiff
West with a majority of 7000 – almost exactly the same as George
Thomas'. The circumstances of his election had forged a particularly
strong bond with his local party – the resurrection of Cardiff West
CLP from the humiliation of the 1982 election was due more to their
joint efforts than any support from outside the constituency: all debts
and obligations were primarily between the MP and his ward parties.
If political push came to party shove, their interests should have first
call on his energy and loyalty.

In neighbouring Cardiff South and Penarth, prospective home to
the Cardiff Bay Development Corporation and the Barrage, a con-
trasting sequence of events was unfolding. Here too, the seat had been
held since 1945 by a senior figure in the Labour Party. James
Callaghan had held all the major offices of state, Chancellor, Home
Secretary and, briefly, Foreign Secretary, before succeeding Harold
Wilson as Prime Minister on the latter's retirement in 1977.

Unlike his colleague George Thomas, Callaghan did not leave the
Commons until 1987, when the tide was running less strongly in the
Conservatives' favour, and his successor was able to retain the seat for
Labour with a comfortable majority. That successor was Alun
Michael, a near contemporary of Rhodri Morgan, but with a very dif-
ferent political history and agenda.

Unlike Rhodri Morgan, Alun Michael had risen through the ranks
of local government: a graduate of Cardiff University, he had worked
as a journalist on the *South Wales Echo*, the local paper, before becoming a youth worker and a City Councillor for the Trowbridge ward.
He had a reputation for dogged loyalty to the leadership of the
Council's ruling Labour group and diligence in attention to the sort
of detail others might find tedious. He was Welsh-speaking, but could
not be described as inspiring in English or Welsh. A harassed supporter was overheard to say during his campaign for the leadership of
the Welsh Assembly, in 1998, 'If there's one thing more boring than
Alun speaking in English, it's Alun speaking in Welsh...' The most
persuasive accolade which Tony Blair could bestow on his protege,
during in the same campaign, was 'One of the most awe-inspiring
sights in Whitehall... Alun Michael with a clipboard'. In the 1987
Election, his Liberal Democrat opponent was Jenny Randerson, an
active and popular local councillor. Mrs Randerson's election address
made her opposition to the Barrage clear: she was the very first politician, local or national, to speak out against the scheme, and she

continued to oppose it, on the City Council and later, in the Welsh
Assembly.

Along with James Callaghan's seat, Mr Michael inherited the backing of his most powerful and influential supporter, Lord Brooks of
Tremorfa. The Star Centre in Splott is at first sight an unremarkable
community centre, typical of many built by local authorities in the
early 70s. It was a combined meeting place and sports centre, offering a bar, badminton court, snooker room and similar facilities, for the
people of Splott, Tremorfa and Adamsdown. But the Star Centre
played a very important role in the political life of Cardiff, for it was
here that Lord Brooks held court, every Sunday afternoon. In the bar,
he would meet with those councillors, would-be councillors, union
officials and Labour party officers, Alun Michael among them, who
had a role to play in his plans for the City. It must be emphasised that
no breath of financial scandal, no whisper of abuse of influence for
material gain, ever touched Lord Brooks' circle. In local government
terms, Cardiff was, and is, a corruption-free zone; a Poulson affair in
the Welsh capital is unthinkable. It was simply made clear to all with
political aspirations in the city, where the main source of real power
lay, and where respect was due. On Sunday afternoons at the Star,
plans were outlined and roles assigned.

Lord Brooks also maintained friendly relations with leaders of the
Conservatives on both County and City Councils – sometimes closer
to that of affectionate sparring partners than political opponents. It
was a basic tenet of Cardiff politics that any favours Lord Brooks
bestowed would, in the fullness of time, have to be returned, as and
when he required. Lord Brooks' support was vital to the success of
any Labour candidate in a south Cardiff election. So it was only natural the new MP would play an essential role in the achievement of
his lordship's pet project, the passing of the Cardiff Bay Barrage Bill.

The first Barrage Bill had fallen victim to the General Election,
which had been called before the Bill could have its Second Reading
in the Commons, so it was not eligible for an automatic 'carry-over'
motion to the new Parliament. The General Election also marked the
end of Nicholas Edwards' career in the Commons and as SoS for
Wales. He was succeeded by the formidable Peter Walker. Mr Walker
and the Prime Minister had made no secret of their many differences
of opinion; he was a Tory 'wet', with little sympathy for the harsh economic neo-liberalism Mrs Thatcher embraced. His many supporters
in the Commons saw his appointment to the WO as a sadistic punishment by exile. As the original Barrage Bill was now, legally speaking,
non-existent, a second Bill had to be drafted from scratch, and South
Glamorgan County Council would have to formally agree to sponsor

it in Parliament, where it was introduced in the Lords by Jack Brooks, in January, 1989.

During the passage of the Taff Crossing Bill, the RSPB had taken full advantage of the Parliamentary convention by which interested parties could present petitions against a Private Bill to Select Committees, of either house, appointed to look in detail at the Bill's provisions. Their petition had persuaded the Select Committee to recommend that a barrage should not be built. But, as the debates on the Second Reading showed, the RSPB could count on the support of a number of MPs well aware that this body had the largest membership of any conservation group in the UK; it made a constituency well worth courting, in political terms. There were also, to be less cynical, many MPs with a strong commitment to conservation in general and the work of the RSPB in particular. Both groups could be counted on to ensure the RSPB case was given a good airing, whenever appropriate.

As the RSPB prepared its case against the new Barrage Bill, they were very much aware that the economic justification for the Barrage, unproven though it was, included the creation of several thousand jobs. To oppose the project on conservation grounds alone would be to open a 'people versus birds' argument which, in the prevailing climate, they could not hope to win. Any case against the Barrage made to a Select Committee would have to be more widely based – chiefly by enlisting the doubts and concerns of local people about the project. MPs would listen much more carefully to the arguments of residents who had lived in south Cardiff all their lives, about the Barrage's threat to their property or health, than to the arguments of bird watchers and conservationists who only visited the area to pursue a hobby or do research.

By this time, Peter Ferns had considerable knowledge of the minutiae of parliamentary procedure. He, and the parliamentary consultants retained by RSPB, knew that Private Bills were not subject to a whip: in theory, MPs and peers could vote on them according to conscience, not the dictates of party policy. However, senior figures in both main parties had expressed support for this particular measure, and would thus ensure that all back benchers with a healthy survival instinct knew exactly how to vote, if required to do so.

The Taff Crossing Bill had included a barrage but the clauses referring to it could be omitted from the eventual Act, in response to petitioners' arguments against them. It was not a mistake Nicholas Edwards intended to repeat: the Barrage had to have its very own Bill, so no future petition, however well argued and justified, could bring about its defeat. With the majority of lobby fodder safely marshalled behind it, this Bill was bound to succeed, no matter how powerful the case against Mr Edwards' whim might be.

There had been much disquiet among the grassroots in Cardiff docklands over the Taff Crossing Bill, largely focussed on the route of the proposed road, and its effects the dangers of heavy traffic for children at nearby schools, the splitting of local communities, etc. These concerns were not sufficiently widespread in the city as a whole to influence council deliberations on the matter, let alone to be focussed on petitioning to a parliamentary Select Committee. However, Mr Edwards' proposals for a barrage on a much bigger scale fuelled these existing anxieties much more – there were concerns about the quality of the filthy water from the Taff and Ely to be impounded behind the Barrage, the threat of rising groundwater and, most of all, the waste of public money on what was seen as a pet project for politicians, with no apparent public benefit. This time, local disquiet about the Bill was more vocal; several councillors, especially those representing wards in or near the docks area were approached by constituents trying to persuade them to look at the proposal with healthy scepticism. As a result, a petition signed by more than 7000 residents of south Cardiff was presented to the County Council, when they met to debate and vote on a motion to promote the new Barrage Bill in Parliament, in October, 1988.

The two hour debate in the council chamber was chaired by Cllr Paddy Kitson, member of the Cardiff Bay Development Corporation, and the debate was opened by Lord Jack Brooks, Leader of the Council and Deputy Chairman of the Cardiff Bay Development Corporation. Of the 45 councillors attending the debate, 40 dutifully voted in favour of the Bill, with one abstention and four votes against. The votes against were cast by three members of the ruling Labour group, Duncan Longden, Mark Drakeford and Jane Hutt, all serving wards in the south of the city. It was Jane Hutt who presented the petition on behalf of their constituents. The fourth 'No' vote was cast by Chris Franks, the County's only Plaid Cymru member, for Dinas Powys in the Vale of Glamorgan. Duncan Longden was a long-serving councillor, who had already announced that he would not be standing for re-election, and therefore had little to lose by opposing the official party line. However he, like Jane and Mark, was duly punished by the withdrawal of the Party Whip.

Labour had won control of the County Council in 1981, with a majority of one. Every member was important, so a *quid pro quo* operated, where the leaders kept the Labour group together by judicious dispensation of goodies to key wards, whose councillors' support was really important to them. However, in the local elections of 1988, when Mark Drakeford and Jane Hutt had won seats, Labour had a much larger majority. Individual councillors were therefore much less important. Benign patriarchal figures like former Council leader Rev. Bob Morgan of Ely and Mike Trickey, librarian and local historian, lost their positions in the Labour Group to Lord Brooks and his supporters; as the numbers changed, the arithmetic of democracy added up differently.

It is important to remember that South Glamorgan included the rural-cum-commuter belt of the Vale of Glamorgan, as well as the purpose-built port of Barry, declining steeply from its brief moment of prosperity early in the century. Councillors from different parts of the County obeyed a self-denying ordinance: Barry councillors didn't have strong opinions about Cardiff matters, Vale councillors didn't make a fuss about what went on in Barry, and Cardiff councillors didn't bother much about either area. The Barrage was not only a Cardiff issue, of no interest to Vale or Barry members, who'd just vote on it as group policy dictated, but a south Cardiff issue – it was expected that members from other parts of the city would not aspire to independent views on it.

Across this geographical fault line ran other divisions in the South Glamorgan Labour Group; the 1988 election had brought in a tranche of younger councillors, concerned at the continuing surge to the right of the Tory government. This led to a philosophical divide. On one side were the believers in a democracy of leadership, where councillors saw themselves as the movers and shakers in their communities, with delegated powers which meant they were under no obligation to consult constituents about specific policies or plans, no matter how great their impact. On the other side, were the believers in participative democracy, who expected to involve the electorate as widely as possible in any decisions that affected them.

The latter tended to represent marginal wards, and to be incomers to the city; there was a higher proportion of women among them and many of them shared a distrust of their older colleagues' liking for large scale visible projects, like the Barrage – the 'plaques on walls' school of local government. In contrast, the 'participative democrats' like Jane Hutt and Mark Drakeford, preferred smaller scale projects, where their communities could be actively involved in change and development.

Longer serving councillors like Jack Brooks, openly congratulated themselves on having a good working relationship with Conservative Secretaries of State, and of being able to take best advantage of Tory plans wherever possible. Their younger colleagues believed they had been elected specifically to protect their communities from the predations of a right wing central government, and responded accordingly, when asked to support a Welsh Office-backed scheme of dubious origin and even more questionable consequence.

To anyone unfamiliar with the inner workings of Labour politics in a large local authority, it might appear surprising that, in the circumstances, only three Labour councillors dared to vote against the motion to sponsor the Barrage Bill. Many of their colleagues did express grave reservations about the project the Group's leaders were backing so strenuously, but in a ruling party with a substantial majority, those leaders' powers of patronage could be decisive. Councillors for wards not immediately affected by the Barrage had much to lose if they were, as their leaders would see it, disloyal enough not to support the proposal. Grants, awards and other schemes to benefit their constituents could easily be directed elsewhere; they could be excluded, perhaps permanently, from the key committees where real power and influence lay. For Councillors Hutt and Drakeford, the Barrage's threat to their wards outweighed these considerations. However, the numbers still added up to Lord Brooks' satisfaction.

There was yet another reason why councillors with serious reservations about the Barrage did not abstain. The Council were not voting, they argued, for or against the scheme itself, but only for or against sponsoring a Parliamentary Bill about it. Ironically, arguments against the Barrage in both Commons and Lords would later be dismissed by its supporters, when they pointed out that the County Council had voted by a very large margin to promote the Bill, and it therefore had the wholehearted approval of most elected members!

The Barrage Bill was eventually re-animated in January 1989. There was sufficient opposition for it to be referred to the Opposed Bills Office, after its Second Reading, so that a Select Committee could examine its proposals. Opposition was provided by MPs who were not interested in giving the Welsh Secretary an easy ride, who were genuinely concerned about the wholesale destruction of an SSSI and who thought the whole Cardiff Bay project would swallow up too much public money, with very uncertain prospects of appropriate return on investment.

Whatever their motives, the way was now open for the RSPB and any other opponents to put the case against the project in full and well-based detail.

3. The Rule of an Engineer

A long time ago, near the borders of Uganda and Sudan, I met an old man…a freelance road engineer. He said to me: 'I will give you a rule for life. It is the rule of an engineer. First find out what is wrong. Then, and only then, work out how to put it right. All the troubles of the world happen because some b.f. starts putting things right before he's found put what's wrong.'

Neal Ascherson in *The Observer*, 18th December, 1988

Norman Robson is a retired engineer, a former student of Ruskin College, stocky, ruddy-faced, a man of great kindness, sharp wit and tenacity. He has lived in Cardiff for more than 30 years, refining his appreciation of good beer, model engineering and the ease with which the powerful so often blur the distinction between their own interests and the public good.

For nearly twenty years, Norman had been deeply involved in housing campaigns in the city. Housing had been a contentious issue in Cardiff since the notorious Hook Road scheme of the late sixties. The scheme would have brought a new main road from the M4 right to the town centre, through north Cardiff, ripping the heart out of Gabalfa and Roath, both residential areas of mostly council-owned or privately-rented working class homes. It required the compulsory purchase of nearly 2500 houses, most of which were then left empty for years while the fine details of the project wended their way through the labyrinthine planning process. While these homes remained unoccupied, there were never fewer than 2500 families on the City's council house waiting lists, and at one point, there were nearly 5000. Opponents of the scheme formed Cardiff Housing Action, which included Labour and Liberal activists disillusioned with the unconcern of many local councillors and MPs. However, one of their most vocal supporters was the Labour MP for Cardiff North, Ted Rowlands.

The citizens of Cardiff were assured by their political leaders that the problems caused by the Hook Road would be only a small price to pay for the prosperity it would bring to the city, just as they were given the same assurances about the Barrage. Eventually, the scheme was narrowly voted out by the then City Council, largely in response to its great unpopularity. However, the desperate lack of affordable housing in the city had been highlighted; in view of the local council's unwillingness to tackle the problem seriously, several Cardiff Housing

Action members formed the city's first housing association. They included staff from the University's Town Planning department, among them Richard and Sue Essex (Sue was later to become a local councillor and chair of the City's planning committee) and John Brookes, who would also be prominent in the anti-barrage campaign. Norman was appointed its Housing Officer, in 1972. The first properties bought by Taff Housing (THA) were in Victoria Park, in the south west of the city, and over the next twenty years, over 500 houses were renovated and made available as homes in neighbouring Riverside and Canton.

In 1986, when he first heard of the plans to build a barrage across the mouth of Cardiff Bay, Norman was living in Riverside, in a small Victorian terrace house near the River Taff, not far from Ninian Park football ground, between the city centre and what once were Cardiff Docks. Riverside, like much of south Cardiff, is low-lying, liable to flood when heavy rain in the Valleys, or even the Brecon Beacons, races down the river to the sea at Cardiff Bay.

Since Nicholas Edwards first suggested a barrage across Cardiff Bay, in 1985, Cardiff Flood Action Committee (CFAC) had been very much aware of the potential problems it would cause, especially changes in the water table. Thomas Rammell's report to the Board of Health in 1850, on Cardiff's water supplies and drainage systems, gave a concise description of the city's geology.

> The substratum of the older, or inland, portion of the town, as far down as Whitmore-lane [roughly where the present city centre meets Butetown] is a gravel, which quickly absorbs the surface water, from this line to the sea, the gravel is overlaid by a stiff black clay. This clay is full 30 feet deep on the shoreline and becomes thinner and thinner as it approaches Whitmore-lane, where it entirely disappears.[1]

As every gardener knows, water moves very slowly through clay, especially the heavy clay Rammell noted between the city centre and the new dockyards; it moves much more quickly through the gravel beneath the city centre itself. In other words, near the shoreline, a layer of clay seals in much of the water table and prevents it from reaching the surface; but further away from the sea, water rises much more freely to the surface, especially when there is a high tide in the Bay, or prolonged and heavy rainfall.

The people of Riverside knew this still, a century and a half after Rammell, when mud and water appeared in their cellars with the spring and autumn high tides, and the heavy rains of winter. They were afraid that this situation could only worsen when a barrage kept water in the Bay at a constant level, near to that of the average high tide.

Floods, usually caused by high river flows, have been a recurring refrain throughout south Cardiff's history, from John Speede's notes on the treacherous 'Tave' in 1610, to the disastrous floods of 1979. That year the flood warning system along the river – supposedly the responsibility of the National Rivers Authority and the local councils – failed, and local residents did not get the intended 3-4 hours warning that disaster was imminent. As a result, floodwater and mud from the Taff damaged hundreds of homes. Compensation from official sources was slow in materialising, and local residents formed CFAC, with Norman Robson as Chair, to press for a just settlement of their claims. The affected area is predominantly working class, and one-to-one legal representation would have been too costly for the victims. Their case was good, but the process was slow, and it was 1988, nine years later, before most of their claims were settled. During their confrontation with officialdom, they gained skills and insights which were to be useful in a very different arena.

In February 1987, Norman chaired what its members hoped would be one of CFAC's last meetings: the main business was to set a timetable for the winding up of the group's affairs, as its purpose, members thought, was all but fulfilled. However, their chairman was very much aware that although this particular fight had been won, an even more demanding battle was looming.

Later that month, Norman had a visit from Peter Ferns, now Chair of the Severnside Conservation Group (SCG), an alliance of voluntary organisations and pressure groups concerned with wildlife conservation in the Severn Estuary, which includes the lower reaches of the rivers Taff and Ely, and Cardiff Bay itself. Peter was fresh from the vigorous struggle over the fate of the Taff Estuary Site of Special Scientific Interest, whose conservation was a significant part of the current South Glamorgan County Structure Plan. The Butetown PDR had endangered a significant part of the habitat of the wading birds that overwintered on the mudflats of the SSSI, but the proposals of the Barrage Bill would destroy it completely. It was concern over the loss of these feeding grounds, defended so vigorously during the passage of the Taff Crossing Act, that led Peter Ferns to contact Norman, when an even greater threat loomed.

Norman had already written to the County Council about the likely effect of the Barrage on the water table; when they had replied that there was no cause for anxiety, Cardiff Flood Action Committee really started to worry… Peter Ferns, although officially appearing before the Select Committee as an expert witness for the County Council, had worked closely with the RSPB; at their suggestion, he contacted Norman as Chair of CFAC. The possibility of flooding, as a result of the Barrage meant CFAC still represented those Cardiff citizens most vulnerable to the Bill's consequences. Letters had already been written to the local press and politicians by CFAC members who were concerned about the Barrage's dubious provenance and possibly dire consequences. With Norman's leadership, the organization also had the necessary campaigning experience, cohesion and staying power to form a working partnership with the RSPB and co-ordinate locally based petitions against the Bill, which would be the most effective way of stopping it. It was clear the more petitions from residents' groups presented to any Select Committee, the better – so, the more residents' groups, the better.

Together, Norman and Peter developed a strategy for the groups they represented, which was to unite their very different interests and skills to achieve very similar ends. They would try to show that the Cardiff Bay Barrage was irrelevant to the real needs of the city, and win national and local political support for the case against it. Both men were experienced campaigners; they knew that the financial and political forces ranged in support of the Bill made its defeat at best unlikely and at worst impossible. They needed a fallback strategy the aim of which was the modification of the Bill so that its worst effects, in terms of rising groundwater, the danger to health of impounding the sewage of the Taff and Ely, and the insupportable public expense, would be mitigated.

To back up their case, the new anti-barrage alliance would need the support of experts in many different fields – hydrology, town planning, environmental science, public health. In the six years of the campaign against successive Barrage Bills, many such specialists would come forward to express their concerns about the project, in Parliament, in the press and at public meetings.

The success of their plans would depend on winning the support of local councillors and, a more daunting proposition, Cardiff MPs. As Chairman of CFAC, Norman had already discussed the problems the Barrage would bring with the Labour County Councillor for Riverside, Jane Hutt, and her colleague, Mark Drakeford, Councillor for nearby Pontcanna. It was necessary for the County Council to vote to approve their sponsorship of the latest Barrage Bill, before it could be formally introduced to Parliament. At meeting on October, 29th 1987, 52 councillors had voted to sponsor the Bill, with two abstentions; the abstaining councillors were Mark and Jane – CFAC already started to reveal cracks in the case for the project. Over the next few months, other local politicians were to be persuaded that there were excellent reasons for opposing the Barrage.

The contributions that experts and politicians alike made to the

campaign were vital, but it was the residents' own energy and commitment that welded such diversity together and gave the whole
enterprise focus, purpose and unity. Without their dedication to what
was to be a long haul, it could have easily faltered.

The first Cardiff Bay Barrage Bill had failed to survive the 1987
general election, so this second Bill was introduced to the Commons
by Alun Michael, the following November. However, the likely costs
of the Barrage were arousing much discontent among MPs for the
south Wales Valleys, lead by the combative Ron Davies, MP for
Caerffili. They believed that the Barrage was just a cosmetic project,
whose benefits, if any, would be limited to the property developers
induced to invest in south Cardiff. They argued that the millions allocated to the scheme would be better spent on reviving the economies
of their own constituencies, where degeneration and poverty were far
more widespread. They threatened to stop the Bill, by a blocking
motion, which would mean that it would fall unless supported by at
least 100 MPs at its Second Reading. Given the opposition to the
Barrage on environmental as well as economic grounds, the government decided to reintroduce the Bill in the Lords, where debate and
votes on a Second Reading would not be muddied by controversial
financial arguments from the Valleys.

The Bill's promoters took advantage of these delays to attempt to
neutralise opposition to the destruction of the SSSI, by including provision for what they referred to as 'alternative feeding grounds' for the
wading birds whose habitat would be destroyed. They also responded
to criticism from local yachtsmen by redesigning the locks in the
Barrage. It was to be expected that they would eventually try to
accommodate anxieties about groundwater damage in the same way.

Meanwhile, fortunately for Norman, the work of setting up anti-
barrage residents' groups was to be much easier than he anticipated –
as it turned out, he was to have an unexpected ally in the apparent
incompetence of CBDC's own public relations department.

The main purpose of all the Development Corporations set up
between 1981 and 1993 was to increase property and land values in
their designated areas, by attracting investors. The theory was that
these increases would then 'trickle down', in terms of better environmental quality and job opportunities, to local residents. So, the sales
pitch, the Unique Selling Point, for any UDC was directed at potential
developers, not at people already living or running businesses there.
CBDC was no exception; from the beginning, its announcements and
media releases were primarily directed at an audience outside the city,
while the interests and anxieties of its residents took second place.
Board members and CBDC management alike tended to assume that

Cardiffians would be grateful to be the raw material for such a bold experiment as the Barrage, and reacted with pained surprise when they were not absolutely delighted by the prospect.

All the local groups that campaigned against the Barrage emphasised at every opportunity that they supported the regeneration of south Cardiff. They appreciated, much better than any member of CBDC, or the many consultants to whom it gave profitable employment, the real needs of the area. Like Neal Ascherson's engineer, they knew that CBDC were magisterially imposing a solution to a problem, without stopping to work out what the problem really was. In their view, a stagnant, sewage-laden lake did not go any way towards meeting the area's requirements for affordable housing, decent jobs and sympathetic development.

So, through the winter and early spring of 1988, Norman chaired packed public meetings, in church halls and community centres, private houses and pubs, where the anxious and angry could discuss the Barrage and how it could be stopped. As a result, anti-barrage groups sprang up throughout south Cardiff.

Unlike the Development Corporation, the anti-barrage campaign was self-financing; meetings and postage and phone calls and press releases were paid for by selling balloons and badges at local carnivals, by appeals for donations from members and, most of all – the fuel which usually powers grass-roots activism in this country – by people putting coins in plastic buckets. Like most popular movements, it depended on people's willingness to venture out on dark cold evenings, stuffing leaflets through letter boxes, street after street, hour after hour, to argue or conspire with councillors at Saturday morning surgeries, to put up posters and write letters. The more routine jobs involved in running the fight against the Barrage were more than compensated for by the adrenaline rush so many campaigners felt; they had a difficult task ahead, but their cause was just and their strategy plain.

Moreover, it was a distinguishing feature of the campaign that everyone who worked for it developed immense respect and affection for their co-workers. This was just as well, for the residents' struggle would demand a great versatility and a wide variety of skills; a social worker learnt to speak with authority about the historical behaviour of Cardiff's watertable, a JP discovered virtually all there is to know about the type of bacteria found in standing urban waste water; an insurance clerk became an authority on the way high tides affect dampness in cellars; a librarian and a professional clown reconnoitred the dark labyrinths of parliamentary procedure, while a baker discovered the hydrological intricacies of urban drainage systems and river flows.

Cardiff Flood Action Committee naturally formed the backbone of the new Riverside anti-barrage group, with strong support from the Taff Housing Association (THA). The Association had played a vital role in refurbishing much of the area's social housing stock, in the previous ten years, and planned to continue doing so. Its members feared that the investment they and their tenants had already made would be lost, if the Barrage went ahead. As John Southern, the manager of the South Riverside Community Centre (SRCC), pointed out, the value of the private homes in south Cardiff threatened by the Barrage totalled about £400 million at 1988 prices; their occupants were having to risk far more on the success of the scheme than any property developer. A large proportion of Riverside residents were first generation immigrants from Pakistan and north India – there were strong Sikh, Muslim and Hindu communities, for which the Community Centre acted as a focus. The SRCC was to speak for them as another institutional opponent of the project.

There were interesting variations in character and emphasis between different anti-barrage groups in different areas. Canton, to the west of the city centre, and neighbouring Pontcanna, alongside the Taff to the north, were, like Riverside, mainly Edwardian and residential. Riverside, however, was still largely a working class area, while Canton and Pontcanna were becoming rapidly more attractive to middle class incomers, offering a larger range of homes, from small terrace houses, whose the front doors opened on to the street, to spacious three and four storey properties on wide, tree-lined Cathedral Road. The anti-barrage groups there included social workers, university administrators and lecturers, retired civil servants and teachers.

In contrast, Grangetown extended south along the west bank of the Taff, from Riverside to the estuary, and its residents were very familiar with flooding problems when the river was in spate. Grangetown's population was just under 12,000, compared to Canton's 8000. Much of the area had been built in the same property boom as Canton, from 1860 to 1910, largely residential, but with a number of factories and businesses, mainly small to medium sized; most of the original residents had worked on the docks, just across the river. However, Grangetown had not enjoyed the gradual gentrification that had benefited Canton; by 1988, many streets, especially to the north west, were dilapidated and decaying.

The Chair of Grangetown Residents Against the Barrage (GRAB) was the redoubtable Stan Perkins, a former coal merchant. Shrewd, dapper and good humoured, Stan had delivered coal to the area for over 40 years, and was proud of his familiarity with every basement, coal hole and cellar in the neighbourhood. His home was a few hundred yards from the edge of the lake to be created by the Barrage, but his main concern was for the many basement flats in Grangetown already below the official water table, and the area's century-old drainage system, which he believed would be incapable of carrying the burden of extra groundwater flows.

In March 1988, CBDC had held one of a series of meetings for local people in the Channel View Leisure Centre in Grangetown. Michael Boyce attended in his supporting role as the County Council's Chief Executive, and Alun Michael was also on the platform, as the Bill's main apologist in the Commons, and the district's MP. Alun Michael's unwillingness to take seriously his constituents' anxieties about groundwater dangers infuriated many of them. At one point, a member of the audience demanded, 'Are you telling us we're going to have this barrage, whether we want it or not?', to which Michael Boyce replied, with uncharacteristic bluntness, 'Yes, you are!' and another anti-barrage residents' group was launched.

The southern part of Riverside ward included Leckwith, a low-lying area of terraced houses around the Ninian Park stadium, home of Cardiff City Football Club. The first Chair of Leckwith Residents Against the Barrage (LRAB) was Dulcie Rees, a cake decorator, wife of Ken, a railwayman. One of the most stalwart of their supporters was the vivid and eloquent Colin Powell. Colin had retired from work as a full-time organiser for the Civil and Public Services Association, at the Welsh Office, because of chronic asthma. However, he still served as a JP and school governor, while he and his wife had acted as foster parents for several years. It was Colin who was to provide some of the liveliest exchanges with successive parliamentary Select Committees, on LRAB's behalf.

Adamsdown also bordered CBDC's designated area; it covered the wards represented on the County Council by Lord Brooks, councillor for Splott, and two of his closest associates, Gordon Houlston, councillor for Tremorfa, and Ken Hutchings, councillor for Adamsdown itself. Surprisingly, given his major roles in the Development Corporation and on the Council, Lord Brooks never appeared at any public meetings arranged by CBDC about their plans, nor did he attend any local anti-barrage meetings from the start of the campaign in 1988 until he was defeated in the local elections of 1993; he did not even attend, most remarkable of all, the meetings arranged by Adamsdown Residents Against the Barrage (ARAB) which included his own constituents. ARAB's first meeting was chaired by Les Baxter, a retired warehousemen, who had lived in one of the small terraces behind Cardiff Royal Infirmary for more than 30 years. As a lifelong teetotaller with an impish sense of humour, when asked for his address he would reply, with an ironic smile, '...like its owner, a dry house, until now.' The meeting was attended by Councillor Houlston, whose apparent determination that no statement from the platform should go unheckled exasperated even the most fair-minded of ARAB's members, and resulted in yet another own goal for the Barrage cause.

The Docks Residents and Tenants Association (DRTA) represented the people of Butetown, the only sizeable residential district within CBDC's operational area. Local anxieties had already been fuelled by the plans for the PDR, and the Association had been formed to negotiate with the local County Councillor, Paddy Kitson. Their spokesman was the articulate and much respected Ben Foday, whose parents had come to Cardiff from West Africa in the early 1950s. Alone among the anti-barrage groups, DRTA's members could expect to benefit directly from CBDC's activities; extra jobs were promised in the construction projects planned, including the Barrage itself, and substantial housing schemes were envisaged. In the light of this, they saw their role as bargaining with the Corporation, trying to offset the difficulties that their activities would bring by negotiating practical favours for the local community – a tactic not available to other residents' groups.

As they pursued a rather different strategy, DRTA did not come under the CFAC umbrella when the processes of petitioning and protesting really got under way. As well as the formally constituted residents' groups, there was another powerful force whose activities became a vital part of the campaign. Glyn Paul was a former marine engineer turned freelance photographer, who lived, and grew roses, in Grangetown. No major event in Cardiff, at least one needing a press photographer, was complete without Glyn's unmissable arrival – a tall, bulky figure in black motorcycle leathers, crammed, with his camera, onto the smallest and oldest Vespa north of Milan, a cigarette protruding aggressively beneath his crash helmet. Glyn with his hot temper and intransigent views, would be the first to describe himself as 'not much of a joiner' – he was the only petitioner against the early barrage bills to do so as an individual, rather than as the representative of a group.

However, he was eventually persuaded to join the movement, and his eagerness to harass movers and shakers in CBDC and the Welsh Office became legendary. He had a unique ability to flush out the sort of official information which, strictly speaking, should be in the public domain, but to which, for their own good reasons, senior civil servants and quango chiefs have great difficulty allowing the public access. It was amazing how often, after a chat between Glyn and some middle-ranking officials at the WO, interesting and useful reports would find their way to photocopiers, and thence into large brown paper envelopes, which in turn appeared on the door mats of CFAC members the next morning. It must be clearly understood that none of the information which circulated like this was legally restricted in any way, Glyn's spirited intervention simply avoided considerable delay and inconvenience.

While the anti-barrage groups were marshalling their forces and preparing strategy, CBDC was planning its future activities. The Corporation's brief was to re-animate the 2700 acres of Cardiff Docklands, not just aesthetically, but economically – profits had to be generated. In January 1988, the consultants Llewellyn Davies Planning (LDP) were engaged to carry out a survey of all existing businesses in the area, their size, trade, number of employees, etc. The object of this exercise was, their representative told the local press, to reassure employers that their views would be taken into consideration in the Corporation's plans for the area.

'We must know what people in the area think, or we might as well just use a bulldozer,' said Miss Hilary Sunman, who led the research. 'There have been complaints, particularly in the London Docklands, that local interests were completely ignored when the redevelopment was carried out, and Cardiff Bay want to avoid any such protests. There is a much better relationship with the local authorities in Cardiff and this survey is part of the efforts to involve local concerns at all stages.'[2]

Although very little cargo now passed through Cardiff docks com-pared to its heyday, the Queen Alexandra Dock and Roath Dock were still open to shipping. The land around these docks belonged to Associated British Ports (ABP), and was not officially part of CBDC's remit, any more than the jobs which they provided. The main sources of employment in the Bay, about 15,000 jobs all told, were based in the Collingdon Road area, near the new County Hall. Collingdon Road had originally been the place where all the trades – engineers, makers of propellers and cables – needed to keep ships at sea could be found. With the decline in shipping, much of their work had disappeared, but engineers are adaptable men, and old tech-niques were altered to fit new trades, like panel beating, HGV maintenance or power boat building. Not only did they survive, but many thrived – rents were cheap and staff training could be done on the job. It must be said that such work places can never be visually attractive, requiring as they so often do easy access to large amounts of recyclable metal, but they provided work and marketable products. Many of the factory units were small and affordable, ideal for starter companies, who moved on to neater, larger, but more expensive trading estates elsewhere in the city, as they expanded.

Consultation exercises like LDP's were to be a distinguishing feature of CBDC's one-way communication with local people. These consultation exercises largely involved telling people, through leafleting or public meetings, what CBDC felt they ought to know, listening to their questions, telling them that they had nothing to worry about, and carrying on exactly as they would have done anyway. This process was perhaps a relic of the military backgrounds of its Chairman and Chief Executive

However, this first major consultation provided CBDC with another of its many self-inflicted public relations wounds. Alas for Miss Sunman's hopes about involving local people, less than two weeks after the survey began, many of the businesses already contacted by LDP for their views on the development, had received official notification from the Corporation that their properties might be subject to compulsory purchase orders.[3] This mistiming showed either CBDC's right hand didn't know what its left was doing, or its plans were subject to change at very short notice, or even that it saw public relations as a purely theoretical exercise. Later events would confirm that all three suppositions were true; whatever the hapless workers of Collingdon Road thought about CBDC's development plans, the bulldozers were on their way.

However, the Corporation did have at least one PR achievement to its name: Lord Brooks had gained the support of a long-standing friend, the editor of the *South Wales Echo*, Cardiff's local newspaper. Geoff Rich was to provide very effective pro-barrage propaganda throughout CBDC's life. As he remarked, looking back on the campaign,

> In the end, it's down to you. The political balance is so fine that if you, through the *South Wales Echo*, oppose it, we won't be able to go ahead... the *Echo* wheeled up its guns in support. I have never regretted it.[4]

It was very lucky for CBDC that Mr Rich, weighed in so often and so heavily on their behalf. Local doubts and fears about the Barrage were provoked, rather than soothed, by inept public statements from the Corporation's representatives; the confident, albeit rather strident, tone of *Echo* editorials on the Barrage campaign was a much-needed counterweight.

Meanwhile, Cardiff Flood Action Committee had also commissioned a report, on the likely effect of the Barrage on groundwater levels in the city, from an independent consultant geologist, Dr Stuart Noake. His report was completed in February 1988. It concluded that the model used by CBDC's own consultants, Wallace Evans and Partners in their 1987 technical feasibility report for the Welsh Office was inaccurate and inadequate, since it did not take into account 'changes in seasonal rainfall, varying thickness of the aquifer or tidal responses', all variables which could affect water flows underground significantly.[5]

Dr Noake concluded that people near Ninian Park Road could find themselves paddling in water outside and inside their homes, and that a lot more money would have to be spent to solve the problems. David Crompton, CBDC's chief engineer, replied on their behalf; they were quite satisfied that their own predictions were accurate. It was clear that unless they were forced to do so, CBDC were not going to respond seriously to residents' legitimate concerns.

At the same time, there was growing concern about the conflict of interest for the councillors on the CBDC board. There were increasingly vocal complaints from councillors not on the board that they were not getting the information they needed. Paddy Kitson, a member of the CBDC board and chair of SGCC, responded in an equally aggrieved tone, 'Even board members sometimes feel things are proceeding without their knowledge'. John Reynolds, Leader of CCC and another member of the board, was frank about resolving the conflicts of his dual role, '... there can be a different perception of what is best and in those circumstances [a conflict of interest between CBDC and the City Council] I would think that my position would be that, as a member of the Bay board, I would have to abide by the majority on the Bay board.'[6] The alienation and resentment that had plagued earlier Development Corporations was alive and well in Cardiff, in spite of SGCC's insistence on a special constitution, designed to avoid just such failures. It is significant that Councillor Reynolds decided to resolve any conflict between his roles as an elected representative and as a paid member of the CBDC board by deciding to act first as a Board member, possibly at the expense of the interests of those he had been elected to serve.

In its early days, CBDC had commissioned 'a full economic appraisal of the 2700 acres of land and water around Cardiff Bay, both with and without a barrage' from the financial consultants Peat Marwick McLintock (KPMG). The document was intended to provide proof of the essential role that the Barrage had to play in south Cardiff's regeneration; it was expected that the confident assertions of politicians and CBDC board members could in future be supported by KPMG's professional opinion, their reliable economic forecasts and impeccable research. It was due for publication in 1988, and was to be presented to the Welsh Office as the final justification for Mr

Edwards' (or, as he had now become, Lord Crickhowell's) whim. His plan would be shown to be not just an idle thought, or flight of fancy, but an instinctive application of economic truths which KPMG would make explicit and concrete.

Unfortunately, the figures obstinately refused to add up in the Barrage's favour, and draft after draft was sent back to KPMG by the Development Corporation for further revision. It is rumoured that as many as seven different 'drafts for discussion' were produced, before the final report could be sent to the Welsh Office for Peter Walker's approval, in August 1988.

KPMG's last effort looked at two possible scenarios: development with a barrage, and development without a barrage. As part of the 'with barrage' assessment, the possible outcomes of three different designs were contrasted, but the main conclusion demonstrated the superiority of the Barrage options overall, in terms of job creation, property values and leverage (the ratio of likely private investment to public investment).

Like all UDCs, CBDC had the specific purpose of increasing land values; this was its main function. For an increase in property values to be realised, investment was needed, beginning with public investment to provide essential services, which would improve the commercial attractiveness of the area and so bring in private money. The more private pounds that were invested for every public pound spent, the greater the leverage, and the more successful the project would be, or so the financial mantra went. Naturally, KPMG saw leverage and higher property values as the main criteria for success.

However, CBDC had made many serious mistakes in its short existence, alienating much local opinion. It could not afford to make any more. If the Corporation continued to present the redevelopment of south Cardiff as a wealth enhancement scheme for property developers, they would risk losing what little local support they still had. So, the Corporation's claim that its plans would also enhance the quality of life for ordinary Cardiff citizens had to be pushed further up the agenda, at least in public. In an area of high unemployment, job creation was the obvious button to press: with a barrage, lots of jobs, without a barrage, far fewer jobs. Therefore KMPG had to include job creation as one of its three success criteria along with higher property values and greater private investment.

Unfortunately, KPMG's report was worryingly restricted in a number of ways. Its calculations specifically left out all development east of the Bute Dock, more than 30% of CBDC's designated area. The excluded area largely consisted of the site of the former East Moors steelworks, and although KPMG projected considerable development, mostly industrial, for this area, they didn't see it as being 'dependent on the Barrage'.[7]

Because of this extraordinary omission, KPMG did not go on to draw the obvious conclusion: if the level of public investment in infrastructure, other than the cost of building of the Barrage, would be the same in all parts of the Bay area, the leverage ratio for the 'without barrage' option would be considerably improved when East Moors was included. The area was too far from both the water front and the city centre for any investor to consider it suitable for retail or residential development. Therefore any jobs created there would be in industrial or business units. KPMG estimated that 50 jobs per acre would be created in 'modern business units' and 52 per acre in 'industrial/warehousing' throughout the rest of the Bay, whether or not the Barrage was built. On this basis, the number of jobs available in the 'without barrage' scenario increased significantly, throughout the designated area, when East Moors was included, a conclusion ignored by KPMG.

KPMG's 'jobs per acre' calculations were to become a central pillar supporting the pro-barrage case from now on; because, they reasoned, more investment would be attracted with a barrage than without one, then more offices, shops and business units would be built, and the more floor space created, the more jobs there would be to fill that floor space. To neutral observers, it seemed a rather crude argument to justify the investment of more than £80 million of public money. The report concluded that 11,000 jobs would be created as a direct result of the Barrage; only 7100 would appear if it were not built. Significantly, the report failed to mention the 15,000 jobs already existing in CBDC's designated area and what would happen to them when south Cardiff was redeveloped; the notices of possible compulsory purchase sent out to businesses in the Bay only a few months before had cast serious doubt on their future.

The report would also admit no alternative development strategy for the area; it was a barrage, or nothing. Certainly, different sizes of barrage were considered, but there was no acknowledgement that there were any other possible centrepieces for south Cardiff's successful regeneration were possible.

So, of the three criteria against which the economic case for the Barrage would based – job creation, leverage and property values – the report's conclusions about job creation and leverage were both seriously in doubt. It must be remembered that KMPG's projections were the main plank in the case for the Barrage; with the Barrage, land values would rise more significantly, more jobs would come, more private investment would be attracted, than without it – KMPG had said so.

The next step in the argument for the Barrage would be to insist, as its supporters often did, that without it the development of south Cardiff would be doomed to the second division; to argue against the Barrage was henceforth to argue against the development.

Moreover, the final report, sent to the Welsh Office in August 1988, had a very significant omission. In an earlier draft, dated 4th May 1988, the following paragraph appeared,

> In recent discussions with the Treasury over our original barrage appraisal report (October, 1987) they have expressed concern that the inclusion of all the betterment effect [the increase in land and property prices if a barrage was built] may lead to an overstatement of the case.[8]

In other words, Treasury officials believed that the Barrage could not be counted on to generate the profits which KPMG and CBDC were hoping for. It must be remembered that when Nicholas Edwards first suggested the scheme to the Cabinet in 1986, the Treasury had so convinced the Prime Minister that it was deeply flawed, that he had to resort to threats to get approval for his scheme. The offending paragraph, which showed Treasury fears about the Barrage were still alive and well, was omitted from the final version, on which all economic justification of the Barrage scheme was to rest. KPMG apparently made no attempt to address those Treasury concerns in their calculations, which remained substantially the same. But because this vital sentence was left out, Treasury doubts were hidden from Parliament and the public throughout the long years of debate that followed. If they had been made public, the financial case for the Barrage could have been seen for the flimsy structure it was, and the entire project would have been very different. As it happened, the May draft did not come to light until the Barrage was almost complete, and it was too late.

KPMG's view of the Barrage's ability to attract employment to south Cardiff were soon to achieve the status of myth. As the environmental problems of the scheme came to light, with inconvenient speed and frequency, over the coming years, so its supporters placed more and more faith in its potency as an economic catalyst.

Peter Walker, before even seeing their final report, was apparently confident that KPMG understated the case; in a written reply to Ron Davies in June 1988, he had said that, 'The projections undertaken recently for the Cardiff Bay Development Corporation suggest that the project there [the Barrage] could stimulate the creation of almost 30,000 jobs and investment of £1 billion'.[9] Even making allowance for that astute politician's careful 'almost', these figures are definitely an enhanced version of the final report's 11,000 jobs and £826 million respectively. Still, 30,000 and £1 billion were satisfying figures that tripped easily off the tongue, so as the months passed they became the official version of what the Barrage could actually do. These figures made it almost impossible for the most well-informed anti-barrage campaigner to argue against something which could bring such prosperity, for who would willingly deny the unemployed of Cardiff much needed work?

The anti-barrage campaign would clearly prove the fallacy of offering the Barrage as a solution to the problem of Cardiff docklands. As a solution to the problem of Lord Crickhowell's reputation as a dynamic SoS Wales, or Lord Brooks' desire to be seen to as a powerful force in the life of the city, it might be acceptable, but for any other purpose, it was irrelevant; a problem which could spawn only further problems.

The 2700 acres scheduled for redevelopment in CBDC's plans included Ferry Road in Grangetown, the site of the City Council's largest refuse tip. Ferry Road had been used as an official municipal dump for 50 years, and as an unofficial industrial one, for about the same time. It covered more than 60 acres, reaching the banks of the Ely, into which its contents leached consistently, lowering the water quality of that polluted river even more. Unofficial tipping had occurred on a large scale, and for a long time, so there was no knowing what might be in the site, or what would happen if it were disturbed. If the area was to be substantially improved, the tip would have to be closed, and its contents removed.

Moreover, a new home would also have to be found for the 300,000 tons of rubbish Cardiff produced each year. The only suitable site would be an extension of the City's other tip, in Lamby Way, to the east of the city. The only direction in which Lamby Way could extend was across the coastline strip towards the Severn Estuary, destroying more than 500 acres of Grade 1 farmland, and the Gwent Levels, also an SSSI.

As well as concern over the use of Lamby Way as an alternative dump, there was considerable disquiet over the future of the contents of the Ferry Road site – should they be sealed in? should they be moved? what exactly was there? how would the large amounts of methane the tip produced be dealt with, if homes and offices were to be built nearby? GRAB members were especially anxious about the answers to these questions, as the tip was a particularly unloved feature of their neighbourhood.

In May the CBDC would present the detailed regeneration strategy for its sphere of influence, prepared by Llewellyn Davies Planning;

it was to be hoped that these issues would be competently addressed.[10] The plans for the docks area were detailed, authoritative and precise, as one would expect from the justification for such a large public investment and the magnet for an even larger private one. There would be a Maritime Heritage Centre, an International Maritime Park, with an aquarium and botanic gardens, a Corniche coastal route for the PDR, a Skytower and a host of other attractions. This was the Barrage's Unique Selling Point, CBDC asserted – without the Barrage at its heart, few of these enticing projects would get off the ground. Unfortunately, even with the Barrage, most of them didn't.

Meanwhile, public concern was growing over the Barrage's likely effect on groundwater levels in the area. On 23rd May, just before these plans were unveiled, CBDC's chief engineer, David Crompton, stated:

> Anyone living south of the main railway line (dividing the city centre from the docks area) may see the water table below them rise... the result of raising the water level in the Bay to just above the level of neap tides will mean a maximum rise in the Grangetown area's water table of about two metres.[11]

This was a highly contentious statement from at least two points of view. The level of water behind the Barrage was to be 'within the range of 4.00 metres to 5.00 metres or thereabouts above Ordnance Datum' – the level of neap tides could reach 6 metres. Also, as CBDC had already admitted, there were wide variations in the way buildings would be affected by changes in groundwater – 'what they are built on, how much load they put on the ground and how deeply their foundations and cellars have been sunk.' Over the 2700 acres of the development area, including Grangetown, there were considerable variations in all these factors; although, according to an article in the *Echo*, 'The Corporation are already doing a detailed survey and they will pay for work needed.'

In other words, although the survey was not yet completed, CBDC were confident of its findings, and could already predict the costs of the remedial work and compensation, totalling £4 million, that would be needed.

The City Engineer, Mr Gerald Mabb, shared the general disquiet. The draft Barrage Bill which Alun Michael had introduced set a two year deadline for compensation claims. But Mr Mabb advised the City Council's Engineering Committee that this was too short, 'as damage to buildings may not be detected for a long time after the Barrage is built'.[12]

In a response in September, CBDC and SGCC quietly indicated

that the deadline for groundwater compensation claims would be extended to six years. The City Council also decided to bring in an independent consultant, Professor Glyn Jones, of University College, London, to look at the public health consequences of the Barrage.

A major problem for the development of the Bay as tourist/invest-ment attraction was the Central Cardiff outfall, which discharged raw sewage into the Taff, near Grangetown. The City Engineer was very concerned about this problem, which, he reported to the Council, would be made worse by plans for 'a cut and cover' route for the pro-posed PDR – the underground section would sever the major drains for Butetown. The re-routing of drains and sewers would cost CBDC an estimated £11 million.

Just as the new residents' groups were making their presence felt, Cardiff Friends of the Earth published a report on the water quality in the impounded lake. 'The Taff Barrage: the pollution problem' was released in June. It claimed that the amount of bacteria in the lake would be up to four times greater than EC standards. Michael Boyce, the Chief Executive of SGCC responded to the report in a statement to the *Echo*, insisting that these standards referred only to bathing water. It was noteworthy that Mr Boyce tacitly accepted that water quality in the Bay would be poor.

Both the Bill's promoters and the embryo Development Corporation regularly referred to water sports, like water skiing, canoeing, dinghy sailing, as among the attractions of an impounded Cardiff Bay: all of these activities involve a great deal of immersion for the participants, intentional or not. Any material produced by CBDC to publicise the delights of the Bay post-barrage, was always illustrat-ed by an artist's impression of yachts and sailing boats of various kinds, scudding briskly across the lake, with wind-filled sails. Opponents were quick to point out that as far as the risk of ingesting dangerously polluted water goes, there's little difference between div-ing into it for a swim or capsizing your dinghy into it. This Jesuitical distinction between 'immersion' and 'non-immersion' water sports was to figure largely in CBDC's defence of water quality in the Bay.

FoE also drew attention to the failure to inform county councillors of these problems when elected members were asked to support the Barrage Bill. Many of these anxieties had already been highlighted in a report prepared for SGCC by a company called Hydraulics Research; this report was not offered for public discussion as readily as FoE's. The LDP strategy was also discrete about any public health problems the Barrage might cause, with only a brief reference to 'the achievement of water quality standards acceptable to the Welsh Water Authority'.

At this time, the Welsh Water Authority announced its intention of petitioning against the Barrage Bill. Like Cardiff FoE, Welsh Water had doubts about the ability of the County Council to maintain adequate water quality behind the Barrage, especially oxygen content and the control of algal growth. Such a petition was the first step in negotiations with the Bill's promoters which would, it was hoped, amend the Bill to the Authority's satisfaction, before a Select Committee would even meet. Nonetheless, the fact that they felt such negotiations were necessary was not reassuring to the general public.

It transpired that the Development Corporation's strategy was already running into problems on another front. The LDP plan suggested converting the Ferry Road tip into a 'parkland for high quality modern business uses'[13]. However, in the wake of a number of serious accidents caused by explosions in housing developments on former tips, government guidelines stated that housing developments should be banned within 100 metres from such sites. At Ferry Road, it was proposed to build on top of the tip itself. In reply, CBDC proposed that the dump 'would be compacted and covered', at a cost of £4.3 million.[14]

The growing public awareness of the problems caused by the Barrage, and the escalating cost of putting them right was turning into serious concern. It was at this time that CBDC and its supporters began to use a defensive technique which rapidly become a familiar part of their response to any criticism of the blocking of the estuary. They pretended that the main argument against the Barrage was a conservation one – based on the loss of the wading birds' habitat. This they weighed in the balance against the thousands of jobs the Barrage would bring, sometimes 30,000, sometimes 20,000, depending on who was speaking, and, naturally, there could be no contest. The arguments about water quality, groundwater, public health and costs were dismissed as mere corollaries to the worries about the birds. For instance, an editorial in the *Echo* on 3rd August, used this ploy very neatly,

> There is great respect for the environmental case but nothing in nature is permanent and natural changes have forced successful adaptation in the past and will do so again... Other problems associated with the barrage, pollution, the higher water table and flooding must all be overcome with confidence and efficiency.

As well as fast forwarding the whole complex and time-consuming business of natural selection on behalf of the Bay's bird population, CBDC would apparently solve all the difficulties the Barrage would bring by good management and force of character. The editorial made no mention of that other essential – money in large quantities – but all over south Cardiff, people were starting to do some adding up, and the totals looked worrying.

Residents' groups had studied the Wallace Evans report on groundwater, with great concern. They were particularly worried that it showed little awareness of south Cardiff's egregious geology, and therefore could not assess the full consequences of the scheme. At a meeting with CFAC in September 1988, the Corporation took the very unusual step of agreeing to commission an assessment of their own report from an expert of CFAC's own choosing. The expert was Stuart Noake, who had already done a report on the Barrage for CFAC. His assessment was highly critical of WEP's methodology, which he considered should throw serious doubt on their conclusions. The City council, too, did not feel able to repose full confidence in CDBC's experts, and sent copies of their findings to its own consultants, Professor J Lloyd of Birmingham University, and Wimpey Laboratories.[15]

As the months passed, more and more of the problems the Barrage would bring came to public view. Due to the large amount of publicity it attracted, and the vigour of the campaign against it, the Corporation had to be seen to be dealing with the problems, all of which would cost money. The disposal of dangerous waste, water oxygenation, pollution control, clearing algal bloom, remedying the damage done by rising groundwater, 'alternative feeding grounds' for wading birds, all would need initial capital outlay, and most would have ongoing costs during the life of the Barrage.

There was also the interesting problem of how such costs would be met after CBDC's legal life came to an end, in 1996 – central government? the Welsh Office? the local councils? In an attempt to allay these anxieties, it was proposed that a proportion of all private investment in the Bay would be allocated to a 'sinking fund' to cover the costs; the proposal did not get an official sanction until the Barrage Bill's Second Reading in the House of Commons, in 1989, when Alun Michael announced, 'Initially the corporation will fund the [barrage] running costs. After its dissolution, it is intended to create a fund from assets to enable the successor body to pay for operating costs.' Nothing more was ever heard of this sinking fund, but the announcement of its possible existence helped to sustain the illusion that the mounting costs of Lord Crickhowell's whim would not be a burden on the public purse.

But many people were still wondering whether anyone in authority was taking the trouble to work out at what point the legendary extra investment attracted by the project would be completely cancelled out by the cost of protecting Cardiff from its ravages. Its supporters maintained a rather loud silence on the matter.

Concern about the effects of the Barrage was spreading to other local groups as well. The Bay was a major sailing centre, with a yacht club of more than 700 members, who used the moorings in the Taff estuary as a base for sailing in the Bristol channel. The 'superb maritime city' foretold by CBDC would have at its heart a barrage which denied ready access to the sea, indeed, one would not be able to even see the sea from Cardiff Bay.

Cardiff Yacht Club, under the leadership of its redoubtable commodore, Mrs Judith Keenor were already making representations against the Barrage, to CBDC. They were joined by the freshwater fishermen of the Taff: members of the Welsh Salmon and Trout Association were concerned at the lack of access Taff salmon would have to the river, when they returned to their home waters to spawn each year, if there was a barrage blocking their route. Certainly, there would be fish passes in the structure, but how would the salmon know where to find them? There were few precedents for such a solution; in spite of CBDC's assurances about the orienteering abilities of breeding salmon, the anglers also went public on their opposition to the Barrage.

The Cardiff Green Party, which had then around 40 active members, was looking for a focus, a way of making its presence felt on a significant local issue, and the Barrage provided the perfect opportunity. It embodied all the things which the Green Party rejected – it was wasteful, unnecessary, environmentally damaging, undemocratic, very expensive and a prime example of top-down policy making. The Corporation prided itself on a policy of open discussion and debate with interested local groups. What this actually involved was anxious local people sitting quietly, they hoped, and listening while CBDC's senior executives tried to set their minds at rest with the maximum of hopeful reassurance, and the minimum of fact and proof. But, it was felt that the Corporation should be given a fair hearing, so, a delegation of three Greens met Barry Lane, the Corporation's Chief Executive, during the summer, at CBDC's offices.

It was an extraordinary exercise in mutual incomprehension. Mr Lane began by trying to establish his own environmental credentials: 'You love trees, I love trees, we're all Green, aren't we?' He was deeply concerned at the lack of homes in Cardiff in the £100,000 range (at 1988 prices) to attract the sort of people the development of south Cardiff needed, such homes were essential; senior managers of the right calibre would accept no less. He was a little vague about where these houses would be built, probably not in Cardiff Bay itself... But the Barrage and the investment it would bring were essential to such residential enhancements for the city. He was also concerned about improving the character of the area round the former goods railway terminus near the East Bute Dock. Mr Lane was relieved to find his visitors were not intimately acquainted with this neighbourhood, which he described as 'a haunt of prostitutes and panel beaters'. This extraordinary combination of livelihoods had apparently captured the imaginations of senior members of the Corporation, who saw it as part of the Barrage's *raison d'être* to banish sex workers and scrap metal dealers, along with the wading birds and an acceptable water table, from Tiger Bay.

During the summer the Greens brought together an alliance of all the groups across the city opposed to the Barrage, to focus publicity and obtain maximum exposure for the arguments against it. The AntiBarrage Consortium included Cardiff Flood Action, FoE, the Severn Estuary Conservation Group, Cardiff Yacht Club, Taff Housing Association and the Anglers. The press launch was held in early September, at the Channel View Leisure Centre, in Grangetown, overlooking the mudflats, with a prospect of small sailing ships at their moorings, and water fowl foraging along the river edge.

The event received sympathetic press coverage, but it was the response of CBDC's Barry Lane, that really attracted attention. He was incandescent,

> What is this consortium? It is not elected as they are self-appointed representatives. You will find they are all unemployed people who spend their life fighting development. They are cynical and I detest cynicism, I want to be positive. If investors are put off by continual whinging, they will go elsewhere... They are mad, absolutely mad. Do they believe they can create a social empire [*sic*]?[16]

Ironically, most the speakers at the launch were constitutionally elected representatives of their organisations; no one had elected Mr Lane. Sadly, the unemployed seemed to be one group not represented among the launch speakers – zoologist, town planner, clerk of works, teacher, computer programmer, librarian... Mr Lane might have been happier with a group he could dismiss as Rent-a-Mob, but the arguments put forward were too serious to be answered so easily.

CBDC feared public dissent about the Barrage, they said, because it might put possible investors off. To justify their reluctance to debate the issues, enticing glimpses were given of the interest shown by developers, in the local press,

Major firms, many of them from overseas, are queuing up to invest in Cardiff Bay, with a variety of projects ranging from a theme park to offices. They are ready to pour millions of pounds into developing south Cardiff, including the building of the most modern planetarium in the world. As well as inquiries from scores of British companies, approaches have been made by Japanese, Saudi Arabian, Canadian, German and Norwegian businesses.

'Their schemes will create many thousands of long-term jobs,' said Mr Barry Lane.

But he warned that investors would quickly look elsewhere if they did not believe the people of Cardiff were totally behind the plans to bring life back to the city's old industrial heartland.

'The only thing which can drive away jobs is the negative attitude of some people in Cardiff, some of whom seem determined to go behind our backs and create doubts,' said Mr Lane. 'It is time for everyone to stand up and be counted – not to try to find fault all the time and force companies to take their jobs to other cities.'

... he said they still regarded as essential the building of a barrage to hold back the waters of the rivers Taff and Ely.

'It is the environment created by the lake that is attracting potential investors, and those who say they want redevelopment but not the barrage are settling for second best,' he added.[17]

It must be remembered that at this point the exact contents of the Barrage Bill had not yet been formally approved by its sponsors, the County Council, nor had they been debated fully in Parliament, let alone become law. As far as potential investors were concerned, there was no guarantee that it would be built anyway, whether there was local opposition to it or not. In strictly legal terms, CBDC had no right to present it as a *fait accompli* to any third party. There was no doubt that the people of Cardiff supported any attempt to revive the Docks, but a substantial number of them had serious doubts about the Barrage, a fact that the Corporation's spokespeople could not bring themselves to accept or accommodate, whether face to face or behind their backs.

In the event, only one Japanese company, Nippon Electric Glass (NEG), set up business in the Bay; their glassworks on the seaward side of the Alexandra Dock, in partnership with Schott Glaswerke of Germany, came to Cardiff because this site offered them essential access to the open sea; so, for them the Barrage was of no account. No Saudi, Canadian or Norwegian businesses followed up those first enquiries.

But Mr Lane's remarks did make one thing clear, the Corporation saw the Barrage and redevelopment as inseparable. The scheme's opponents feared that no matter how many faults were found, the whole project would go ahead. It was a test of the city's nerve, of its machismo – only wimps had doubts and wanted their questions answered. It seemed the Barrage was not a matter for debate. There was no going back; it could be shown to be economically unjustifiable, wasteful and dangerous, but, by God, it would be built; too many important people had taken this whim too seriously, too publicly, for it to be abandoned, no matter what its flaws might be.

In October, the County Council set its final seal of approval on the scheme, by voting to sponsor the Private Member's Bill, by which it would eventually become law. There had been no doubt that this first hurdle would be successfully passed, but CBDC must have been gravely concerned at the amount of lobbying of councillors the AntiBarrage Consortium (ABC) was doing. ABC's case was implicitly endorsed by two reports produced for the City Council in the weeks leading up to the crucial council vote. One confirmed the high cost of dealing with the waste dumps in the redevelopment area, which CBDC insisted the City Council should meet. The other, from the City's Environmental Services Director, gave details about the probable effects of algal bloom, which would increase water toxicity in the impounded Bay; water quality was among the public health responsibilities of the City Council.

However, the Council debate and its pro-barrage vote had an interesting sequel, less than a week later. The South Glamorgan and Cardiff sections of the Labour Party, representing the rank and file membership of the party locally, as well as Labour councillors, published their own response to the Corporation's development strategy. It made clear that the vote by most Labour councillors was not an accurate reflection of members' views on the issue. In a statement to *The Western Mail*, Mike Harries, Secretary of the Cardiff City District Labour Party said,

> Currently, the CBDC has no fallback position and, worse still, is offering a hostage to fortune. If, owing to CBDC's publicity, investors see the bay with the barrage as the necessary green light, they will see the bay without a barrage as a failure from the start. The Labour Party wants this redevelopment to succeed and we cannot believe the CBDC can be so short-sighted as to have no plans without the barrage.[19]

That the local Labour party should take up a position of such scepticism about the Barrage, albeit sympathetic scepticism, says a great deal for the AntiBarrage Consortium's credibility and campaigning strategy. They could face the parliamentary tests to come confidently and in good heart.

4. The Barrage Bill in the Lords, or, Pulling a Cow up the Matterhorn

I give credit to the promoters for their pertinacity, but when thinking of this proposal I was reminded of a remark I heard in my
younger days, when I did some modest climbing in the Swiss Alps,
'You can pull a cow up the Matterhorn if you are prepared to pay
enough guides, but is it worth it?' There is no doubt that one can
clear the algae, divert the midges and do all those other things if
one is prepared to spend vast sums of money; but one must ask
oneself whether it is worth it.

> Baroness White during the Second Reading debate in the
> House of Lords on the Cardiff Bay Barrage Bill, 23rd
> February, 1989

One cold December evening in 1988, the most important meeting in
the anti-barrage campaign so far was held in the offices of the Taff
Housing Association in Lower Cathedral Road. It was attended by
representatives of most of the Residents' Groups who wished to petition against the Cardiff Bay Barrage Bill, due to have its Second
Reading in the House of Lords in February. As the Barrage would
block a navigable waterway, it would require a specific Act of
Parliament to permit its construction. This process excluded any possibility of the public planning enquiry which contentious projects on
such a scale would usually require, so petitioning, and appearing
before, parliamentary Select Committees would be the only chance
opponents of the scheme would have to stop or delay it.

The meeting was chaired by Kevin Standring, Deputy Head of
Conservation Planning at the RSPB, and its purpose was to decide on
joint strategy. Kevin was an accredited Parliamentary Agent; he was
recognised, in the words of the Private Bills Office, as 'in every way a
respectable person', who was entitled to appear before Select
Committees of both Houses of Parliament. In the hearings of Select
Committees, Parliamentary Agents could take on the role of solicitors
or barristers in a law court – presenting arguments, examining and
cross-examining witnesses, generally orchestrating the presentation of
a case. RSPB, as one of the UK's largest and most active conservation
groups, found it useful for several senior staff to be accredited in this
way. They played a vital role in mitigating the potential environmental damage of much recent legislation; the Barrage Bill, with the

inevitable destruction of the Cardiff Bay SSSI, was a perfect example.

The RSPB was well aware that the politicians who sat on Select Committees, or who read their subsequent reports, were much more inclined to listen sympathetically to the case made by local people against bills like the Barrage Bill, than the arguments of conservationists with few or no local connections. Hence Peter Ferns' earlier liaison between the RSPB and the Cardiff Flood Action Committee; as a result, the RSPB was prepared to provide the residents' groups with the services of a parliamentary agent.

It was clear from the start of the meeting that Kevin relished this particular role, just as, over the next four years, he was to thoroughly enjoy working with the members of Cardiff's lively and varied anti-barrage movement. He was an impressive, compelling character, physically compact, active and purposeful, with a bristling moustache that seemed a powerful energy conductor, a penetrating gaze which missed little and a vigorous, easy laugh. Like most of the Bill's opponents, he appreciated the pleasures of argument and debate, especially when, as in this instance, the case was good and the opposition was vulnerable on a wide range of issues.

Everyone else at the meeting looked to Kevin for advice and information on how to make their way through the parliamentary minefield opening up before them. He confirmed that the system was inflexible and not exactly user-friendly. Select Committees and their clerks followed a strict timetable; notice of intent to petition, the petitions themselves and the fees for doing so ($£2$ for the petition itself, and $£2$ for each day the Select Committee would take to consider it) had to be presented at the Private Bills Office on pre-arranged dates. The clerk to the committee would require that a timetable of appearances was drawn up and strictly adhered to. If a petition was to be presented in person then the petitioner had to appreciate that he or she was there on sufferance: no one had the right to appear before such a Select Committee. The assumption had to be that if committee members found a petitioner's behaviour or language unacceptable for any reason, they were under no obligation to listen further or to give reasons for refusing to do so.

As Kevin described in detail the esoteric and often arcane rituals of parliamentary procedure, it began to dawn on his audience that they had acquired not only a friendly adviser, but also a vital combination of shepherd and sheepdog. The whole petitioning process seemed specifically designed to remind those who invoked it of the power and majesty of Parliament, rather than to help them get a fair hearing.

It was quite clear what the substance of their petitions would be.

The reports by CBDC's consultants, Wallace Evans, had clearly shown that potentially damaging changes in the water table would take place as a direct result of the impoundment of the Barrage. Reports by the City Council's Planning Officer and the Welsh Water Authority had shown that the water quality in the impounded Bay would be poor enough to be a risk to public health. If enough well-argued, well-presented petitions were put before the committee, with support from expert witnesses, requiring appropriate safeguards against these threats, then the inadequate protection measures already in the Bill would have to be beefed up considerably. This would add substantially to the cost of building and maintaining the Barrage.

The most recent report on the effects of the Barrage supported this theory. Under an EC Directive of 1985, (85/337/EEC), and the UK's Town and Country Planning (Assessment of Environmental Effects) Regulations 1988 (SI 1199) all major development projects had to be the subject of an environmental assessment of their impact on 'human beings, flora, fauna, soil, water, air, climate, the landscape and the interaction between any of the foregoing.' Although such assessments were not yet compulsory for any projects instigated by Private Bills, in April 1988, WEP, on behalf of CBDC and the County Council, had commissioned such a report into the environmental effects of the Barrage from the Environmental Advisory Unit of Liverpool University (EAU). Their findings were published in February, 1989. The main conclusions were not comforting for the Bill's promoters. For instance;

> The impacts of alternative project options were not included in our terms of reference. Possible alternatives to the proposed barrage did not fulfil the objectives of the Promoters, or were rejected on economic grounds. They have not, therefore, been subject to a full environmental assessment, although it appears that some alternatives would offer fewer environmental costs and more environmental benefits than the proposed scheme.[1]

Once again no other possible centrepieces for the regeneration project were envisaged – it was a barrage, THIS barrage, or nothing.

When the EAU looked at the fate of the birds whose habitat the scheme would destroy, and the alternative feeding grounds suggested for them, they concluded,

> It cannot be expected that the birds displaced from Cardiff Bay will be accommodated elsewhere in the Severn or another estuary... The creation of new intertidal mudflats as a mitigation measure must be regarded as an innovative, but essentially experimental technique... The lagoon does not provide a complete

compensation for the loss of habitat in Cardiff Bay.[2]

In other words, the expense of constructing and managing alternative feeding grounds could well be wasted.

The petitioners believed that, at some point, someone in CBDC,
the County Council, the Welsh Office or even Parliament itself, would
have to notice that all these costs – groundwater protection, water
quality improvement, alternative feeding grounds – would outweigh
any financial benefits of the scheme, and less damaging alternatives
would have to be considered.

The wording of the petitions had to follow a prescribed format,
which was splendidly orotund, magisterial in its authority and confidence; it seemed more appropriate to the age of Robert Walpole than
that of Margaret Thatcher.

> To the Honourable the Commons of the United Kingdom of
> Great Britain and Northern Ireland in Parliament assembled.
> THE HUMBLE PETITION of ... SHEWETH as follows:-
> A Bill (hereinafter referred to as 'the Bill') has been introduced
> and is now pending in your Honourable House intituled ...
> YOUR PETITIONERS therefore humbly pray your
> Honourable House that the Bill may not be allowed to pass into
> law as it now stands and that they may be heard by their Counsel,
> Agents and witnesses in support of the allegations of this Petition
> against... the property, rights and interests of your Petitioners and
> in support of such other clauses and provisions as may be neces-
> sary or expedient for the protection, or that such other relief may
> be given to your Petitioners in the premises as your Honourable
> House shall deem meet.
> AND your Petitioners will ever pray &c...[3]

It referred to a world far removed from groundwater levels, midge
infestation and the development potential of Cardiff Docks, but it was
the only language in which the anti-barrage case could be put, just as
a Select Committee was the only available forum in which that case
could be heard, so the campaigners would have to make the best of it.

The Second Reading of the Bill in the Lords was planned for
February, 1989, so a Select Committee of the Upper House would
probably consider it in March or April. This meant that a great deal
of work had to be done very quickly by the campaigners. Requests to
petition had to be prepared and sent to the Private Bills Office; the
petitions themselves had to be drafted, presentations to the
Committee had to be got ready, and expert witnesses chosen and
briefed. As well as being eminent in their particular fields, witnesses
for the petitioners would have to be prepared to appear for very modest fees, or even no fee at all; fortunately, there were several willing to

do so. Simultaneously the anti-barrage arguments had to be kept
before the increasingly apprehensive people of Cardiff, and potential
sympathisers in the Lords had to be canvassed and briefed.

It was impossible for Kevin to co-ordinate the preparation of all
the petitions – so the work was delegated to particular members of the
petitioning groups, to firm guidelines set out by the RSPB, based on
experience in earlier campaigns. As for keeping the campaign in the
public eye, further community meetings were arranged, and it was
deemed that the movement needed a clearer identity, an image to set
alongside CBDC's logos and glossy publicity leaflets.

Here the anti-barrage campaign was very fortunate. Sue Pomeroy,
a graphic artist and illustrator from Florida, had recently moved to
Pontcanna, with her husband Boyd, a double-bass player in the
National Orchestra of Wales. Both had embraced the campaign with
enthusiasm and Sue had generously put her skills at its disposal. Her
elegant designs, based on the birds of the estuary, appeared on T-
shirts and balloons, posters and letterheads, car stickers and leaflets,
enhancing the image of the anti-barrage campaign immensely, giving
it grace and authority. Sue's presence at any public meeting or debate,
always brought a certain piquancy to the proceedings – to hear
Cardiff's present attractions and future development discussed with
vigorous commitment and enthusiasm in a Florida accent could
entrance even the most entrenched pro-barrage supporters.

The task of identifying possible sympathisers in the Lords and
ensuring they attended the Second Reading Debate, as well as briefing them fully on all barrage-related matters fell to Cardiff Green
Party members. Political parties as such could not petition, unless, like
Riverside Ward Labour Party, they were based in the area affected by
the Bill. So, getting briefing notes out to peers whose known concerns
meant that they would take more than a passing interest in the Cardiff
Bay Barrage, was their role. Kevin was able to pass on a core list,
drawn from previous campaigns, and a trawl through the latest edition
of *Dods* produced some more environmentally sensitive peers. Of
course, CBDC had been doing exactly the same thing, backed up with
more personal contact. Lords Brooks and Crickhowell must have had
a quiet word with many of their colleagues in bar and tea room; Mr
Inkin had confided in fellow quango members, and thus several influential minds were, as their replies confirmed, quite made up.

The debate in the Lords was formal and concerned, rather than
passionate or rigorous. As fifteen petitions against the Bill had already
been received, it would automatically be considered by a Select
Committee, which would have much more time than their Lordships
to assess its provisions. The main purpose of the debate was to high-

light issues which the Committee was advised to consider in more detail, rather than to thrash out the worth of the Bill *per se.*

Lord Brooks moved the Second Reading and spoke in support of the Bill, with a lengthy endorsement from Lord Crickhowell. As expected, they presented the Barrage as an essential economic catalyst, creating jobs and bringing prosperity, not just to Cardiff, but to the whole of south-east Wales.

The chief speakers against the Bill, Lord Moran and Baroness White, were clear about their support for the redevelopment planned for Cardiff Bay. Yet both adopted a tone of polite scepticism about the need for a barrage and expressed grave doubts about its ability to attract enough investment to justify its costs.

Lord Moran had had a long and distinguished diplomatic career, had won the Whitbread Prize for biography in 1973 for a book on Henry Campbell-Bannerman and, more germane, was Chair of the NRA's Regional Fisheries Advisory Committee for the Welsh Region, President of the Welsh Salmon and Trout Angling Association and Vice-Chairman of the Atlantic Salmon Trust. He was therefore very knowledgeable about matters like water quality and conservation, which were a significant part of the anti-barrage case. He declared,

> I am not convinced that such a barrage is an indispensable part of the development of Cardiff Bay... Much of the area being developed is not round the estuary at all, but to the east of it... I think we should not agree to their [the existing landlords in the Bay, such as ABP, British Rail and the city council] making money at the expense of the quality of life of other people... The barrage appears to have been planned before there was a full understanding of the environmental problems...[4]

As a member of the Lords sub-committee of the European Communities Committee concerned with the environment, he was anxious about the fate of the SSSI.

> For this House to agree the destruction of a very important SSSI on grounds other than overriding national necessity would, I believe, be bad in itself and an extremely unfortunate precedent.

In a full and well-informed exposition of the other problems the Barrage would cause, his lordship noted,

> It [the Select Committee] should make sure that the water quality problems can and will be solved and the necessary finance provided now and in the years to come when the CBDC may no longer exist and local people and their councils may be left to foot the bill.

He concluded

> A tidal exclusion barrage is not the only solution. Alternatives should be very carefully considered. Just before the debate started I had a very swift glance at the environmental study [the Liverpool University environmental impact assessment]. On page 73 it mentions alternatives to the proposed barrage. The advisory unit did not conduct full environmental studies of them and says that these studies have not therefore "been subject to a full environmental assessment, although it appears that some alternatives would offer fewer environmental costs and more environmental benefits than the proposed scheme." The Committee should take note of that.[5]

Only time would tell whether the Committee's members would fulfil Lord Moran's high expectations.

Baroness White spoke more briefly, but her concerns over water quality in the impounded lake carried equal force, as she had a home in Riverside herself. She too was anxious about the costs of maintaining 'the kind of fresh water lake that people will want... if one is prepared to spend vast sums of money; but one must ask oneself whether it is worth it'.[6]

There was a certain symmetry in the interests of the supporters of the Bill, and those of the two main objectors. Lord Crickhowell and Lord Moran both held office in the NRA, and were keen fly fishermen: Lord Brooks and Baroness White both lived in Cardiff and were highly influential in the Welsh Labour Party. But unlike their fellow peers, neither Lord Moran nor Baroness White had staked their considerable reputations on the Barrage, and thus could afford the luxury of open minds and pertinent questions.

The debate included an interesting intervention from Lord Trefgarne, who set aside his usual brief as Minister of State for Defence Procurement to make plain the government's grounds for supporting the Bill. He faithfully trotted out the CBDC case,

> The Government have weighed these environmental costs – and we certainly accept that they are costs in respect of lost feeding habitats for the birds – against the paramount importance of realising economic, recreational and other benefits that can be expected to arise from a barrage.[7]

Lord Crickhowell's response to the points put by Baroness White and Lord Moran was also predictable, 'Given the choice between the possible loss of some waders and the huge gains in terms of living conditions, employment prospects and economic health of hundreds of thousands of people in a region that has suffered for too long, I come down on the side of the human beings.'[8] Of course, His

Lordship was too modest to mention the huge gains for landowners in the area, like ABP, of which he had the great good fortune to be a director. He also, as so often in this story, failed to map out the exact route the people of Cardiff were meant to travel, from the Barrage to the goal of greater quality of life.

He reminded his audience that, where Private Bills such as this were concerned, the burden of investigating its full implications should fall on the Select Committee; his lordship was apparently very happy for matters like water quality, groundwater changes and public health to be left to its members. Like Lord Brooks, he did not refer or respond to Lord Moran's plea that feasible alternatives to the Barrage should be explored.

As the Bill was to be considered by a Select Committee, there was no vote at the end of the debate. However, Lord Moran had been concerned that the petitions already lodged did not refer to two issues which he felt the Select Committee should consider – water quality and fish migration. He could speak with considerable authority on both issues, as Chair of the NRA's Regional Fisheries Advisory Committee for the Welsh Region. It was known that his views about the NRA's role in supporting the future of fly fishing differed significantly from those of its Chair, Lord Crickhowell, which added a certain edge to the debate. Parliamentary procedures allowed the Lords to instruct select committees to examine matters referred to during Second Reading debates, and on his suggestion, the Instruction was agreed. Afterwards, the House moved on to discuss the Code of Recommendations for the Welfare of Goats.

The first Select Committee on the Cardiff Bay Barrage Bill – there were to be four on the various Barrage Bills altogether – met on 11th April, 1989, in the one of the imposing committee rooms at the Palace of Westminster. The Committee Chair was Lord Elibank, a Conservative, former barrister and personnel consultant. He was supported by two other Conservative peers, the Earl of Halsbury and Lord Belhaven & Stenton, with Lord Foot, a frontbench spokesman for the Social and Liberal Democrat Party, and Lord Galpern, a Labour former Provost of Glasgow, a man who, like Lord Brooks, had risen through the ranks of local government.

The RSPB, the other naturalists' groups and Cardiff Flood Action, would be represented before the Committee by John Popham, a colleague of Kevin Standring, who was temporarily occupied elsewhere. John Brookes would speak for Taff Housing and the South Riverside Community Centre: Peter Davies, a Cardiff barrister, for the Docks Residents and Tenants Association: Susan Hamilton for the NCC, and Mr Glyn Paul, as always, for himself.

Before the Select Committee proceedings began, the anglers reached an accommodation with CBDC over the design of the Barrage fish passes and withdrew their petition. During the hearing, it was announced that the Yacht Clubs had also withdrawn their petition, after CBDC agreed to build an extra lock in the Barrage and protect moorings in Cardiff and Penarth.

But first, the Select Committee was to hear the case for the promoters. Their legal team of three barristers was headed by Peter Boydell QC, one of the leaders of the planning bar. He would have been familiar with Cardiff, as he had appeared for the developers at the public enquiry into the ill-fated Ravenseft development in the early 70s, when ambitious and locally unpopular plans to gut and completely rebuild the city centre had been defeated. More recently, he had appeared for Bristol City Council at another House of Lords Select Committee, deliberating on the plans of the Bristol Urban Development Corporation.

The main thrust of his argument was that the Barrage was essential to the development of south Cardiff; in particular, the attraction of the lake it would create would make a significant difference to private investment in the area, and any problems it would cause could be dealt with quite satisfactorily, by adaptations to the Bill. A number of witnesses were called to testify in support of this case. An important part of their argument was by now very familiar; companies which would relocate to Cardiff Bay if there was a barrage, would not do so without one.

No representative of any such company was brought before the Select Committee to support this claim. Instead, the sponsors found their expert witnesses among their own employees and appointed advisers, including Barry Lane, the Corporation's CEO, Michael Boyce, South Glamorgan's CEO, Sir Christopher Benson, Chair of the London Docklands Development Corporation and an adviser to CBDC, Paul Orchard-Lisle, a surveyor specialising in work for UDCs, Richard Porter of KPMG, who had worked on the economic appraisal of the Barrage for the Corporation and the WO, and Michael Richardson, Chairman of N.M. Rothschild and Sons (Wales), financial adviser to CBDC. It is interesting to note that the Rothschild office in Cardiff opened shortly before the Bill first appeared, and closed shortly after Mr Richardson's subsequent appearance before the Commons Select Committee on the Barrage Bill. Perhaps they were afraid not enough of the entrepreneurs attracted by the Barrage could afford their interest rates.

Most of Mr Boydell's questions to his witnesses dealt with the betterment of the area which would flow from the Barrage, corroborated by their experiences with similar projects, and figures from the latest of the many drafts of the KPMG economic appraisal.

Counsel and agents for the petitioners took the opportunity to cross-examine each witness, and made a number of telling points, such as the alarming discrepancy between the private/public investment leverage of 4:1 suggested by Richard Porter of KPMG and that of 10:1 calculated by Michael Richardson of Rothschild, or the fact that successful developments were already underway in London Docklands, Liverpool and Bristol, all overlooking large expanses of mudflats, without benefit of barrage. They also made much of revisions to likely costs and benefits in successive versions of the economic appraisals, some with apparently very little substance; as Susan Hamilton pointed out in her cross-examination of Richard Porter, the whole issue of betterment of land values in a 'with barrage' scenario, the main justification for the project, was 'a matter of judgement, of assessment and experience... It is not something we can find a real figure for.' John Popham pressed the point further in his cross examination, 'These assumptions often have a strong degree of subjectivity, especially with regard to the issues [land use] we are talking about here?', and Mr Porter could only agree.[9]

During his appearance, Geoffrey Inkin was keen to establish the source of funding for the Barrage. John Popham asked, 'Do I understand that £250m will come straight from government funding and the £150m will come from increased land values?' Mr Inkin replied, 'No. £75m-£125m is the sum, to be precise'. One could only hope, for the sake of the Development Corporation's financial health, that its Chair did not really believe that a possible variation of 75% in funding was a sound basis for their activities, or that it was actually a 'precise' figure.[10]

Given the complexity of the financial case for the Barrage, it is perhaps natural that the Committee did not pursue the many contentious points aired in cross-examination. However, their lordships did respond to a suggestion from Mr Popham that the authors of the KPMG report would have felt bound to produce figures favourable to the 'with barrage' case. Lord Foot asked Richard Porter '...your calculations are all based on material which is provided to you by the Development Corporation?' To which the reply was, 'Yes. It is provided by them and, of course, provided to them by professional advisers.'[11]

In a supposedly wealth-generating project, like the Barrage, the objectivity of experts and advisers whose evidence is used to demonstrate its viability should always be a mater for debate. It must be much more so when its promoters, like Lord Crickhowell and Lord

Brooks, have made it clear that the entire Cardiff Bay regeneration could not succeed without it. In such circumstances, can one imagine a geologist, town planner or economist telling the body that paid their fees, and offered the possibility of further work, that their dream could not be realised? But to raise such a question, in particular circumstances like these, about particular individuals, would be to cast doubt on their probity, and so a vital note of caution could not be sounded explicitly to their Lordships. However, as their Lordships' final report on the proceedings showed, they would not have been very receptive to such a suggestion.

There were also exchanges which neatly illustrated the wide gap between the world of the Promoters, where big money chased even bigger money from one ambitious scheme to another, and the more modest, down to earth concerns of the petitioners. At one point, Lord Galpern asked Michael Richardson of Rothschild's if he was a bird watcher; he replied, 'I don't think I can say I am. I sometimes shoot pheasant...'[12]

On the eighth day of the Committee proceedings, it was the turn of the petitioners to present their case. The RSPB and the other conservation bodies took the line that the Barrage was not essential for redevelopment, and therefore the destruction of the SSSI in Cardiff Bay was unnecessary. They were therefore concerned to emphasise the flaws in the pro-barrage case presented by KPMG, and provide evidence to show that successful development was possible with the saltmarsh and mudflats of the Bay intact.

The first petitioner to be heard was Peter Ferns, on behalf of the RSPB, and local naturalists' groups. He emphasised the importance of cleaning up the waterfront and the tidal mudflats, to present the Bay as a local nature reserve, an attraction in its own right. In his cross-examination, Peter Boydell pointed out that the Taff estuary was not mentioned in certain bird-watching guides for the UK; Dr Ferns replied that such guides would direct people to the most appealing sites, and, at present, Cardiff Bay, 'with the poor quality of the immediate surroundings, the industrial dereliction, the refuse-strewn foreshore', was certainly not one of them.[13]

The Committee questioned him about the possibility that ducks and other waterfowl would colonise the impounded lake and replace the wading birds on the mudflats. He contrasted the present status of the two species, 'waders, despite the high level of protection they have, as we have heard, in the form of SSSIs, are not doing so well. They are the group of species that require more protection at the moment and that is why we do not regard the replacement of the waders by freshwater wildfowl as being something that is worthwhile.'[14] The

Barrage Bill included provision to a replacement feeding ground for the waders at Wentloog on the Gwent Levels, but, as Peter Ferns commented, it would be only a third of the size of the mudflats.

In support of his petition, Dr Ferns called Anthony Goss, a consultant on planning and urban design, and a former professor of town planning. Mr Goss had a longstanding connection with Cardiff, and was convinced that the former docklands were already being redeveloped successfully, and there was no need for a barrage. He pointed out that, far from being depopulated and vacant, the area had a population of 5000, and about 1000 which firms provided 15,000 jobs. (It is significant that these figures were not contested in cross-examination). He was convinced that south Cardiff did not need a regeneration strategy of its own; such plans 'should be within a wider planning context, a wider planning strategy for the city as a whole, and for its hinterland.' He felt strongly that 'the democratic consultation process is… being pre-empted by the Cardiff Bay regeneration strategy… Even though we are told the strategy is a vision and that it is infinitely flexible, it has taken the form of a plan in my opinion; a non-statutory plan with barrage [*sic*] as a fixed point'.[15]

Mr Goss was followed by John Bowers, Senior Lecturer in Economics at Leeds University, and an expert in cost benefit analysis on long-term environmental projects, who counted several government departments among his clients. His submission was a comprehensive destruction of the KPMG appraisal, on which the whole economic case for the Barrage rested.

Mr Bowers pointed out that all government departments, including the Department of the Environment and the Welsh Office, had to follow Treasury guidelines in evaluating projects like the Barrage, or produce their own, more detailed, guidelines. He believed KPMG had fallen short of Treasury requirements on several counts. The most important of these was that 'the mechanism by which the project achieves the stated objective has to be made plain and alternative means of meeting the objective stated and evaluated.'[15]

If, as the Bill's promoters asserted, the main objective of the project was the regeneration of the Bay, the appraisal should therefore have explained exactly why and how it was necessary. As Mr Bowers pointed out, none of the many versions of the economic appraisal included such an explanation. He added, 'It is very important that this mechanism should be spelt out so that it may be examined and exposed to criticism.'[16] The implication was that the mechanism had not been spelt out, because such a mechanism did not exist.

To illustrate the confused thinking which resulted, he quoted KPMG's final version, which showed, 'the consequence of building

the Barrage… is a rise in the density of office development on average from 42,000 to 70,000 square feet per acre. One could ask how
does the building of the Barrage bring this about? It is not explained
and it seems to me that obviously building the Barrage does not bring
about such a change in density at all. The higher density could clearly be achieved without a barrage. It may be that average rentals will be
lower if the office development were at the greater density without the
Barrage, if firms are, in fact, willing to pay a premium for proximity
to a lake in contrast with proximity to an estuary, but I think this illus-
trates the point. Since it has not been explained what benefit the lake
confers we have no constraint whatever on what is assumed.'[17]

Mr Bowers went on to examine KPMG's assumptions about the
Barrage's importance as an attraction for investment. He emphasised:

> It is well-known that the bulk of investment attracted to inner city
> areas… is simply transferred from elsewhere within the country,
> much of which is, in fact, relatively short distance moves. Often,
> they are within the region and, in some cases, moves from very
> short distances within the local area… much of the investment
> which is long distance which is attracted as a result of such
> schemes would otherwise have been located in another develop-
> ment area… I do not think this fact of transference is in dispute,
> since the consultants largely admit as much.[18]

He defined the hypothetical benefits brought by the Barrage as:

> … the industry which would not have existed elsewhere in the
> country if the barrage were *not* built. This would be only a small
> part of the total economic activity in the Cardiff Bay area. (My
> italics)[19]

At this point, Lord Elibank broke in to ask, 'If the investment came
from Japan, would the same apply?' Mr Bowers replied, 'No, my
Lord, but the consultants', Peat Marwick McLintock, report says (at
least the original version, not the revised version) that virtually none
of the investment is expected to come from abroad.'[20]

In the event, Mr Bowers was proved perfectly correct – a large
majority of the firms which appeared in Cardiff Bay post-barrage had
relocated from elsewhere in south-east Wales, many of them only
short distances within Cardiff itself.

Under intensive cross-examination by Mr Boydell, Mr Bowers
stuck to his guns, insisting that the economic case for the Barrage
failed to satisfy the Treasury's own requirements. In reply to a question from Lord Galpern, he said 'The Treasury does not ensure that
all cost-benefit analyses conform to guidelines. It asks the parent
departments concerned to do that, as I understand it. The Treasury

view is that it does not have the expertise in land drainage or flood protection or roads or whatever is the appropriate field, to do that. It asks the Departments concerned to do that.'[20]

In other words, it had been the responsibility of the Welsh Office, as 'the parent department concerned', to ensure the guidelines were followed in this instance. As Mr Bowers had shrewdly noted, in a previous reply, 'There may be a political decision to carry out the Cardiff Bay Barrage despite the economic appraisal. My judgement, and I stick to it, is that this economic appraisal does not accord with Treasury guidelines and does not constitute a proper cost-benefit analysis.'[21]

Later, towards the end of the Select Committee's deliberations, Mr Boydell introduced a group of civil servants from the Department of the Environment and the Welsh Office to support the promoters' case on the exact status of SSSIs and any requirements for their protection. It is important to note that he did not call their Treasury colleagues to support the promoters' case on the exact status of the KPMG economic appraisal and any requirements for rigour and consistency.

The next petitioner to appear before their Lordships was Norman Robson, on behalf of Cardiff Flood Action Committee. For the past year, Norman and Charles Burris of CFAC had discussed the draft Barrage Bill, as published in June 1988, with CBDC and the County Council. One of their main concerns was the lack of protection it gave against possible groundwater damage to local properties, especially as it contained clauses offering two of the largest firms owning property in the area, Wiggins Teape of Ely and Associated British Ports, substantial compensation in the event of barrage-related damage. However, the version of the Bill which was presented to the Lords by Lord Brooks, and was currently before the Select Committee, had been revised in an attempt to appear to address some of the issues they had raised.

The most significant addition was Clause 12, which detailed the conditions under which the promoters were prepared to undertake 'remedial works' on property affected by groundwater changes, or other barrage-related damage. This new version of the Bill was accompanied by a plan of south Cardiff, on which two lines had been drawn, dividing the area into three zones; the line nearest the shoreline was called 'the Protected Property Line', and the other 'the further Protected Property Line'. The areas they defined corresponded to the districts which according to CBDC's own reports, were at greatest risk from groundwater changes – those within 'the Protected Property Line' being most at risk, those within 'the further Protected

Property Line' at less risk. All buildings in the area between the shore-line and 'the Protected Property Line' would be surveyed, at the promoters' cost, before impoundment, and again two to five years after impoundment. Any owner or occupier of a building between 'the Protected Property Line' and 'the further Protected Property Line' could request pre- and post-impoundment surveys from the promoters. Claims against the promoters as a result of these surveys could be made up to twenty years after the completion of the Barrage. The owners and occupiers of properties outside both lines would not be entitled to surveys at the promoters' cost, nor was there any provision for them to make claims for damage against CBDC.

When questioned by John Popham, Norman emphasised residents' fears about the inadequacy of the bore-hole readings which WEP had used to define the 'protected' and 'further protected' property areas. Stuart Noake, the groundwater expert brought in at CFAC's request, to scrutinise these findings, would be giving evidence on this later, so, for the time being, Norman described an alternative 'Protected Property Line' which would be more acceptable to CFAC, from Blackweir, where the Taff ceases to be tidal, to the north, to the river Rumney, on the east, to Penarth Cliffs on the west, and bordered by the sea to the south. He also pointed out the unfairness of the twenty year limit on claims for remedial work, in view of the unlimited indemnity the Bill offered ABP and Wiggins Teape (whose paper works on the Ely were one of the area's largest employers). He emphasized the unacceptability of Welsh Water's belief that the Barrage would actually improve flood defences in the area. Norman justified his scepticism by pointing to an official statement that 'The return frequency of these events [severe flooding from the Taff] is in excess of 100 years' – in fact these 'not twice in 100 years' occurrences had already happened twice in the last twenty years.[2]

In his evidence, Dr Noake expressed concern about the failure of the WEP tests to take into account the effects of prolonged rainfall on groundwater levels, especially in the areas where it was admitted groundwater would be 0.5m below the surface post-barrage. He also poured scorn on the rather primitive 'bucket chain' methods used to obtain data from the test boreholes.

Mark Drakeford appeared in support of Riverside Branch Labour Party's petition. He represented Pontcanna ward on the County Council, and was one of the councillors suspended for voting against sponsoring the Barrage Bill. Counsel for the promoters made much of the fact that when SGCC had first voted on the Barrage, he, with Jane Hutt, had voted in favour; but, in November 1988, after Cardiff Flood Action Committee had so successfully revealed the scheme's flaws, they had both voted against it. However, in the most recent vote, in January, with elections to the Council due in only a few weeks, they had once more abstained. To have voted against the Bill a second time, would have been to court expulsion from the County Labour group – certainly they would have forfeited the support of the party in fighting the coming election.

One of the unique planks in Mark's case against the Bill was the absurdity of the 'protected', 'further protected' and unprotected zones. He said

> ... within the area I represent, within less than a five-minute walk you can traverse through all three zones laid out in Clause 12. The same street will have three different sorts of compensation schemes applied to it. Immediately adjacent neighbours will find themselves falling into different zones within the clause.

Nor was he satisfied with the way the lines had been decided on,

> Our problem with that is that having said to us on the earlier occasion that they are perfectly satisfied with their evidence they have subsequently found themselves not to be so satisfied and prepared to change the zones... we do not believe the promoters have an accurate knowledge of the geology of the area. I am sure your Lordships will be aware of Professor Lloyd, who is the City Council's advisor... in his reports he has specifically, specifically, – indicated that the geology of the Pontcanna and North Riverside area is inadequately understood and inadequately explored by the promoters. As a consequence, I think their capacity to draw lines and zones on maps is adversely affected.[23]

As well as supporting her fellow councillor's views, Jane Hutt, the next witness, representing Riverside on the County Council, put forward the particular concerns of her own ward. She referred to a survey done by Wallace Evans, at the request of the Cardiff West MP, Rhodri Morgan, a feasibility study of housing in south Riverside. It suggested that '109 out of the 142 properties that they looked at, in one little block by the river, would be affected by dampness as a result of the Barrage... and would require remedial work.'[24] She added that the resulting uncertainty was a source of great anxiety to people already at risk from poverty and poor housing.

Duncan Longden, the third Labour County Councillor to refuse to vote for the Barrage Bill, appeared before the Committee next. Councillor Longden was not standing for re-election, and so was less indebted to his party leaders than Mark or Jane. He briefly repeated the general points made by his colleagues, but expressed an interesting view of the Barrage's begetter, Lord Crickhowell.

Lord Galpern tried to soothe Councillor Longden's anxiety about water quality – 'I listened to the speech of Lord Crickhowell, Chairman Designate of the National Rivers Authority, on the second Reading of the Water Bill. There is no doubt about it, he is a tough driving chief executive who will get things done. I am certain this new River Authority is going to be an effective body.'²⁵ Either the noble Lord did not know that Lord Crickhowell was the progenitor of the Bill they were considering, which is most unlikely, or he did know, and was sending out a clear signal that he and his colleagues had worked out exactly what conclusions they were to reach about the Bill's future, in view of its begetter's tough, driving qualities. Fortunately, Councillor Longden was not inhibited – he knew Lord Crickhowell too well, in his earlier incarnation as Secretary of State for Wales, to let the matter pass unremarked. He informed Lord Galpern that, as South Glamorgan's representative on the Welsh Regional Land Drainage Committee, he had heard Mr Edwards announce 'that the majority of major work with regard to land drainage had already been carried out and he would expect local land drainage committees would have fewer expensive schemes and be asking for less in government grants'.²⁶ This statement made an interesting contrast with the millions of pounds from government funds that Crickhowell had sought for his own pet project, but their lordships let it pass without comment.

The final witness to support the Riverside ward petition was Councillor Sue Essex, who represented the area on the City council. She was Chair of the City Planning committee, and a professional town planner, with Mid Glamorgan County Council. She made it clear that as a planner, she shared John Bowers' concern at the lack of a proper cost-benefit analysis of the Barrage project, and Stuart Noake's anxiety about the inconsistency of the Wallace Evans findings on groundwater. Mr Boydell took the opportunity, in cross-examination, to remind her that the City Council had decided not to petition against the Barrage. He, in turn, was reminded that the votes he referred to were about whether or not to petition, not about the Barrage itself.

When questioned about her view that the quality of the water in the impounded lake would make it unsuitable for swimming, she crisply informed him, that

> My comments were taken after discussion with our environmental health officers and they, at the end of the day, will make the decision as to what will be allowable or will not be allowable in terms of the situation.²⁷

It was a neat and pointed reminder of where the final responsibility for public health in the area lay: let CBDC, Welsh Water and their experts say what they wished, the environmental health officers of the City Council would have the last word.

The well-informed, carefully researched presentations by Councillors Drakeford, Hutt and Essex made a very dramatic contrast to that of the Councillors who had appeared for the promoters, Martin Davies, deputy Leader of the Conservative group on the County Council, and Peter Perkins, Labour's deputy leader of the County Council, who had represented Grangetown since 1981. The 1985 version of the County Council's structure plan set out its clear commitment to the preservation of the Cardiff Bay SSSI. Cross-examined by John Popham, Councillor Davies confirmed he knew nothing of the Bay's SSSI status until the Barrage was proposed. However, Councillor Perkins had been a member of the Council at the time the Structure Plan was approved, and Susan Hamilton, cross-examining on behalf of the NCC, asked how he reconciled its proposals with the inevitable destruction of the SSSI. His replies made it clear that he had not read the Structure Plan, and, like Councillor Davies, had no idea of the Bay's status until the Barrage was proposed. This was a significant admission – not only did the Plan set out the Council's responsibilities in conservation matters, but also its plans for housing, transport, and any other areas involving construction and physical development. For councillors to admit such ignorance was a serious matter. It is not surprising that on his return to Cardiff, Councillor Perkins had to face a very angry meeting of 50 members of Grangetown Residents Against the Barrage, who had already announced they would be putting up their own candidate against him in the forthcoming council elections.

The witnesses supporting Riverside Labour Party petition were followed by petitioners presenting their own case to the Committee. John Brookes, as a housing activist and a lecturer in town planning, spoke to the petitions of the Taff Housing Association (THA), and the South Riverside Community Development Association (SRCDA). Like Norman, he was particularly concerned about the implications of Clause 12, apparently cobbled together by the promoters to try and defuse at least some opposition. However, the THA petition was more concerned to simplify the process for local people to claim damages under the terms of the Bill, than with the technical flaws in CBDC's groundwater mapping. Likewise, the SRCDA petition wanted the residents of south Cardiff to have the same claim on CBDC for groundwater damage as homeowners in mining areas had on the Coal Board for damage due to subsidence. In such cases, the onus was on

the Coal Board to prove that they were not at fault, and it was felt that
the Development Corporation should have the same responsibility.
But, Dr Brookes added,

> Sadly, our experience in discussions with Cardiff Bay
> Development Corporation over the last nine months suggests that
> the amendment will meet with a predictable negative. I will not be
> surprised to hear that, for the undertakers, the premium costs of
> indemnifying themselves against such claims... would be prohibi-
> tive... should the undertakers put up such a cost argument, this
> would be my reply:
> If the undertakers cannot persuade an insurance company to
> indemnify them against a risk which they claim to be negligible,
> how negligible can it be, in fact?[28]

As Dr Brookes was not cross-examined, the promoters did not
have the opportunity to answer this argument.

Glyn Paul's petition was largely based on his lifelong knowledge of
the area, and on personal investigation. Like all the local petitioners, he
was deeply unimpressed by the superficiality of CBDC's researches.
He referred to the opinion of Dr John Miles, a groundwater specialist
at Cardiff University, that a full, reliable study of south Cardiff's
groundwater should take at least five years, not the one year that
WEP's had lasted.

He produced evidence to show that statements by the promoters
on important matters like the current erosion of the banks of the Taff,
the frequency with which the river was dredged and the backfilling of
basements in the area, was inaccurate. He also pointed out that he had
brought several errors in the WEP groundwater report to the authors'
attention, in the previous October, which they had accepted, and he
also offered proof of their apparent inability to answer pertinent questions he had raised in a letter nearly eight months before, which was
still unanswered.

The petitions from local residents' groups were unanimous in their
opposition to the Bill in principle. They were also all agreed on the
need to provide owners and occupiers with protection against
groundwater damage. The Docks Residents and Tenants' Association
(DRTA) added a request for compensation for depreciation in property values as a result of such damage. With relatively minor
variations, anti-barrage groups had been consistent in the points they
made to the Committee, in the hope that the repetition of the same
well researched and deeply felt arguments would mean their concerns
were sympathetically addressed.

One of the last witnesses to appear was Maelgwyn Watkins, for the
Nature Conservancy Council (NCC). He was questioned by Susan

Hamilton, the NCC's agent, and cross-examined by Peter Boydell, about the status of the Cardiff Bay SSSI. Mr Watkins confirmed that it was included in the South Glamorgan County Council Structure Plan revision in 1986, where it was referred to as the Cardiff and Penarth Tidal Flats, and designated an area of scientific and natural interest. The Plan was passed to the Welsh Office for the SoS's approval and modification. It was confirmed by a Welsh Office panel in 1988, and passed to the SoS – Nicholas Edwards' successor, Peter Walker, – who then deleted any mention of the Tidal Flats from the final report, as 'inappropriate having regard to SGCC's promotion of a private bill to enable the construction of a Cardiff Bay Barrage.' In other words, Mr Walker had single-handedly modified the area's status, apparently making the passage of the Bill easier, by reducing the legal protection to which it was entitled.

There was also a revealing reference to the report of the Commons Select Committee on the Taff Crossing Bill. Mr Boydell commented, 'Although the Committee took the view it would be a major disaster for the bird life of the Taff estuary, nevertheless the Bill passed, did it not?'[29] This is, at best, a misreading of that Committee's final report. The scheme that they concluded would be a disaster for the birds of the Taff was Nicholas Edwards' recently proposed barrage from Penarth Head to the Alexandra Dock, not the much smaller Taff Crossing barrage they were actually considering. The barrage proposed in the Taff Crossing Bill was actually removed from the final Act, specifically because that Select Committee believed it to be too expensive and environmentally damaging! It is quite understandable that counsel for the promoters would not want such details brought to public attention.

On 9th May, the members of the Committee visited Cardiff, to see the Bay and the planned site of the Barrage. On their return, they heard the summing up by counsel for the promoters and the petitioners. Mr Boydell put forward another version of Clause 12, amended, the promoters confirmed, to take into account the petitioners' main concerns. The revised clause was much longer and even more complicated than the original. It included provision for the promoters to publish their proposals in a local newspaper and circulate them to over 12,000 properties within the 'further Protected Property Line'; the contents would have to be approved by CFAC before publication. A code of practice on actually implementing Clause 12 would be drawn up, in consultation with local councils, and CFAC. All properties within the further Protected Property Line would be surveyed before impoundment, at the promoter's cost, but significant distinctions remained between 'protected' and 'further protected' properties

– for instance, the occupiers of 'further protected' properties had to apply for surveys, 'protected' occupiers did not. The revisions included the appointment of an independent expert, a surveyor who could arbitrate in disputes between the promoters and individual residents.

Mr Popham, for the petitioners, replied that the alterations, although a significant advance on the original Clause 12, did not really address his clients' concerns; they felt that the same remedies should be available whether they lived within the 'protected' or the 'further protected' lines. Their Lordships agreed that in the interests of ease of understanding and fairness, such a change in the Bill should be made, and recommended as such, in their final report.

Unfortunately, that final report also fully endorsed the need for a barrage as the centre of the regeneration of Cardiff Bay. One of the most disappointing aspects of the Select Committee's conclusions was the absence of any substantial examination of the scheme's costs, a significant plank in the case against it.

Paragraph 14 of the report set out clearly their Lordships' view of the Barrage's real financial justification:

> ... the Government had approved the cost/benefit analysis... and were prepared to commit large sums of money to the project because they accepted that this scheme would provide the greatest financial return. There was no evidence to suggest that such sums would be granted for any alternative scheme.[30]

In other words, Mr Edwards' barrage appeared to be the only option for Cardiff Bay, because that was the only scheme his former colleagues in government were willing to finance.

The anti-barrage campaigners were not surprised by the outcome: their opponents had been playing on their home turf, before the Select Committee, where the interests of Cardiff residents could be outweighed by the supposedly larger issues of redevelopment, property investment and political ambition. Their Lordships were at ease with ambitious projects and the apparently cavalier use of public funds; to point out that these things did not necessarily contribute to the well-being of many local people was obviously a truism easily ignored in this high-powered, but unworldly setting. Indeed, the rather lacklustre Third Reading debate in the Lords in July, was remarkable only for the richness of the compliments paid by their Lordships to the skill with which Lord Elibank and his colleagues had conducted the business of the committee.

However, the campaigners were confident that, as the Bill wended its way through the parliamentary process, its flaws would be become increasingly obvious, with emasculation, at worst, or defeat, at best, as the most likely outcome. But whatever the result, it would now depend on the House of Commons, for, as an article in *The Western Mail* put it, on 30th May, 'the Bill still has a long way to travel, with plenty of ambushes along the way'.

It was now rather late in the Parliamentary year, and so the Bill would have to be formally 'carried over' to the Commons after the opening of Parliament, and the Queen's speech, in October. For this, a carry over debate and vote in the Lower House would be needed. The first major vote would follow its Second Reading there, a few weeks later. As it was a Private Bill, it would have to be supported by at least 100 MPs to close the motion. If it did not have enough support, opposing MPs could 'filibuster' – just keep the debate going, until it ran out of time, and was defeated. Such debates on Private Bills usually took place late at night; even with the strong government support it enjoyed, the promoters might fail to muster enough lobby fodder, and as every prosperous highwayman knows, ambushes work best on the dazed and sleepy.

It was known that the Valleys' MPs, led by Ron Davies of Caerffili, were preparing to scupper the Bill, if at all possible. They were confident that the wealth its promoters insisted would be brought to Cardiff would definitely not trickle up to the Valleys, and precious investment which could have saved their struggling communities would be frittered away on a concrete dam and a stagnant lake. But, as the Bill was being introduced to the Commons by another Labour MP, Alun Michael, many Labour members outside Wales thought the debate could be seen as a local dispute, which they would do their utmost to keep out of.

The old Valleys/Cardiff split was a significant issue throughout the Barrage debate, as it always has been in Welsh politics at large. Ron Davies, Ted Rowlands and Kim Howells could bang on to their heart's content about the iniquities of the Development Corporation and its costly schemes. The voters of Caerffili, Pontypridd and Merthyr believed it was an important part of their MPs' job description to make sure Cardiff's gold was fairly shared with the rest of cash-starved post-industrial Wales. For a MP from Cardiff itself to support such a stance, as Rhodri Morgan was asked to do, was a much riskier enterprise, where he could be seen to be arguing against a wealth creation scheme right in his own backyard. Before he came out against the scheme, he would need assurance of the reality of its threat to the homes of many of his constituents, as well as solid support from his own constituency party and, above all, evidence that there were no real economic arguments for the scheme.

The Cardiff residents' groups, as well as the RSPB, were preparing to present an even more powerful case in the Commons than in the Lords. With much stronger and more coherent opposition from the Valleys, they hoped for a more rigorous debate, followed, if necessary, by a more searching examination from a Commons Select Committee.

Meanwhile, elections for South Glamorgan County Council had taken place on 4th May. Anti-barrage candidates had stood in two wards, The Marl, in Grangetown, against Councillor Perkins, and Butetown, against Councillor Kitson, both leading supporters of the Barrage. In Grangetown, a former bus inspector, Anthony Baber, had the support of the newly-formed Grangetown Residents Against the Barrage. None of the 50 or so members had any experience of party politics or fighting elections, and it was not until three weeks before polling day, that they decided to put up a candidate at all. Lacking the financial support of an established party machine, they had to spend much valuable campaign time collecting money on street corners and at public meetings, to pay for leaflets, rosettes and all the other impedimenta of electioneering. Fortunately, they were allowed, free of charge, to set up their committee rooms in a former fish and chip shop, near Grangetown's main shopping area. Filling envelopes and writing election addresses among the empty fish fryers and chip vats, they were heartened to realise they were causing their pro-barrage opponents some anxiety, when posters began to appear advising the voters of Grangetown to 'beware of single issue candidates!'

In Butetown, Ben Foday put his hat in the ring earlier in the campaign, also with no political or election experience, against a long-serving councillor, with a party machine behind him. Meanwhile, in Pontcanna ward, where the anti-barrage group had been particularly active, all three of Mark Drakeford's opponents also declared themselves against the Barrage – Conservative, Social & Liberal Democrat and Plaid Cymru! There could be no greater tribute to the effectiveness with which Pontcanna Residents Against the Barrage had put their case.

When the results were declared, it was clear that the Labour anti-barrage candidates had been returned with substantially increased majorities. The two 'single issue' candidates had polled on average more than 50% of the votes given to the Labour victors in their wards. It was clear that the campaign was beginning to make a real impact on public opinion in south Cardiff; the election results and the concessions won from the Select Committee had given its supporters a taste of greater advances they could make in the future.

There was still one major uncertainty in the campaign – no Cardiff MP had yet declared outright opposition to the Barrage. Rhodri Morgan had taken a stance of determined objectivity, while trying to

address his constituents' concerns about groundwater and flooding;
by demanding the survey of dampness in homes in Riverside, which
Jane Hutt had mentioned in her evidence to the Select Committee, for
instance. But, for anti-barrage arguments to get a sympathetic hearing in the Commons, an MP with *locus standi* would have to put the
case. This was particularly important in view of the stout support the
Barrage Bill would have from Alun Michael, MP for Cardiff South
and Penarth.

One of Rhodri Morgan's main concerns was the apparent diver-
gence of expert opinion on local groundwater changes, as a result of
the Barrage – Wallace Evans drew one conclusion, from their surveys,
while Stuart Noake not only disagreed with their conclusions, but was
also sceptical about their methods. Rhodri had told his constituents
that he would read all the evidence presented to the Lords, before finally making up his mind. While he was doing so, two polls took place in
west Cardiff, both of which might have been calculated to remind him
just how his many supporters really wanted that mind to be made up...

The first was a vote by his own constituency party, of 17-4 against
the Barrage, in late June. The second was a house-to-house poll in
Pontcanna, Mark Drakeford's territory, run by Pontcanna Residents
Against the Barrage: it covered six streets, outside the 'Protected
Property Line', and none of those questioned were in favour of the
scheme – more than three-quarters said they were willing to write to
Rhodri Morgan opposing it. As a relatively new MP, in a city where
most of the powers that be in his party not only supported the
Barrage, but claimed it as their own, he would need a substantial jus-
tification for coming out against the project.

In one of many 'Cardiff Bay Supplements', in the *South Wales Echo*,
the Leader of the Opposition, Neil Kinnock, had spoken admiringly
of the work of CBDC.[30] While studiously omitting any mention of the
Barrage itself, he quoted with obvious approval projected 'with barrage' figures of 30,000 extra jobs, and millions invested. To fly in the
face of such an endorsement would do a fledgling political career no
good at all – only if his constituents were clearly seen to give him no
alternative, could his opposition to the Barrage be in any way justified;
but even if justified, it might still be unacceptable. However, those
constituents had done their very best to oblige, to good effect. At the
next PRAB meeting, on 3rd July, the newly elected City Councillor
for Riverside, Jane Davidson, read out a letter from the Cardiff West
MP, who could not attend, because of business in the Commons,
finally pledging his support for the anti-barrage campaign.

In a typically swashbuckling article in the *Echo*, setting out the reasons for his stance, Rhodri said,

... There is no place for the grandiose and pretentious in Cardiff. Capital city we may be, but capital cities have to make a living too. We have to fight for every new job we can get into the city and to keep the existing jobs as well. This strategy for wholesale clearance of so much of the present fabric of Docklands, just to make way for the Brave New World of Nicholas Edwards' Golden Pond, is far too big a risk for my taste...

[Collingdon Road is] a seed bed for small businesses... we need places like that in Cardiff, but under the CBDC proposals, it's all to be demolished... Those 300 businesses employ many thousands of people. They probably pay on average of £1.50p per square foot a year in rent. Wherever they move to, they will on average be paying double that... How many will accept financial compensation and close down altogether?

... On the one hand, you have the promise of a new Marbella-on-Taff destroying some jobs and creating others in offices that could be located elsewhere in Cardiff.

On the other, you have the possibility agreed by a distinguished professional geologist of harm being caused to the living conditions of a large swathe of the older parts of my constituency.

Is the risk worth the benefit? You know my answer is No.[31]

The anti-barrage campaigners might have lost the first round of their Parliamentary battle, but their efforts had won them a formidable ally in confronting the second.

5. An Extravagant Nonsense in the Commons

A vote in the House of Commons has more authority when it's a
free vote than when it's a whipped vote.
Rt. Hon. Alun Michael, M.P. in an interview on the *Today*
programme, BBC Radio 4, 1st July, 2003

The anti-barrage campaign gained new impetus after Rhodri
Morgan's declaration against the scheme.

One of most tireless campaigners was Charlie Burriss, of
Pontcanna Residents Against the Barrage, and Taff Housing
Association. Carpenter, weight lifter, amateur brewer and Clerk of
Works to THA, he had resigned from the Labour Party when George
Thomas, as Labour SoS Wales in the mid-sixties, had accepted a
place on the board of Julian Hodge's controversial Bank of Wales.
Since then, he had directed his formidable knowledge of left wing politics and the housing conditions of south Cardiff to afflicting the
comfortable among the city's political elite. In CBDC, he felt he had
an adversary, not exactly worthy of his skill, but at least well worth the
trouble of humiliating, a task he relished.

When Norman Robson and Charlie had first contacted CBDC
about the inadequacies of the WEP reports on groundwater, the
Corporation's chief engineer, David Crompton, was quick to realise
that here were two opponents whose skills and local knowledge could
be very useful. Not useful, in the sense of pointing out hitherto
unseen flaws in the project itself, but in providing guidance about how
better presentation of the Barrage case could be used to defuse public opposition – the wording of leaflets, the conduct of public
meetings, etc. But this was a game the *enfants terrible* of Taff Housing
were not prepared to play. Instead, they used their access to CBDC's
inner engineering counsels to try and increase the levels of protection
available for residents, through the Barrage Bill.

The aim of the anti-barrage campaign was, of course, to prevent
the Barrage being built. The preferred means of achieving this was to
prevent the Barrage Bill becoming law, through arousing and focussing
public opposition, convincing MPs of the power of the arguments
against it and through local people putting the case against as frequently and vigorously as possible to Select Committees considering
the Bill. If rational argument failed to convince the project's supporters, then another tactic could be employed – successive representations

to CBDC, the Welsh Office and Parliament itself, would lead to the inclusion in the Bill of so many protection measures and remedies for groundwater damage, poor water quality, midge infestation, fishery maintenance, etc, that the supposed financial advantages bestowed by the Barrage would be more than cancelled out by its cost, and it would not go ahead. It was this latter tactic that Norman and Charlie were pursuing in their discussions with the Development Corporation, trying to negotiate the inclusion of more and more potentially expensive clauses in the latest, post-Lords, version of the Bill.

The Parliamentary year begins and ends in autumn. Any piece of business uncompleted – bills still to receive the Royal Assent, for instance – have to be the subject of a successful carry over motion. In other words, the House currently considering it must formally agree that it is in a fit state for its passage through Parliament to continue in the next session. The Barrage Bill was due to have its Second Reading in the Commons in July, 1989, so that, with a little luck and absolutely no opposition, it could theoretically have been completed in the 1988-89 session. However, Ron Davies put down a blocking motion, which meant that there could be no carry over debate until the House resumed after the summer recess, in October. So, the anti-barrage campaigners had a further breathing space to prepare their case for the next Select Committee, in the Commons, and to continue the debate with CBDC.

By the end of July, 1990, the final date for submissions, more than 70 petitions had been notified to the Parliamentary Private Bills' office – a record for a Private Bill, with more than 50 being lodged by individuals. This was a tribute to the efforts of Norman and other members of CFAC. Not only had they put the arguments against the Barrage accurately and forcefully, they had also persuaded their neighbours that the expense and effort of the very demanding petitioning process was worth it, if the Barrage was to be defeated. Their success was confirmed by the increase in the number of petitions since the first Select Committee, in the Lords, when just fifteen had been heard.

Significantly, CBDC's protestations before their lordships about the groundwater threat had not reassured major landowners in the area. The Welsh Rugby Union were petitioning, as the sacred turf of Cardiff Arms Park was vulnerable; Wales Gas was petitioning, because subsidence due to groundwater changes might damage pipelines: property developers Crest Nicholson were petitioning, because increased dampness would affect the homes they planned. Changes to the water table were no longer just an anxiety for people living in the Victorian terraces of south Cardiff, but were a major

concern for national companies planning to make significant investment in the area.

In early August, the County Council announced that the plans for
the Peripheral Distributor Road (PDR) linking south Cardiff with the
M4 were now complete. More than five years earlier, the PDR had
been proposed as vital for the area's redevelopment, long predating
what Rhodri Morgan had called 'Nicholas Edwards' Golden Pond'.
The whole debate about the role of the Barrage in the regeneration
project was complicated by the plans to build the PDR, as it became
impossible to calculate whether increased land rentals and higher
property prices were due to the Barrage or the road which provided
the fast transport links essential for prosperity. In the unlikely event
that the ambitious targets for betterment set out in KPMG's in their
economic appraisal were achieved, would they be achieved because of
the Barrage, or because of the PDR? The coincidental timing of the
two projects made it impossible to prove the unique wealth-creating
properties of the Barrage alone, fortunately for the reputations and
peace of mind of its supporters.

The cost of the PDR was estimated at £100 million; it was hoped
that at least 50% of this would be met by a grant from the European
Commission, and the Welsh Office was due to conclude negotiations
with the EC in October. However, the success of the Greens in the
European Elections had lead to changes of emphasis in road building
policy. So, only a few days after the Council's announcement, the
European Regional Development Fund (ERDF) declared that new
priorities meant it was unlikely the money would be forthcoming.
Uncertainty over the financing of the road scheme put a large question mark over the whole regeneration project, while arguments about
whether it would finally be paid for by the Welsh Office, the
Development Corporation, the ERDF, the County Council, or all of
them combined, rumbled on alongside the Barrage debate for many
months.

Meanwhile, Rhodri Morgan's declared opposition to the scheme
had polarised opinion within local Labour Party groups. In August,
his constituency party tabled a motion against the Barrage at the
monthly meeting of the South Glamorgan County party, listing nine
reasons why the party should oppose the scheme. It was defeated by
28 votes to 9. In September, a similar motion was defeated by 31 votes
to 10, at a meeting of Cardiff City Labour Party. It is interesting to
speculate if it was one of these meetings that Lord Brooks referred to
in an interview he later gave to Mike Ungersma,

One night... I was fed up with anti-barrage resolutions and we had

a meeting of the party with another one of these on the agenda. I
looked around the meeting and I was outnumbered.

Democracy, don't forget, is all about numbers, about arithmetic. This chap got up to move the resolution and I thought:
'What am I going to do?' I looked up and saw I was under the
smoke alarm. Now, no smoking is allowed in the meetings, but I lit
my pipe, and said 'Oh, sorry,' and blew the smoke straight up into
the alarm. The bloody thing was making a hell of a racket all over
the building. The porter rushed in and said: 'Everybody out!' Two
fire engines arrived. I knew the young fireman in charge and he
looked at me and asked, 'What room are you in?' I said never mind
about that, how long will it take you to search this building from
top to bottom? 'That's a two hour job,' he said. I told him: 'You
start at the top and work your way down.' We all had to go home.[1]

Even if neither of the meetings was the relevant one, the incident
gives striking insight into Lord Brooks' view of the way in which
Labour Party business should be conducted, and informed debate
carried on, at the lower levels of the Party hierarchy. Moreover, the
incident is also remarkable as a unique instance of a member of the
public appearing to give instructions to a senior fire officer at the
scene of a potential fire – instructions which that senior fire officer
then seems to obey. Did the Council Leader apparently see the city as
his personal fiefdom? What he wanted for Cardiff should, it seemed,
be what the Labour Party wanted for Cardiff. Given his influence, it
would be a brave member who challenged him over the Barrage issue.
Votes at County and City group meetings were taken on a show of
hands – no secret ballot; in the circumstances, it is a matter for con-
gratulation that as many as 19 votes were cast against Jack Brooks' pet
project. As the MP Jimmy Hood later commented in his report on the
Bill to the Commons, there were, fortunately for Cardiff, several brave
party members ready to oppose such municipal big guns.

However, although the votes in the City and County meetings
were lost, some at least of the arguments were won; a few weeks later,
Cardiff Central Constituency Labour Party voted to oppose the
Barrage. Interestingly, their MP, Jon Owen Jones, also a protege of
Lord Brooks, chose not to represent that view in the House; he did
not take part in the debates, and did not vote either way on the
Barrage Bill after its Second Reading in the Commons, a month later.

However, just as the City Labour Party vote was taking place,
another report on the Barrage's likely effect on the water table
appeared. It was prepared by Dr Gordon Saunders, one of the UK's
most respected hydrologists, at the request of Cardiff Flood Action
Committee. His report was intended to form the basis of his expert
witness in support of CFAC's petition against the Barrage Bill.

Dr Saunders was highly critical of the original Wallace Evans report on groundwater, whose 'simplistic and outdated research' had failed to give sufficient attention to the relationship between groundwater levels below ground, and changes in the level of still or running water on the surface, such as lakes or rivers. Throughout the debate so far, CBDC's engineers had sought to make a distinction between rising groundwater and excessive surface water – such as high river flows or a lake of 400 acres. This latest report confirmed what anyone living on low-lying land in a river valley in time of heavy rainfall knows – in certain geological formations, like those in south Cardiff, a high water table and surface water will interact, causing flooding, dampness and subsidence.

For CBDC, this was simply the latest in a long series of challenges for their public relations machine. They responded by distributing over 50,000 leaflets throughout the city, entitled 'Groundwater – the facts', in an attempt to allay increasing local anxiety. It was significantly vague about the current water table in the area, referring to it as 'between three and five metres below ground level', and describing the likely rise as 'Very near the edge of the Bay... about 2.5 metres', which if the water table below your Bayside home was already three meters, was not an entirely reassuring prospect, that is assuming that CBDC's assessment would not be have to be revised yet again following anti-barrage evidence to the forthcoming Select Committee, as it had been after the previous Committee. There was no mention in their leaflets of south Cardiff's geological eccentricities, which Stuart Noake had earlier criticised them for ignoring, and which could influence the movement of groundwater so much: nor was there any mention of the uniqueness of the scheme itself. The deliberate impoundment of 400 acres of standing water in a very low-lying area, only for cosmetic reasons, was something of an experiment, and, had they realised this, the people of Cardiff would have been very interested indeed to see how it would all turn out.

October 1989 would be the 150th anniversary of the official opening of Cardiff docks; the Commons debate on the Second Reading of the Barrage Bill was due to take place in mid-November. CBDC took the opportunity to use the anniversary for a celebration of the regeneration project as a whole. Part of the celebration would consist of a presentation to over 100 MPs, who were invited to Cardiff for the weekend as the Corporation's guests, and accommodated in the city's most comfortable, and costly, hotels at CBDC's expense.

The Bill's opponents pointed out that this meant that MPs would have been well-primed with pro-barrage arguments, before the debate even began, and that their resources did not give them the same

access to the country's political decision makers. They retaliated with
their own anti-barrage propaganda weapon; a model ark made by
supporters, plastered with CFAC's signature posters – 'This house
against the Barrage' and 'Stop the ~~dam~~ barrage' – which was paraded
round the parts of the city vulnerable to groundwater changes. They
also tried to counter CBDC's 'entertaining' manoeuvre, by a postcard
campaign, where all MPs and peers likely to take even a passing interest in the Barrage Bill were informed of what was at stake and asked
to vote against the measure – anyone in Parliament who had anything
to do with conservation, environmental protection, town planning or
water quality was asked to give their case a hearing. There were some
encouraging replies, and some rather disheartening ones, like that
from the former chief of the Welsh Tourist Board, who was convinced
that the Barrage and a successful development were inextricably
linked, Geoffrey Inkin had told him so...

Building arks, even model ones, canvassing by post, leafleting and
public meetings were a constant drain on the limited resources of the
campaign. RSPB were generous in their help with the Select
Committee process itself, but spreading the word, and supporting the
campaign in Cardiff had to be done unaided; so there had to be raf-
fles and street collections, floats at carnivals and local festivals. Badges
and balloons had to be sold, as well as the real campaign business of
groundwater reports to be assessed, construction costs to be scrutinised and petition statements to be prepared and researched.

Leaders of the campaign remember this period, the four years
from the Commons Second Reading debate to the final passage of the
Act in November 1993, as one of hectic 36 hour days fuelled by the
adrenaline of comradeship and the knowledge that they were right –
CBDC had a case to answer, and in all justice, a democratic society
should require that they answer it. Unfortunately, it required phe-
nomenal energy and commitment from some members of that
democratic society to ensure that they did.

The debate on the carry over motion began in the Commons, at
7pm on 14th November, 1989. A carry over motion must have the
support of a majority of MPs present, if the bill concerned is to proceed. Naturally, the motion was proposed by Alun Michael. He began
by rehearsing the usual arguments about how important the Barrage
was for attracting investment to south Cardiff, and laid great emphasis on the job creation aspects of the scheme. He tried to get his
retaliation in first on the vexed issue of investment for Cardiff being
at the expense of investment for the Valleys, by repeating the pious
hope that 10,000 of the legendary new jobs 'will be filled by workers
from the rest of the region'.[2]

Of the MPs opposing the motion, Rhodri Morgan had the greatest local interest, so he responded first. His main point was a rather
unexpected one – the Bill did not deserve to be the subject of a carry
over motion, as it had reached the Commons, from Another Place, in
a very flawed state. The alterations to the original Protected Property
Line had been one of the most significant changes that the Lords had
made to the Bill. The accompanying plan giving its exact route was
essential to a clear definition of the relevant clauses, and an integral
part of the proposed legislation. But, unfortunately, Lord Elibank,
who had earlier received the congratulations of his fellow peers for his
effective chairmanship, had managed to sign five copies of the wrong
plan. The Protected Property Line (PPL) had been incorrectly shown
on the plan passed to the Commons for their consideration.

As Mr Morgan pointed out, the incorrect plan had implications
for would-be petitioners. His constituents would have decided to petition, or not to petition, on the basis of whether they lived inside or
outside the Protected Property Line –

> What could easily have happened to all or any of the 850 homes
> and few businesses in the area affected is that if they had proceed-
> ed on the basis of the document on which... they were relying [the
> incorrect plan] they would have proceeded on the basis that they
> did not need to petition because they were within the line. They did
> not therefore petition. If they then find that they are outside the
> line and want to petition about that fact, they have lost the right to
> do so. [24th July was the final date for submitting petitions]

The wording of his constituents' petitions had to reflect where
they were in relation to the PPL – 'Someone within a protected property zone must frame his petition making it clear he is a householder
or the owner of a business within the zone. If the property or business
is on the other side of the line, the petition must be phrased differently
to be in order'[3].

Alun Michael, in contrast, saw the problem as solely one of parliamentary procedure, which could be easily solved '... the Chairman of
the Lords committee can sign a new plan, or an amended plan can be
put to the Commons Committee.'[4] He seemed unaware of the importance of the petitioning process for those Cardiff people who were
anxious about the Bill, and how they might have lost a important
opportunity, through Their Lordships' error. It would be inappropriate to suggest that Mr Michael, as a spokesperson for the promoters,
would not be very interested in the petitioning process, except insofar
as the fewer petitions before the Committee, the quicker the Bill
might get on the statute book.

In the event, the Deputy Speaker ruled that the carry over debate would have to continue, as the Examiners, who assessed the suitability of Private Bills, had already agreed that it could. This meant that members would therefore vote on the Bill's fitness to proceed at the close of the debate.

The debate followed a predictable pattern: most of its substance had already been aired at length before the Lords, or in the local press. With strong support from Valleys MPs like Ron Davies, Kim Howells, Allan Rogers and Ted Rowlands, its disputed credentials as a job creation scheme, poor water quality, groundwater changes, etc. were thoroughly eviscerated. Rhodri Morgan was keen to point out that the support of the two local authorities for the Bill did not invalidate any of the arguments against it, nor was it a sign of strong local support for the Barrage. On the contrary, their early recruitment to the cause of a Conservative Secretary of State meant that

> ... when dissent emerged in the community as more facts became known, it was more difficult for the supertanker of local authorities and the government, aiming straight for the Titanic, to turn themselves round in time, because dissent was seen not merely as the result of new information but as a breach of the code of lèse-majesté or hara-kiri or omerta.[5]

The support of the two Labour councils for the scheme was a major obstacle for any Labour MPs opposing it, and this was the best possible justification for his pro-barrage council colleagues that the MP for Cardiff West could devise, faced with yet another public split in the party.

When he went on to outline the water quality problem, Sir Anthony Meyer interjected,

> I do not know whether the hon. Gentleman has been to Venice. It smells pretty nasty, but it is still an extremely attractive place.[6]

Sir Anthony had a long-standing involvement in the Barrage Bill: he had been chair of the fourth Standing Committee on Statutory Instruments in 1987, which granted Nicholas Edwards' wish to adapt the UDC principle for Cardiff, including local councillors on CBDC's board, and the building of the Barrage as part of its remit.

The comparison of Cardiff Docklands, present or future, with the Jewel of the Adriatic was dismissed with the amused contempt it deserved, but the reference caught the public imagination in the city; for the next few months, no stand up comedian in a Cardiff pub or club felt his act was complete without references to the Roath Rialto or the palazzo of Butetown. Local singer Frank Hennessey was inspired to write what would become the signature tune of the anti-barrage movement, 'The Grangetown Gondolier'.

Sir Anthony Meyer later spoke again, with magisterial generality,

> The plain fact is that the combination of our procedures for deal-
> ing with private Bills and with public inquiries is one reason why
> we have such difficulty carrying through any great enterprise in
> this country,[7]

and he drew comparisons, to Britain's disadvantage, with the way such things are handled in the rest of western Europe. Many Cardiff residents would have responded that the doubtful quality of the enter-prises proposed might have a great deal to do with public reluctance to support them.

Ron Davies presented his case with his usual energy, reinforcing Rhodri's argument that this could not be presented as a Labour scheme; as the member for Caerffili, well outside the remit of South Glamorgan County Council, he could adopt a more combative tone about Cardiff's local councillors' 'sweetheart relationship' with Nicholas Edwards, and assert

> ... for every unit of the party supporting the scheme, at least one
> other opposes it.[8]

Allan Rogers, an engineering geologist, as well as MP for the Rhondda, had studied CBDC's statements on groundwater, and the Wallace Evans' reports, with attention. He did not think much of them. An information leaflet for MPs attracted his particular ire and he quoted its inaccuracies, omissions and vagueness with gusto.

> The leaflet says 'What is the present groundwater level? It varies
> throughout Cardiff but is much lower underground than in many
> parts of Britain'. That is a lie... There is no such thing as an aver-
> age level [of groundwater]. It is misleading to suggest that the
> groundwater level in Cardiff is much lower underground than in
> many parts of Britain.

Echoing Baroness White in the Lords' debate, he concluded 'this is riddled with inaccuracies. I am not saying that problems cannot be overcome, but there is no need for them.'[9]

Kim Howells, MP for Pontypridd, contributed a lyrical disquisi-tion on water quality, 'Meanwhile, stinking flows the Taff, miserable are the views that it provides, and scientifically fascinating is the qual-ity of its water and the debris that it bears down to the proposed site for the Barrage.'

Gwilym Jones, Conservative MP for Cardiff North, weighed in

with an enthusiastic defence, including apposite quotations from KPMG's economic appraisals, and a remarkably ill-informed response to Allan Rogers' criticisms of CBDC's groundwater leaflet.

> I imagine there will be some percolation [*sic*] of groundwater, but surely groundwater must still obey the laws of gravity... groundwater can emerge from a mountain, but that is because gravity causes water to flow down inside the mountain. I have not seen mountains in south Cardiff.[10]

Such interventions in parliamentary debates reinforce Virginia Woolf's comment that conversation doesn't really exist – there are really only intertwined monologues; in any arena where one speaker really had to answer the points raised by another, or be ignored, there would have been no place for Gwilym Jones' contributions.[11]

But Gwilym Jones also referred to his blocking motion on the earlier South Glamorgan (Taff Crossing) Bill, which had meant that it, and the Barrage it included, were delayed for at least six months, giving Nicholas Edwards time to prepare the political ground for the much bigger barrage he preferred. That motion had, Mr Jones claimed, been based on a concern for the future of the Cardiff Bay SSSI, which would be diminished by the Barrage-as-road crossing proposed in the Bill. Now, three years later, the total destruction of that same SSSI had become only a matter of 'deep regret'.[12]

One of the most effective speeches of the debate was the last, by Ted Rowlands, MP for Merthyr and Rhymney. He was concerned with the lack of information about the scheme's 'huge and significant public expenditure consequences... The House is being asked to pass a carry over motion for a bill whose public expenditure implications have not been explained.' Alun Michael responded rather weakly that these matters would be investigated by the Select Committee. Ted Rowlands pointed out that the original Bill had carried a financial memorandum, which was missing from the current Bill. The original financial memorandum had quoted a cost of £85 million; the Select Committee had heard evidence that the Barrage would cost £113 million, with land reclamation costs of £15 million, depollution costs of £60 million and road schemes of £118 million. Where were the total costs of more than £400 million to come from? Where were the detailed costings? He added

> Even according to the promoters, there will be a net operating loss of £652 billion [*sic*]. Who will fund that? Will it be funded by the ratepayers or will the Welsh Office make an on-going contribution?[13]

He reminded the House of the disastrous development plans for

Cardiff in the 1960s, defended before a public enquiry by the same Peter Boydell QC who now spoke for the promoters of the Barrage. That scheme had also been justified as vital to the city's prosperity and to job creation but had been defeated, so that

> Today, Cardiff city centre is one of the finest of any city. That hap-
> pened... because we turned our backs on huge developments and
> went for the sensible, progressive, organic development of the
> city.[14]

Ted Rowlands was still speaking when the debate's deadline was reached, at 10 pm. Two votes now followed – the first on whether the Bill was in a fit state to be carried over, and the second on whether it was actually to be carried over.

Despite the late hour, the public gallery was crowded with CFAC supporters in their distinctive canary yellow sweat shirts, emblazoned with Sue Pomeroy's logo of a redshank in flight. They counted about 30 MPs in the House, at 9.50, with a large anti-barrage majority. Inexperienced in the ways of Parliament, they began to hope that the carry over motion might be defeated. But, as ten o'clock approached, the payroll vote came in to take their places on both sides of the chamber. Officially, Private Bills are unwhipped; MPs are supposed to make up their own minds on the issues under debate. However, the Welsh Secretary had put his weight behind the Bill and the Leader of the Opposition had spoken favourably of its aims – all career politi- cians would know what side their bread was buttered on. At this point in his career, Rhodri Morgan couldn't offer anyone a cabinet seat, Ron Davies and Kim Howells couldn't influence the siting of facto- ries or hospitals, they had nothing to trade with in the larger political world outside south Wales. So they had to sit and watch while Edwina Currie and Norman Tebbit, Sir Nicholas Fairbairn and Neil Hamilton, Rhodes James and Anne Widdecombe arrived to cast their votes for the carry over motion on a bill of which they knew little and probably cared less. The bill was approved as fit to be carried over by 192 votes to 58, and the carry over motion itself was passed by 183 votes to 48.

However, another useful weapon was added to the anti-barrage armoury, when an alternative development strategy for Cardiff docks was unveiled at a crowded public meeting in the elegant Edwardian baroque City Hall. Called *The Living Waterfront*, the scheme had been prepared by consultants for the Save the Taff Group, which included Cardiff Flood Action Committee, Taff Housing, the RSPB, Cardiff Naturalists and other interested local groups. The City Hall meeting was presided over by the RSPB's national Chair, and chief inquisitor

of BBC's *Mastermind*, Magnus Magnusson. He shared the platform
with Rhodri Morgan, Sue Essex, Chair of the City Council's Planning
Committee, John Brookes of Taff Housing Association and Norman
Robson of CFAC.

The Living Waterfront had grown from John Brookes' discussions
with the RSPB about the possibility that the SSSI itself could form the
centrepiece for the development, rather than an impounded lake
which would destroy it completely. So, this was the brief to which
Chris Baines, a landscape consultant specialising in environmentally
sympathetic developments, was asked to work. The scheme he produced would cost £60 million, about half the going price of the
Barrage.

On *The Living Waterfront*, a seawall would be built across the
mouth of the Inner Harbour, which would still allow the sea tides
access to the Bay: a lock for shipping would be included. The mudflats themselves would be cleaned up by the removal of the debris and
rubbish which fouled them. A visitors' centre, with a watch tower,
would be built, so that tourists could observe the wading birds at close
quarters. Walkways and cycle paths would be laid out, to allow easy
access to the SSSI, without disturbing the redshank, dunlin and
curlews feeding there. New leisure facilities would be built – playing
fields at Penarth Moors, and a quality park on the Marl – both open
areas currently underexploited. Most of Cardiff Bay would remain
open to the sea, there would be no risk of groundwater changes, and,
as neither the Taff nor the Ely would be impounded, there would be
no additional water quality problems. Cardiff would at last be able to
capitalise on its unique asset – an urban wildlife park of more than
300 acres.

The unveiling of the scheme meant that anti-barrage campaigners
could no longer be accused of condemning the 'ugly' mudflats of
Cardiff Bay to remain exactly as they were. There was an alternative
to the Barrage; more to the point, that alternative was cheaper, safer
and more attractive. What Chris Baines was not qualified to predict,
even if it had been included in his terms of reference, was the extent
of the government's commitment to the Barrage. As the complex revisions and rewrites of the original KPMG economic appraisal had
shown, this was the be-all-and-end-all of the project. Nicholas
Edwards had presented the Barrage as an essential magnet for development money, with the whole regeneration of south Cardiff
dependent on it.

CBDC announced it would reserve judgement on *The Living
Waterfront* until the project had been thoroughly examined.

Meanwhile, the battle of the groundwater experts was intensifying.

Stuart Noake and John Miles, a groundwater hydrogeologist at Cardiff University's Department of Civil Engineering, had both severely criticised the quality of the research undertaken by Wallace Evans and Partners for CBDC. The poor quality of the computer modelling on which it was based had particularly concerned Dr Miles, as well as the ignorance of the unique geology of south-east Wales that it displayed. In response to these concerns, Alun Michael and Peter Perkins, councillor for Grangetown, had commissioned yet another report, from Glyn Jones, director of postgraduate studies in hydrogeology at University College, London. His report was published on 20th November: predictably, Professor Jones said that the remedial work planned by CBDC would be 'more then adequate' to deal with the 'dampness or wetness' which would be the most likely result of the Barrage's impoundment.[15] By coincidence, the very next day Rhodri Morgan had arranged a meeting between CBDC and Dr Miles, with Dr Gordon Saunders, now lecturing at Goldsmiths' College, London. Dr Miles was also an expert in the computer modelling of groundwater, the use of computer software to forecast the likely movement of water and soil in particular circumstances. Both men were firmly convinced that CBDC's modelling was, as John Miles said, 'no more than a first shot. The Bay and their consultants ought now to proceed to a full and thorough groundwater modelling exercise using the latest technology.' Dr Saunders added that 'the borehole study and conclusion drawn by the CBDC and its consultants is nowhere near adequate.' Dr Saunders obviously shared Stuart Noakes' contempt for the WEP technique of plastic buckets lowered down a hole on a rope, on which they placed such undeserved trust.[16]

During the Commons Second Reading debate, late in the evening of 19th December 1989. Alun Michael reprised his role in the carry over debate of a few weeks before, when, alone among Welsh Labour MPs, he had loyally spoken to his pro-barrage script. This time, he enjoyed the vocal and humorous support of Paul Flynn, of Newport West, with whom he shared a Commons office and a London flat. Unfortunately for the promoters' case, Mr Flynn's contributions to the debate were more remarkable for their enthusiasm than their substance. He responded to Ron Davies' informed and passionate statement of the RSPB's case, by commenting with heavy irony,

> The RSPB is campaigning and putting Cardiff's prosperity at risk because it wants to fight the line at Cardiff. It knows that if it can win its case in a bay as ugly as Cardiff's, it can fight and win in the Mawddach estuary, the Towy estuary and other beautiful estuaries...
> One of the fauna that exist in great numbers on the marl [sic] and foreshore of Cardiff bay is the rat. If one wants to see a living

waterfront, one should go to certain areas – I shall not name them
now – at high tide, when rats come over the sea walls...[17]

The implication was that with the Barrage, the rodent wildlife of
south Cardiff would become an endangered species, like the Bay's
dunlin and redshank. Alas, Mr Flynn's worst fears were not realised,
the rat population of Grangetown and Cardiff Bay flourishes still. No
other Welsh Labour MP was moved to speak in favour of the Barrage,
ironically or otherwise.

For the Bill's opponents mainly MPs from the Valleys supported by
colleagues like Alan Williams and Win Griffiths from more westerly
Welsh constituencies the debate was an opportunity to attack the economic principles behind the development of Cardiff Bay, often to the
exclusion of any mention of the Barrage itself. They were keen to point
out that CBDC's activities were financed from a limited Welsh Office
budget – by implication, at the expense of their own constituencies.

In this spirit, Denzil Davies, MP for Llanelli, revisited Ted
Rowlands' earlier criticisms, in the carry over debate, of the Welsh
Office's unwillingness to give details about what their grant-in-aid to
CBDC was actually being spent on. He pointed out that the
Corporation's plans for housing in the Bay meant that three quarters
of the residential property there would be 'up-market private sector
housing', and so the WO's contribution of £100 million over three
years for infrastructure costs was, in effect, a subsidy for private housing in particular, and property developers in general.[18]

Ted Rowlands himself took the argument even further, pressing
the Under Secretary of State, Ian Grist, for more details about the
Welsh Office's contribution to CBDC's overall capital costs. Mr Grist
reminded the House that

> ... my right hon. Friend the Secretary of State for Wales
> announced on 11 December that he was making £31.5 million
> available to the Cardiff Bay development corporation next year,
> and that, over the next three years, government funding would
> total £100 million, bringing the total amount given, or announced,
> to date to some £150 million. Beyond that, we will ensure that suf-
> ficient funding will be made available to enable the corporation to
> carry through its task... the total cost to the development corpo-
> ration is estimated ... to be some £402 million.[19]

The Member for Rhymney and Merthyr was equally persistent in
his attempts to drag out of the Bill's supporters the running costs of
the development, especially the Barrage. Understandably, Mr Michael
was not eager to respond; but when it eventually came, his answer was
to haunt him and his allies for more than a decade. He replied

> Initially, the corporation will fund the running costs. After its dis-
> solution, it is intended to create a fund from assets to enable the
> successor body to pay for operating costs.[20]

This was a particularly neat grammatical construction by the
future First Secretary to that 'successor body' – the Welsh Assembly.
It efficiently conceals who is doing the intending, who will do the creating, how the assets will be realised and who will decide what the
operating costs will be. These uncertainties would be exploited to the
full by Mr Michael in his later role.

His splendidly vague assurance did not inspire Mr Rowlands' confidence, and he demanded, in vain, of Ian Grist, 'Let me ask the
Minister again. He just got up and said the Cardiff Bay development
corporation [*sic*] will be able to raise money because it will sell houses and assets and develop its land. Does that mean that, if there is a
nice large surplus, it will come back to the Welsh Office and pay off
the £400 million initial investment?' When Ian Grist failed to reply, he
went on, 'Will the Minister answer the question? As he has not risen
from his seat, we must make the simple assumption that the £400
million is all grant and that if the CBDC earns lots of money as a consequence of the scheme, the money will not come back to the Welsh
Office. That is the simple lesson to draw from our series of
exchanges.'[21]

Mark Drakeford later summarised the thrust of Ted Rowlands'
argument very neatly, 'Wouldn't it be quicker, simpler and, in the long
run, cheaper, just to hand a Welsh Office grant-in-aid of £400 million
straight to the present and future landowners of Cardiff Bay, and not
bother with a barrage at all?'

Rhodri Morgan made several powerful contributions to the
debate, adding focus and specificity to the anti-barrage case.
Referring to the consequences of the recent decision on European
support for the PDR, he said

> A report by Coopers and Lybrand pleads the case for the
> Butetown link being given European regional development and
> Welsh Office support… The report makes it clear that there would
> be development in Cardiff Bay if the Butetown link is built. That
> is far more important than anything that the barrage is likely to
> contribute.
>   There is absolutely no other way of interpreting the statement
> in paragraph 549 of the report. After interviewing people in the
> property development industry, the writers of the report said:
>   'A majority of interviewees not yet committed to investment
> would still consider investment in the wider area if there was no
> barrage.'
>   Remember, the report is talking about property developers –

'However, this would significantly influence the timing and
scale of their investment, the quality and value of activity in their
choice of location either within the Bay or elsewhere. None of
them interviewed would invest without improvement in road links
in the Bay area.'

Mr Morgan went on

The Butetown road link is the critical factor... Not only Coopers
and Lybrand say that the barrage is not as important as other
essential factors. For example, in the December 1989 issue of
Housing magazine there is an interesting quotation...
'Barry Melhuish, Sales Director of Barratt, South Wales, con-
firms this. "Our development [the Windsor Quays development on
Ferry Road] is planned as a waterside development... which can
cater for the barrage happening or not happening". He says, "We
are proceeding without a care for the barrage."
... Sam Pickstock of Tarmac South Wales said he did not intend
to wait for the barrage and that his investment decisions had nothing to do with whether the barrage went ahead – and that was the
view of the largest housing developer in Britain.

In other words, the scheme's supporters might not be able to produce developers willing to declare a barrage was essential to their
plans, but its opponents had a number of big names prepared to say
that it definitely wasn't.

The Cardiff West MP enthusiastically revisited CBDC's apparent
inability to produce accurate plans of the vital Protected Property
Line. After the earlier fiasco, revealed during the carry over debate in
November, when the Chair of the Lords Select Committee had
signed the wrong maps to accompany the Bill, it now appeared that
'further uncovenanted changes' had appeared. The secretary of
Pontcanna Residents Against the Barrage (PRAB) had discovered
that the plans accompanying the Bill, and the plans CBDC had sent
out to local residents, differed – in the smaller scale plans, nine houses in Severn Grove in Canton had still 'been omitted from a list in
which – according to the original plan put before the House of Lords
– they should have been included'. Not only had the rights of those
living in Severn Grove to protection under the Barrage Bill been com-
promised, but even more worryingly, the competence of CBDC had
been called into question yet again.

PRAB's secretary was Ruth Dennis-Jones; she had lived in
Canton, just round the corner from Severn Grove, for nearly ten
years. She was not a cartographer, surveyor nor an engineer, but was
blessed with the ability to master any new subject that interested her,
with professional speed and thoroughness. Since graduating in Life

Sciences from Swansea University in the late seventies, she had been successively a university administrator, a pig farmer and had run a media company producing Welsh language videos; she was currently training as a Sub-Postmaster. She had also learned Welsh as an adult, progressing from scratch to a good honours degree and perfect fluency in less than six years. Fortunately for the other residents of Pontcanna, she could also read maps, and was prepared to put this skill at their disposal, *gratis*. The Development Corporation, on the other hand, was apparently paying lavish salaries for rather embarrassing inadequacies in this field. As Mr Morgan concluded, '...the Titanic was built by professionals, whereas Noah's Ark was built by inspired and very committed amateurs.'[22]

Ron Davies again made the environmental case against the Barrage, as he had during the carry over debate. He sounded the first serious public warning about the scheme's possible illegality under European law:

> The EEC directive on the conservation of wild birds requires the protection of species and especially of migratory birds... Article 2 of the treaty does not say there shall be a balance but that priority shall be given to ecological needs... if the Bill reaches the statute book, that will not be the end of the matter. We shall find ourselves before the European Court of Justice charged with a breach of article 2.[23]

His warning was soundly based and very timely. But, like Alun Michael's plans for using profit from asset sales to meet the Barrage's running costs, the words would come back to haunt him when he in his turn occupied the Welsh Secretary's office in Cathays Park.

The current incumbent, Peter Walker, had already agreed the date of his departure with the Prime Minister – he would return to the back benches in May 1990, when he would have been SoS for nearly three years. Since taking over from Nicholas Edwards, he had made very few public statements about the Barrage itself, in spite of the rapidly widening public debate on the issue. He apparently saw it is an integral part of the successful development of south Cardiff, but this in turn was seen as part of a general revival of post-industrial south Wales,

> Particularly startling has been the success of Wales in attracting investment from abroad and from other parts of the UK – a success in which Cardiff has shared.[24]

Walker had come to the Welsh Office from the DTI, where he had orchestrated the government's strategy for the steel and coal industries. The subsequent battles had ended in the decimation of heavy industry in south-east Wales, with a legacy of deep bitterness and distrust towards the Conservative government. As a result, in 1987, the new SoS had had serious public relations problems. He tried to deal with them, and the economic deprivation of the area, through the Valleys Initiative. This programme sought to co-ordinate public and private schemes for development in the Valleys, ensuring projects and investment were distributed consistently: Walker had thrown his considerable energies into the scheme. His efforts had won him a certain amount of grudging, partial respect, even from the hard left councillors of the Rhondda and Merthyr. However, this respect was to a great extent because he so clearly wasn't Nicholas Edwards.

> In Rhondda, they recall Edwards visited once, Walker seven times last year alone. 'Edwards was an abrasive bastard you wouldn't want to be in the same room with...' said a local editor.[25]

For Edwards, the redevelopment of Cardiff Bay had had the highest priority; Walker had wider horizons, and tried to promote Wales itself, on his trips abroad. Speaking to businessmen in Chicago, he did an impassioned hard sell,

> You are welcome, particularly in Wales. Wales is the most transformed economy in Western Europe... We would like to have every kind of American company in the Principality.[26]

The very few public references to the Development Corporation Walker made were cast as admonition, rather than encouragement:

> Welsh Secretary Peter Walker has warned planners and developers not to make a mess of the Cardiff Bay regeneration. He told them on Friday: 'There is no excuse for doing this badly. It would be deplorable for Cardiff and for Wales if this opportunity was lost'.[27]

When articles in *The Western Mail* or the *Echo* mentioned the Barrage and the Welsh Office, they were usually accompanied by photographs of Nicholas Edwards, rather than his successor. It was almost as if Walker was discretely distancing himself from the scheme. In his autobiography, Walker surprisingly makes no mention of Cardiff Bay, the Development Corporation or the Barrage, although he dwells at length on his time at the WO, and the Valleys Initiative, which absorbed considerably fewer of his department's resources[28]. Significantly, he has been the only SoS Wales to date who has founded and run a major business successfully, as opposed to simply taking a seat on the board of an established company. His curriculum vitae makes it clear that he is a man who can read a balance sheet, who

would know very soon after meeting the members of the board
whether it was worth his investing in their enterprise.

Peter Walker would have read the balance sheet for the Cardiff Bay
Barrage, he would have met the members of the CBDC board, and
one has the strong impression he did not approve of what he saw. But,
like Nicholas Edwards, the Welsh Office was his swansong on the
national political stage; there was no mileage in criticising or rethink-
ing the project – he just did what was necessary to prevent it
becoming unacceptably embarrassing, and got on with what were
would appear to be more rewarding matters elsewhere.

Perhaps, as a shrewd capitalist, he would have secretly agreed with
his political opponent, Allan Rogers the left wing Rhondda MP,

> … Someone came up with this scheme and ever since it was moot-
> ed all that we have done is to try to shoehorn all the facts to fit the
> scheme…[29]

Mr Walker was not among the payroll vote who shoehorned the
Bill through its Second Reading, by 112 votes to 16.

6. Moments of Conflict and Controversy

Do not judge men in moments of comfort and convenience. They are best judged in moments of conflict and controversy.

Martin Luther King, quoted by Jimmy Hood MP on his minority statement on the report of the Commons Select Committee on the Cardiff Bay Barrage Bill, May 1990.

The Commons Select Committee on the Barrage Bill, in its latest 1990 manifestation, had four members, two Conservative, two Labour. The Chair was Robert Hicks, Tory MP for Cornwall South East; unusually for a Member of Parliament, Mr Hicks was a science graduate, and a member of the Royal Geographical Society, which probably enabled him to follow some of the more esoteric debates about groundwater modelling or mapping more easily, and critically, than most MPs would have done. His fellow Conservative was Gary Waller, who had been in the Commons, representing a Yorkshire constituency, since 1979. Both were conscientious, apparently industrious back benchers, strangers to controversy, loyal to the party line.

Their Labour colleagues were both ex-miners, members of the NUM and former local councillors. Michael Welsh, MP for Doncaster North since 1983, had won his Commons seat relatively late, in his early fifties, and seemed to enjoy a comparatively quiet life, in Parliamentary terms. For Mr Welsh, the proceedings on the Barrage Bill must have induced strong feelings of *déjà vu*, as he had been a member of that earlier Commons Select Committee, which in 1986 had considered the South Glamorgan (Taff Crossing) Bill and firmly rejected the Barrage it had proposed for Cardiff Bay.

Jimmy Hood, elected for Clydesdale in 1987, was a much more abrasive and outspoken character, who had frequently attracted the attention of party whips as a result. Mr Hood is one of those politicians who seem incapable of remaining neutral or disinterested about any serious issue which attracts their notice. So, typically, he brought his experience as a Trade Unionist, (his low opinion of CBDC's economic case was clear from the beginning) and his miner's knowledge of the unpredictability of underground water movement to the questions before the Committee, with forthright clarity.

The fifteen petitioners against the Bill in 1989 had swollen to over 70 in 1990 and the Committee graciously agreed to the petitioners' request that some sittings be held in Cardiff, so that older or poorer

residents would not be forced to travel. This was the first time for
more than a quarter of a century that a Select Committee had met
outside Westminster.

As they convened for the first time in Commons Committee
Room 5, on 1st February 1990, the four MPs might have been for-
given for assuming they would just have to listen to a reprise of the
arguments heard by their colleagues in Another Place, the previous
April. They would have been very wrong. Those arguments had
widened and deepened in the meantime. Groundwater changes, water
quality and the destruction of the SSSI were still key issues, but the
anti-barrage campaign was attracting support from an increasing
number of experts of national and international reputation, eager to
contribute to the debate on the future of Cardiff Bay.

However, most of the counsel and agents for promoters and petitioners had been heard by the Committee's predecessors in the Lords:
Susan Hamilton for the Nature Conservancy Council, John Popham
and Kevin Standring for the RSPB and CFAC, with Peter Boydell
QC for the promoters, although Mr Boydell was now supported by
another eminent planning QC, Charles Sullivan.

Many of the petitioners were appearing before the Committee as
individuals. Others represented the five anti-barrage groups, with several hundred members between them, which had sprung up in the
city, under the aegis of Cardiff Flood Action, and Norman's leadership. These representatives, from Canton or Pontcanna or CFAC,
brought expert witnesses with them.

The anti-barrage groups were wholly reliant on donations by their
supporters, few of whom were wealthy, to function at all. The promoters, in stark contrast, had apparently limitless access to public
funds, to pay as many consultants as they wished to speak to the
Honourable Members on their behalf. But, by dint of persuasion, persistence and excellent argument, the anti-barrage groups had
recruited one of the most eminent musters of volunteers to appear
before any Parliamentary Committee.

The RSPB's agents had to consequently orchestrate an unprecedented number of individual and group petitions. Not only did they
have to deploy the complex arguments of expert witnesses like John
Miles and Kenneth Rushton on groundwater, or Geoffrey Barker on
waste disposal, they also had to stage manage appearances by more
than twenty private petitioners, most of whom were making their first,
rather nervous, venture into public life. To make their task even more
interesting, it had to be achieved without any money to pay even
experts' travel expenses, let alone their professional fees. The RSPB
was generous with the services of its agents, but even their resources

as the largest conservation pressure group in the UK seemed the merest drop in the Development Corporation's apparently bottomless buckets of 'grant-in-aid'.

All this had to be accomplished within the corset-like constraints of strict Parliamentary procedure, whose arcane protocols and etiquette could daunt even the most assiduous student of Erskine May. Acting as parliamentary agent for petitioners before a Select Committee is definitely no easy ride; it requires the abrasive professional flair of a barrister in a high profile court case, with the stamina of a Ph.D. student, when presenting a thesis to four, often cantankerous and always demanding, professors, in a *viva voce* exam lasting several months. It's a role needing the endurance of a ox, as well as the inquisitorial skills of Socrates and the versatility of a quick change artist.

Much of the evidence to be brought before the Committee was highly complex and technical; examination and cross-examination of witnesses often revealed the need for further detail, more data, supplementary reports. These had to provided forthwith, by petitioners or promoters, working to the Committee's requirements and strict timetable; if you were given 30 minutes to read and summarise a 3000 word report, then you did it in exactly 30 minutes, and produced 20-odd copies of your summary, to boot. In a court case of similar length and character, teams of junior lawyers and clerks would sit behind the leaders, to make and pass notes, assemble evidence, re-schedule witnesses and produce reports to order. Counsel for the promoters, of course, had such support in abundance; the Petitioners' agents had no-one. Even John Popham and Kevin Standring, gifted as they were with apparently limitless energy and an insatiable appetite for hard work, could not do everything themselves. So, they recruited voluntary, unpaid clerks from among the anti-barrage campaigners. Thus, Francis Maxey of Canton Residents Against the Barrage, professional juggler and circus tightrope walker, was approved by the Clerk to the Private Bills Office as 'a fit and proper person' for this role, which gave him privileged, if temporary, access to the telephones, photocopiers, fax machines and lavatories of the Palace of Westminster. During the Committee's two week sitting in Cardiff, Ruth Dennis-Jones, map reader extraordinaire and secretary of PRAB, took on the role, in the only slightly less august surroundings of South Glamorgan County Hall, foregoing several performances by her beloved Welsh National Opera, to do so.

As it turned out, their function often combined the skills of circus ringmaster and opera impresario, as they orchestrated petitioner appearances to deploy the wide variety of opposition to the Bill to best

effect – the bioscientist and the retired railwayman; the shy elderly
widow, speaking in public for the first time in 60 years, and the ambitious career politician: the museum curator and the town planner; the
young mother with her toddler dozing in a pushchair and the management consultant with an international reputation. Everyone had a
different perspective, everyone had the same aim – to stop the
Barrage.

In addition to hearing a greater number and variety of petitioners,
the Committee had to consider many issues not discussed before their
noble colleagues. One of the most controversial was the future of the
Ferry Road waste tip. Nothing could be more daunting to the
schemes of an imaginative town planner than a large, active, open
landfill site, prominent and unignorable, bang in the middle of a redevelopment. Landfill sites smell: they look awful: every day they are
visited by long processions of large, grimy vehicles, which tip even
more malodorous waste on them: there are very tight restrictions on
what can and cannot be built near them: even when they are finally
closed and cleared, there is a constant risk of explosions by methane
leaking from their decomposing contents. Ferry Road was a fine
example of all these woes, but, in addition, it shared a site with the
former Grangetown gasworks, still ennobled by two mammoth gas
holders, and its very own, possibly cyanide-enriched, waste tip. The
area had only been referred to very briefly in the representations to
the Lords Committee, but in the ten months since then, it had
become a matter of major concern in Cardiff, particularly to the people of Grangetown.

The tip covered over 60 acres of south Grangetown, on the penin-
sula between the Ely and Taff estuaries, and was Cardiff City
Council's biggest landfill site, active since the 1930s. By no stretch of
the most vivid imagination could it have a place in CBDC's plans for
'a superb environment in which people will want to live, work and
play'.[1] None the less, it had to be dealt with somehow in the development strategy Llewellyn Davies Planning LDP) prepared for Cardiff
Bay in 1988. One can only admire their courage and flair in grappling
with this planner's nightmare; it would be, they said,

> ... reclaimed for a park – 'Moorland Park'. This should have a new
> interesting land form and create a series of natural and semi-nat-
> ural woodland habitats. In the distant future, development could
> proceed – selected high quality campus projects within the park-
> land setting.[2]

The 'interesting landform' could be either the huge hole that
would be left if the tip was completely removed, or the huge mound

that would be created if its contents stayed where they were and the site was sealed off; knowing themselves to be on dangerous ground, in every sense, LDP wisely left the prospect rather vague.

The phrase 'in the distant future' was at least a realistic acknowledgement of the dire state of the tip, and the amount of time that would have to elapse before it could be judged safe to build there, given current regulations about the development of contaminated land, which the tip certainly was. LDP wisely did not touch upon another, even more vexed, question – where would Cardiff's domestic rubbish go when 'Moorland Park' was under construction? The only available alternative tipping site was at Rumney Moor, on Lamby Way, off Newport Road, east of the city centre. However, even the Lamby Way site would have to be considerably extended, southwards, if the three million tons of domestic rubbish Cardiff produced each year was to be disposed of. Unfortunately, this would entail the destruction of yet another SSSI, one of the few areas of marshland used for grazing in south Wales.

Even more worryingly, the latest in the succession of economic appraisals from KPMG had revealed that it would be necessary to realise the maximum value of all available land in the Bay area, including Ferry Road, as soon as possible, if the Barrage as a magnet for investment was to be justified. Building development there could no longer wait for some distant future.[3] Also, as Nigel Mason, a KPMG consultant, told the Committee, there were likely to be major transport problems in the Bay if commercial developments were concentrated in the Inner Harbour area – it would be necessary to spread them out a little more – with a 'second node of development in the Ferry Road area.'[4]

It was clear the original plans for wooded parkland had to be abandoned, and the need for 'campus' offices took their place. If building there was to begin in the lifetime of the Corporation, it could not wait for the site to be decontaminated; the 30-year-old tip would have to be completely removed.

The cost of the Ferry Road project, and its effects on public health and the environment were thoroughly aired before the Select Committee. The petitioners believed that the costs of making the area safe and attractive had not been properly estimated by CBDC. The state of the tip and its contents had not been fully investigated, and their plans for removing the waste were vague and over-optimistic. As a result, any costings they had provided were bound to be unreliable. The whole scheme was driven by the need to maximise land values in the area as quickly as possible; in contrast, the more gradual development proposed by the RSPB's *Living Waterfront* scheme would allow

more time to plan the tip's future and as well as creating suitable alternatives. A similar problem existed just across the Ely, at Penarth
Quay, where a much smaller domestic waste tip would also have to be
cleared and removed, to allow housing development and a marina to
go ahead, albeit at slightly less cost.

Promoters and petitioners alike acknowledged that Ferry Road
could not remain as it was, and that improving the site would be
expensive. But the petitioners believed that the need to maximise
profit, and justify the building of the Barrage, meant the promoters'
plans involved too much risk, too much money, too little thought and
too little time. They were certain that without the need to justify the
Barrage-as-investment-magnet, the whole project would become
more manageable, in terms of cost and timescale.

As a result, there were petitions on five areas of concern, which
were to be spoken to throughout the hearing: the destruction of the
SSSI; Ferry Road tip; the quality of the water in the impounded lake;
rising groundwater in south Cardiff; the flawed economic case for the
Barrage. For three months petitions on these themes were presented
with evidence from expert witnesses and personal testimony from
individuals. The clinical, scientific, coolly rational approach of the
experts was given colour and immediacy by the statements of ordinary Cardiffians.

As John Popham deftly reminded the MPs, the petitioners' main
arguments were closely interwoven: the economic case for the Barrage
demanded maximum land values, which forced the redevelopment of
the Ferry Road area and its tip with indecent haste; the Living
Waterfront scheme had to be assessed against the desired investment
returns set out in the KMPG appraisals; the promoters would not
agree to meet the costs of remedying damage from rising groundwater if these would impinge too heavily on the scheme's profits, and so
on.

Groundwater

The promoters' case remained unchanged; Nicholas Edwards' dream
of a 'superb maritime city' could only come true if the mudflats of
Cardiff Bay were covered by a freshwater lake, to make an attractive
centrepiece for massive, profitable redevelopment. The Bill set the
impoundment level, the height of the lake's surface above sea level, at
between 4 and 4.5 metres, as recommended by WEP.[5] However,
CBDC had recently overruled that advice. They estimated that, if the
'ugly' mudflats and saltmarsh of the Bay were to be completely con-
cealed, the impounded lake would have to be at least 4.5 metres deep.

Anti-barrage campaigners knew that setting impoundment at this level would only increase the risk of damage from raised groundwater. If the water level was set at only 4 metres, it might still be possible for at least part of the high water table round the Taff and Ely estuaries to drain into the Bay; at the level now demanded by the promoters, even this modest safety valve could not operate. Petitioners believed that, as a result, the whole question of any remedial works or protection measures for groundwater damage in the Bill had to be completely overhauled.

As John Miles said,

> My concern is the way the barrage investigation has gone about it from the wrong end. You should do the groundwater investigation and then say what impoundment levels will be.[6]

Unfortunately, the whole concept meant the project could only be approached 'from the wrong end'. The Secretary of State, and those Cardiff councillors who so readily adopted his dream as their own, had already announced there would be a barrage, so all the harsh realities of geology, river flows and tidal ranges could not be allowed to cloud that vision. If drowning the mudflats meant dangerous changes to the water table, so be it.

In the months since the Lords Committee, Norman Robson, Glyn Paul and Charlie Burriss had continued to meet with the Corporation to convince them of the need to rethink. All three men had experience in the building trade, all knew Cardiff's peculiar geology, and were confident enough to deal with the promoters on many issues. However, as the arguments over groundwater became more technical, they felt greater expertise was required.

Glyn had been doing regular door-to-door campaigning in his part of Grangetown, keeping neighbours up-to-date with developments. During one of these doorstep sessions he met an engineering student at Cardiff University, who had just moved into a nearby flat. When Glyn started to explain about groundwater, the young man suggested he should talk to a senior lecturer in the University's Engineering Faculty, Dr John Miles, an acknowledged expert in that field.

In October 1989, Glyn arranged a meeting between Dr Miles, Norman and Charlie. By coincidence, in 1987, when WEP were beginning their groundwater research, they had invited Dr Miles to work on the project. He had refused, as he would have had to devote more time to the work than his existing commitments allowed.

However, as he listened to the three campaigners, he had to agree there were serious causes for concern; the promoters had a case to answer, and he was willing to help the petitioners make sure they were forced to answer it. He looked at all the available work on groundwater and the Bay, and met with Ray Hornby of WEP, and Rowland Edwards, their groundwater consultant, several times. As a result, he agreed to give evidence for Cardiff Flood Action, without payment.

As he told the Committee Chair, '...these were lay people, a lot of them with no great knowledge, and they were obviously struggling and they could not afford experts and I felt sorry for them... The case that I gave to them was, I am not anti-barrage, and they were quite happy to proceed on that basis'.[7]

So, the man who was the Corporation's own first choice as specialist, while still apparently in favour of the Barrage, was convinced by current evidence that its begetters were incapable of carrying it through with the necessary technical rigour. He also persuaded his fellow groundwater experts, Professor Rushton of Birmingham University and Brian Connorton, Groundwater Resources Manager for Thames Water, to look at the anti-barrage case; they shared his view of WEP's work, and they too offered to appear as witnesses for the petitioners, also without payment. Barry Lane's band of mad, unemployed cynics had now been joined by the elite of British hydrology, and knew they were, more than ever, a force to be reckoned with.

Dr Miles was an expert in the computer modelling of groundwater. For obvious reasons, it is very difficult to observe the movement of groundwater, and practically impossible to reproduce its behaviour experimentally. The uncertainties these problems caused had long been a stumbling block for civil engineers, until the advent of computer modelling. This innovation meant that software became available specifically to replicate groundwater movement and the events which could change it, so that engineers could have much more reliable information about possible changes in flow and volume under particular conditions, like the building of the Cardiff Bay Barrage.

Since the first programmes were developed, in the late 1980s, no major engineering project where groundwater was a significant issue could proceed without this sort of modelling. Because of the complexity of the software needed, and the amount of specialist knowledge of system design, mathematics and hydrogeology needed to use it successfully, experts in this field were few – Dr John Miles and Professor Rushton were among that tiny group, and many of the rest were their former students.

The petitioners had three worries about groundwater – the poor quality of the promoters' work on changes to the water table, obvious even to laymen, which Dr Miles and his colleagues would deal with, their lack of appreciation of the importance of the 'made ground' (i.e.

land which has been raised above sea level by tipping waste material on it – made ground is present throughout most of south Cardiff) and the sections of the Bill which were meant to protect them from those risks, which Norman spoke to. Acting as more intimate, counterpoints to these themes were the heart-felt pleas of private petitioners.

Hilary Robinson, for instance, spoke movingly of her family's terrible experiences in the floods of 1979. A former office cleaner, Hilary cared for an invalid husband suffering from a severe stroke and a sister with Downs Syndrome. She was also a volunteer playleader at the local multi-cultural playgroup in Riverside. Of all the petitioners' statements heard by the committee, hers was the most powerful argument for the redrafting of Clause 12.

> The front and the middle living room were... about eighteen inches under water, but then there were three steps down to the third living room and kitchen where we lived and all these rooms were four feet under water. It was up over our mantlepiece...
>
> There was no official communication with us that night or the following day, but various volunteers came round offering soup and sympathy...
>
> Slowly the water seeped away and after 36 hours it had gone, leaving behind a carpet of mud and sewage... I shall never forget the smell... Our front room carpets which had remained downstairs were ruined by soaking and sewerage [*sic*] and they were dumped out in the street to be carried away. The next few days were spent mopping up... Everyone's possessions were out in the street; it was terrible.
>
> My daughter Ann, who was 15 at the time, became very ill with bronchitis and had to be evacuated – everywhere was so damp...
>
> We received a total of £166.72 from the Lord Mayor's fund and EEC contributions. That was because we were not insured. Then a public meeting was held in the City Hall with a packed audience. Everybody was demanding compensation, a public inquiry; they were very angry. After the councillors left the stage, the Cardiff Flood Action Committee was formed with a representative from every street that had been affected, and Norman Robson was elected unanimously as chairman and he has my full support.
>
> There were many problems with the insurance companies. We had building insurance with Sun Alliance which partly covered the damage to the structure of the house, but we had no contents insurance; we could not afford it. Because we had a duplicate [*sic*] policy, the original being with the City Council as we had a City Council mortgage, the insurers would not accept our claim and said we were not covered for flood damage. Many people in our area had similar problems with insurance.
>
> After great difficulty, they finally agreed that after all we were covered for floods but then the loss adjusters appeared and instead of the estimated £6,000 for remedial work, we were offered half

that – £3,000. Later they upped it to £3,750, and I was told I could do the decorating myself, which I did...

I began going to meetings and found people were angry at the lack of compensation and at the authorities for not issuing warnings, and even after two ombudsmen reports the authorities are still blaming each other...

After taking legal advice on the strength of the ombudsman report, my husband and I started legal action for damages... there were many obstacles to overcome before the case finally came to court in October, 1987, 8 years after the floods... Mr Justice Michael Davies found Cardiff City Council two-thirds responsible and South Glamorgan County Council one-third to blame for failing to warn residents in the Cathedral Road and Riverside areas of the impending danger from the great flood of 1979. South Glamorgan County Council appealed the decision and final settlement was not until November 1989, nearly 10 years after the floods...

So this Bill causes even more confusion. Who will be to blame if there is a further flood? There are no guarantees in this Bill...[8]

Colin Powell, retired trade union official, magistrate, school governor, foster father and secretary of Leckwith Residents Against the Barrage, also looked back to the 1979 floods – his wife's grief at the damage to the home they had worked so hard to make, the discomfort of being without heating or cooked food, for several days, in a cold December. However, with typical good humour, he also described the anguish of their dog, obviously thoroughly housetrained, confined to the first floor by the flood water, and unable to get outside to do what a dog has to do.

My daughter asked me this morning not to mention this bit, because 'I get embarrassed, dad', but I said, 'no, it has to be said.' I can remember my wife at the top of the stairs, laying down newspaper... saying to our dog, 'Come on, boy, pick up your leg and have a go!' He could not get out anywhere. That sticks in your mind, trying to pick up the dog's leg saying, 'You know what you have to do.' It didn't happen; he didn't go for three days.[9]

The provisions of the infamous Clause 12 of the Bill, had been changed slightly to accommodate the proposals of their Lordships. The most important alteration was the removal of the 'further protected property' area – in the current version, there was just one 'protected property' line. The owners and occupants of buildings within that line were entitled to a survey assessing the dampness of their property, to be arranged by the promoters, before the bay was impounded, and a further survey in the second year after impoundment. Any deterioration due to groundwater revealed by the surveys would entitle them to require CBDC to carry out remedial work.

Owners and occupiers of property outside the line would have to arrange such surveys at their own expense. If there was any deterioration due to raised groundwater, CBDC would be required to carry out remedial work, and refund the cost of the surveys. In both areas, any claims had to be made within twenty years of impoundment. No money would change hands, there was no compensation in cash or kind, residents would have no say in which surveyors would enter and examine their homes or when; no wonder that Hilary, Colin and so many of their neighbours had lodged petitions.

Knowing the technical flaws in the promoters' case could be left in the safe hands of Dr Miles and his colleagues, Norman described the elaborate and complex Code of Practice (CoP). The purpose of such codes, when accompanying a parliamentary bill, is to set out how its provisions were to be put into practice and to define its terms. Codes of practice are not considered part of the Act they refer to, and may be altered, without further legislation, by those responsible for the Act concerned, in this case, the Development Corporation or its 'successor body' – whoever would take charge of the Barrage after CBDC's demise, in the late 1990s.

The Barrage Bill's Code was very significant; it defined conditions, like the level of the impounded lake, and procedures, like those to be followed by surveyors assessing 'protected' properties. If the Bill became law, its terms would be as important for any householder making a claim as those of the Act itself. However, while the Act could only be altered by further legislation, the CoP could be changed unilaterally by the undertakers, the Corporation. No matter how carefully the Code was drafted, or how much its terms protected local residents, it could still be altered, at any time, even after the Royal Assent, and the people of Cardiff could be left with no redress whatever. CFAC were particularly anxious about this possibility, because, Norman told the Committee, 'if we do not get this right, if the Barrage Bill is allowed to pass, we will be in a very powerless condition. They will be able to do whatever they like with us, quite frankly'.[10]

He outlined the many talks he, with Charlie Burriss and Glyn Paul, had had at CBDC's offices; they had been looking at the Barrage proposals for more than two years. As a result, they felt the Protected Property Line was unworkable, given the gaping holes in the promoters' case. 'We would hesitate to put a line on the thing given the uncertainty about groundwater levels and so forth,' he added.[11] They felt strongly that, where groundwater damage was suspected, the onus of proof should lie with the promoters, not local householders, because, Norman insisted, 'we have not asked for this barrage, we have not asked for it and all the problems it brings with it and it will bring with it...'[12] They were being asked to carry the can for something they didn't want, and felt very bitter about it all.

There was further concern about the effect the threat of groundwater damage might have on the value of their homes. With hindsight, given the steep rise in property values throughout Cardiff, including Riverside, Grangetown and Canton, in the next ten years, that fear seems totally misplaced; it seems much more rational when seen in the context of the property market in Riverside following the flood of 1979, so graphically described by its victims. There it had actually been impossible to sell a perfectly acceptable six bedroomed house on the Taff Embankment for more than £500. With such memories, 'barrage blight' was not an empty phrase, and it was felt the promoters should be made to pay for such losses.

CFAC were also concerned about the methods likely to be used in the surveys. The promoters' Code of Practice suggested electric moisture meters, but Cardiff Flood Action and Taff Housing had members with much experience of renovating older buildings in south Cardiff. They knew that most houses built there between 1880 and 1950 had been plastered with black mortar, which contained high levels of carbon, and was therefore an efficient conductor of electricity. In such circumstances, it was very unlikely the electric moisture meters proposed by CBDC would be accurate. Instead, Norman suggested the use of piezometers, recommended for measuring dampness by the highest national authority on such matters, the Building Research Establishment.[13] Of course, the more sensitive and accurate piezometer would be rather more expensive than the promoters' method, although no doubt the fees charged by Messrs Boydell and Sullivan would have paid for all the piezometers the petitioners could possibly desire.

Another major concern was the complexity of the Code of Practice itself. Norman commented, 'It really is a very difficult thing. It is too complex to be argued in front of the Committee... It seems obvious we will be discussing it with the promoters for some time.' He went on, 'At present there is no provision for arbitration in the event of any dispute between us... they [CBDC] could impose their will on us, and there is nothing we could do about it.'[14] He suggested that the Bill should be amended to include a complaints administrator, appointed by the Secretary of State for Wales, to deal with disputes over the implementation of Clause 12, and also that, if the Bill became law, then the Code of Practice could not be amended by the promoters, without the consent of the groups representing the petitioners.

Mr Popham pointed out that there was a precedent for such a complaints administrator – the Channel Tunnel Bill had included just such provision. In that case, the arbitrator was supposed to deal with complaints by the public, where it was unclear which of the many public bodies and private companies involved in building the Tunnel were responsible for the matter complained of. As Hilary and her neighbours had had to wait more than ten years for derisory compensation after the fiasco of 1979, while various bodies played pass the parcel with the blame, this seemed little enough to ask.

Norman ended with a heart-felt appeal to the Committee, 'we must plead with you that the Barrage Bill is not allowed to proceed... We are concerned about prosperity, we do want to see the docks develop, but we do not see any connection between building a concrete wall 30 foot high, enclosing a dubious lagoon, and development.'[15]

The next witness for the petitioners was Dr John Miles, who carried out a thorough, neat, professional demolition job on the research done by CBDC's own groundwater consultant, Mr Rowland Edwards. Mr Edwards, whose final report to CBDC had reassuringly concluded that there was no evidence groundwater levels would change dramatically post-barrage.[16]

Much of the evidence on which this conclusion was based had been gathered by a method startling in its simplicity. Test boreholes were sunk in those parts of Cardiff where, the Corporation's engineers believed, the groundwater level might give cause for concern. A chain was then lowered into each borehole, with small buckets attached, 18 inches apart. When inspection showed a particular bucket contained water, it was assumed that this indicated the current groundwater level at this spot. This technology was probably no more sophisticated, or accurate, than that available to Thomas Rammell, for his investigations in the same area, 150 years earlier, but it was the basis for the groundwater contouring of south Cardiff on which Mr Edwards placed such faith, and on which decisions about a multi-million pound development, involving potential damage to over 12,000 homes, were to be made.

Dr Miles had become familiar with Mr Edwards' research methods at the meetings he had attended with Norman, Glyn, Charlie and CBDC. Wallace Evans in particular had deferred to his expertise and reputation, and given him full access to their work. As a result, he was able to produce a daunting list of their errors and omissions. The most significant of these were:-

- The computer programme, the Wallingford Procedure, employed by Mr Edwards and his colleagues had been used inappropriately and inaccurately; it was just not designed for the purpose to which they had been put it, and therefore any results derived from it could not be relied on.

• Too few boreholes had been sunk in the Bay area itself; it was therefore impossible to assess how the tides and groundwater flows interacted at present, and how those flows would run when there were no longer any tides, after the Barrage.

• Data had only been collected in those areas where WEP thought there might be problems – in gravels. The much riskier made ground of Grangetown had been ignored. As a result, the role of the city's sewers in modifying groundwater flows in made ground was still not assessed; Dr Miles believed that it was only the capacity of Grangetown's sewers to absorb groundwater that kept the area dry enough to be habitable, as it was.

• There seemed to be no good geological reason why the northern boundary of the 'protected property area' had been set where WEP had put it. Many homes beyond this line would be at risk, post-barrage.[17]

The Committee did not have to take the word of John Miles alone on these very grave failings. Professor Rushton, one of the other eminent groundwater experts appearing for the petitioners, was unable to attend the Committee, as he was working on a project in India. However, Dr Miles spoke to his colleague's proof of evidence. He confirmed that Professor Rushton was the leading groundwater expert in the UK, and went on, 'I do not think there is anybody nearly as good', adding modestly, 'I include myself in that'.[18] The Professor had worked on groundwater computer models for, among others, the Anglian Water authority, Thames Water Authority, North-West Water Authority, Severn-Trent Water Authority and many more.

Dr Miles emphasised that the Professor agreed with the points he had already made on WEP's apparently unprecedented use of the Wallingford Procedure, and their failure to quantify the impact of the Barrage on the groundwater system's capacity to drain away inflows.[19] Professor Rushton's evidence, based on his own work creating a groundwater model for Liverpool, endorsed Dr Miles' own views on the importance of including sewers and water mains in such plans.

The Committee had already heard the evidence, for the promoters, of Mr Glyn Jones, author of the report on CBDC's groundwater studies commissioned by Alun Michael and Peter Perkins. Mr Jones had repeated his endorsement of this work, and Mr Boydell emphasised his credentials, including work on a groundwater project at Riyadh, in Saudi Arabia, with Professor Rushton.

Mr Popham had referred to this project in his cross-examination of Mr Jones when he established that the groundwater modelling for that project had been done by Professor Rushton alone, Mr Jones had played no part in it. Kenneth Rushton was keen to emphasise that Mr Jones had none of the modelling skills essential for this sort of work. In other words, he did not have the experience or qualifications to make any reliable assessment of the promoters' work on groundwater. The Professor's other main concern was that WEP's work did not 'include any time variant responses' – it did not cover a long enough period, with varying rainfall, river flows and tides, season by season. As Dr Miles commented, 'you have to produce history before you can go on to predict.'[20]

Summing up his own evidence and that of Professor Rushton, Dr Miles said that the WEP report had 'been undertaken by somebody who is not experienced in groundwater flow modelling... Given the current level of understanding, you cannot really safely proceed with the Barrage.' He advised that 'if you brought in somebody who really knew what they were doing, if they worked flat out, they could do that [an accurate groundwater flow model for south Cardiff] within a year, so it would not involve a massive delay...[until then] you cannot say what the effect of the Barrage will be.'

This view was endorsed by Brian Connorton, a specialist in water flow modelling and Groundwater Resources Manager for Thames Water Utilities, when he was examined by Mr Popham. Mr Connorton had been responsible for modelling groundwater changes in London, for the building of the Thames Barrage. He also believed another year's work was necessary, to provide the reliable data the promoters had singly failed to come up with, so far.[21]

Popham asked what the consequences would be if the Barrage went ahead, as set out in the current Bill. Dr Miles commented, 'You could effectively turn Cardiff into an urban swamp. There would be problems of rising damp in houses, you could have water levels above ground level.' He added 'How this would work, I find it difficult to conceive, because nobody has ever tried doing this to a city before... it [a correctly designed and tested model] would show you... where the problem areas would be.'[22]

Dr Miles' impressive evidence for the petitioners was given even greater credibility by his apparent support for the Barrage itself. 'I think no civil engineer could be against it, it is a smashing civil engineering scheme but you have to do the thing properly, and the work which has been undertaken [by WEP] really is not quite up to standard...'[23] Some years after, he was to confess that this support for the Barrage was only careful stage management by John Popham; he felt, rightly as it turned out, that the Committee would listen more sympathetically to a professional scientist in favour of the promoters' ends, but whose high standards lead him to question the sloppiness of their means, than to one prepared to launch a frontal attack on the whole scheme.

The Chair was obviously impressed by Dr Miles' abilities and his evidence. He asked, 'Why did not the Corporation seek some other specialist, i.e. a groundwater modellist [*sic*] rather than go down the path they did?' John Miles modestly suggested that CBDC might not have heard of any. But Mr Hicks persisted, 'I cannot understand why the Corporation who have if anything been criticised for being too extravagant with public funds... did not go to the right people.'

He went on, 'To me, as a layman, you have not been questioning their [CBDC's experts] technical competence in their own spheres but in effect saying that they know damn all about this particular aspect.' When Dr Miles agreed, Mr Hicks added 'Which is quite a damning indictment, if I may so.'[24] At this point, the anti-barrage campaigners listening to the hearing, felt they were nearer to achieving their aim than at any time since their fight began.

The Chair went on to confirm that Dr Miles was still acting for the petitioners without payment. 'Yes', he answered, 'I am losing about £200 today in train fares!' He was asked how and why he became involved in the petitioners' campaign: 'So you were willing to do quite a lot of work without any real motivation, except the wish to be able to make some sort of judgement?'[25]

Even the sharp and combative Peter Boydell could not shake Dr Miles' confidence in his assessment of the promoters' groundwater reports. The QC suggested other bodies whose experts, on the other hand, had apparently found WEP's work quite satisfactory. He asked what the National Rivers Authority's view had been. Dr Miles' reply was a perfect justification for the lawyers' dictum that counsel should never ask a question to which they do not already know the answer. He said, '...National Rivers Authority is an interesting case, they have just been set up, and I know that they at the moment do not have a groundwater specialist, because in December they phoned me up and said they were setting the post up and would I be interested in it and how much would they have to pay me to fill the post! So who they have got to make these comments, I am not quite sure.'[26] At this point, petitioners who had already suffered at the hands, or rather the wit, of Mr Boydell, were strongly tempted to get up and cheer.

It was clear that this relentless exposure of the promoters' negligence and ignorance was destroying the Barrage Bill before the

Corporation's very eyes; they had to do something – anything – to preserve it. So, in an extraordinary eleventh hour attempt to limit the damage, while Dr Miles was still being cross-examined by their counsel, on 27th March, two months into the Committee hearings, they commissioned yet another assessment of WEP's groundwater work, from Hydrotechnica Ltd. John Miles had earlier referred to this company as highly reputable groundwater modelling practitioners. Here David Crompton, CBDC's director of engineering, had seen an opportunity to win back some of the credibility lost by their disastrous performance so far. If the Committee had listened with such admiration and sympathy to Dr Miles' evidence, then would they not have to listen with equal admiration and sympathy to experts he approved of, if only they could be produced to speak on behalf of the Barrage...

Amazingly, Hydrotechnica's report was presented in evidence to the Committee a mere six days later. The MPs agreed to consider it, only on condition that Dr Miles be recalled to read and comment on it. He was not impressed.

> I think it is a ludicrous thing that we are talking about something that is going to affect a city centre and all these houses and costs millions and millions of pounds of public money and the Promoters have brought someone in who had a glance through reports and decided it was probably alright.[27]

As he pointed out, among many other important omissions, Hydrotechnica had not even looked at the contentious groundwater modelling issue.

In his summing up, John Popham drew three conclusions from Dr Miles' evidence – a year's further research was needed; an impoundment level could not be set until that research was complete; a Protected Property Line could not be set until that research was complete. The alternative had been suggested by John Miles himself, with wry humour,

> ... I think the claims resulting from it [the barrage] and the fact I have stood out against it would attract to me a lot of consultancy...[28]

Ferry Road

The story of Grangetown's Ferry Road tip provided still further evidence that the demand for a barrage had been allowed to distort the whole regeneration strategy for south Cardiff. Nicholas Edwards' vision made it necessary to recast the economics of the development so that projected increases in land values had to include an area, like Ferry Road, which was not yet ready to offer such returns. For development in the district to show enough profit to justify the Barrage, it would have to be cleaned up at frantic speed. The Corporation's plans for doing so were thrown together hurriedly, without adequate preparation, research or consultation.

As it became clear that CBDC were planning to excavate and remove the contents of the tip, public concern grew at the prospect of the inevitable noise, smell and public risks. Before the Select Committee first met, Rhodri Morgan wrote in January 1990 to the Department of the Environment for their comments on this prospect. David Trippier, Minister of State at the DoE, replied, in a letter dated 16th February, 1990. His response did not make comfortable reading for the Corporation:

> The excavation of landfill site should be undertaken under the most rigorously controlled conditions and is generally not to be encouraged...
> The removal of very large quantities of old refuse from the Ferry Road site is likely to be difficult. Such removals have taken place elsewhere... where the waste has only been moved a short distance. Other schemes... have generally involved small sites... where the high costs... can be justified...
> It is unlikely that any... sites in Wales would be prepared to accept the old refuse... This means that the waste would, almost certainly, be sent to a private sector site... involving long haulage routes.

In short, translated out of the careful language of the civil servant who drafted Mr Trippier's reply, it said 'This could be a dangerous, complex and expensive thing to do.'

The DoE were not alone in their worries about the consequences of removal. Cardiff Flood Action had sought the advice of Geoffrey Barker, a former Assistant County Engineer to Surrey Council, now a consultant on waste management. On the 2nd February, he met with David Crompton, CBDC's Head of Engineering, Owen Glyndwr Thomas, CBDC's engineering consultant, and Norman, in Cardiff.

At this meeting, a number of facts about the tip, and CBDC's plans for it, were established. The Corporation estimated it held 3,500,000 metres^3 of refuse. They were considering a pilot scheme, removing 115,000 metres^3 over nine months, but planning permission from the City Council would be needed to move any more of the contents. The best way to move the waste to its eventual destination would be by rail, using a disused coal delivery terminal nearby; about 1000 tonnes could be moved per train load which, as the Corporation spokesman tastefully expressed it, 'would be odorous'. As one Cardiff

Flood Action supporter commented, 'It may be odorous in Cardiff Bay, but it'll stink to high heaven in Grangetown.' The work would be put out to tender, and the successful contractor would be responsible for finding a site to dispose of the waste. The former clay pits and brick fields of Bedfordshire were apparently being investigated as suitable depositories. Mr Crompton had written to Bedfordshire's County Surveyor, Tony Brown, sounding out their likely response.

It also emerged that the former tip would eventually be used for industrial development; residential use was uneconomic, with so many more attractive sites available in the area. However, the Corporation's advisers believed the increased value of the land would make the costs of removal (which CBDC did not divulge at this point – probably because they had absolutely no idea of what they were) just about feasible. The site was also wet; the river Ely had originally meandered in deep twists and turns right across it. Tipping had filled these meanders, and thirty years' rainfall had left the site thoroughly waterlogged. This resulted in constant leaching into the already heavily polluted river. The Corporation appreciated the need to dry out the tip, to stop this leachate reaching the waters of the Barrage-impounded lake; they planned to dewater the site, section by section, then pump the leachate out into the Bristol Channel through a long outfall. Apparently, no treatment plant of sufficient capacity to cope with it existed.

Barry Lane was cross-examined about the details of the Corporation's plans for transporting the contents of the tip to Bedfordshire; the plans were shown to be rather vague. Mr Popham asked '…it is a round trip of 400 miles is it not?' Mr Lane replied 'I have not done the sums'. He also appeared to be ignorant of the recent public outcry in Bedfordshire, when plans to accept waste from Europe had been announced – so great was the outcry that the plans had to be abandoned. Jimmy Hood questioned the Chief Executive about any backup plans CBDC might have for dealing with the waste. He answered with airy grandeur, 'We do not accept that the heart of Cardiff should be left with methane generating material. There must be ways of removing it…'[29]

Sitting quietly at the back of Committee Room 5, listening with great interest to this exchange were members of FoE's Cardiff and Penarth groups. Penarth FoE were taking a very close interest in the Corporation's plans for the tip. They had good grounds for believing that that quantities of low-level radioactive material from Amersham International's Cardiff factory had been dumped there, over the years. In their view, the tip's contents should not therefore be classified as 'domestic waste'. They wondered if the people of Bedfordshire knew

exactly what was coming to them; it was felt the CBDC's performance in the frankness and accuracy stakes so far had not been
reassuring. So, just to make sure, one of them slipped out, to find a
telephone. He spoke at some length to his opposite number in
Bedford FoE, who was most interested in what he had to say. He, in
turn, made more phone calls; the most fruitful were to a senior member of Bedfordshire Council, and to a producer at Radio Bedford,
who gave the matter a thorough airing on their early morning news
roundup.

As a result, the future of Ferry Road was raised at a stormy meeting of Bedfordshire Council's Minerals and Waste Sub-Committee,
on 19th February, a few days later. Several of the councillors on the
sub-committee made it clear they would not be at all happy to accept
the tip's contents. They were particularly angry that in doing so, they
would be colluding in the destruction of an SSSI, to which the majority of them were opposed on principle. In his correspondence with
their County Surveyor, David Crompton had somehow omitted any
mention of the drowning of Cardiff Bay: the waste disposal practices
of Amersham International also seem to have slipped his mind. It
began to look, very unlikely that Bedfordshire clay pits would offer a
home to Ferry Road's waste.

Rowland Edwards had seen his professional reputation tested
almost to destruction over groundwater; he might have drawn a little
consolation from watching the same thing happen to a fellow expert
witness as John Popham cross-examined Owen Glyndwr Thomas
about Ferry Road. Mr Thomas was responsible for the Corporation's
plans for dealing with the tip.

John Popham quickly established that Mr Thomas had no specific
qualifications or experience in waste management, that he had no
experience in dealing with still-active tips, like Ferry Road, and that
he had not carried out any substantial investigation of the tip itself.[30]

Worse was to come when Mr Popham introduced the petitioners'
own waste disposal expert, Geoffrey Barker. He was concerned over
the lack of control over what had been dumped at Ferry Road, and
said 'I am very glad that in my career I never had the difficult job of
filling up a landfill site that contained such large meanders in such difficult circumstances.... The whole site must be a kind of pudding now
in the river area.'

He was critical of the promoters' view of the result. 'The pollution
has been found and is clearly stated. The extent of it, however, has not
been quantified and this, I think, is a matter of concern.' He described
how, as the site was saturated and had a high water table, pollutants
moved horizontally through it rather than vertically, as they would in

drier conditions. This meant that the tip would be further contaminated by the contents of the neighbouring gasworks. Mr Barker pointed out that the promoters' own proofs of evidence included 'some pretty horrendous examples of the sort of pollution they found in trial boreholes under the [gasworks] site... Spent oxides have been dumped in the past on this site and they are likely to contain cyanide and other substances.'

Mr Barker went on to describe the problem of costing removal of the tip's contents. 'At the moment, I consider such information as has been provided by the promoters with regard to the proposed methods of transportation and proposed place of disposal is not clear enough and certainly a contract could not be drawn up on the figures as prepared at the present time.'[31]

He estimated the cost of clearing the Ferry Road and Penarth Quay tips at £94.7 million, compared to the promoters' figure of £80 million. Mr Barker's figure did not include costings for 'uncertainties', such as preventing the escape of pollutants from the gasworks site, delays in transportation, extra costs for excavating the river channels, or the costs of dealing with any additional pollution discovered under the site. He felt it might be necessary to allow a further £3 to £5 million to cover these contingencies. These expenses would, have to be weighed against the possible benefits of redevelopment, but there was no evidence that CBDC had done any of the necessary sums.

Mr Barker's professional caution was in stark contrast to Christopher Benson's blithe optimism on behalf of the promoters, 'I think it will be extraordinarily difficult to see that area [the tip] developed adequately unless some higher land values are attributed elsewhere to allow them to be subsidised...'[32] So much for the harsh economic realism of the property developer – but then, with the substantial grant-in-aid from the Welsh Office at its disposal, perhaps CBDC could afford to be a little vague.

Mr Popham referred to the £6.5 million CBDC had offered the City Council as a contribution to the City's waste treatment costs, following the loss of the tip. The Council were considering the installation of an anaerobic digester plant to dispose of the city's refuse, in place of the landfill site; this, Mr Barker estimated, would cost around £19 million, and he allowed a possible net income from the recycled waste the digester would produce, which was 'unlikely to exceed £10 a tonne'. He agreed with Mr Popham that the City Council would have to find the subsequent shortfall in costs.[33] In other words, the City Council would be heavily subsidising CBDC's rush to maximise profits from the development of the site.

It also appeared that Bedfordshire County Council were not the only local authority whom the Corporation had apparently not briefed fully about waste and its disposal. On 28th March, Councillor Ian Brown, an enthusiastic member of the City Council's Engineering Services Committee, gave evidence in support of Riverside Ward Labour Party's petition.

The councillor was deeply concerned about the assumption of this for the promoters, that tipping on the Ferry Road tip, would end in mid-June, 1990, and that, from then on, the City's waste would be dumped at the Lamby Way site. Although a member of the council committee responsible, he knew nothing of this plan, or any formal agreement to it. The member for Rumney, a Conservative, also sat on this committee, and he had had no formal notice of any development of the Lamby Way/Rumney Moor tip, in his ward, either.[34] Yet again, CBDC had ridden rough-shod over local democracy and local sensibilities.

Mark Lintell, director of Land Use Consultants, a multi-disciplinary environmental consultancy, was cross-examined by Mr Sullivan, about his suggestions for the future of the tip, in support of *The Living Waterfront* proposals. These proposals assumed that tipping would have to continue at the site for six to eight years. Mr Lintell described the advantages: '... a long period in which to research the alternatives is obviously of great value to the city. It means they are not rushed into consideration of an alternative site or alternative method of treatment... also... the costs of disposing of waste to landfill are infinitely cheaper than any of the other disposal methods.'

He added a third benefit, an example of the much wider context in which the petitioners saw the whole development issue, 'the deferment of impact elsewhere [whichever site the Ferry Road waste would have to be transported to] is actually a benefit, can be seen as a benefit.'

When pressed by Mr Sullivan about the lower private investment and lower returns to the Corporation in the area, that would result from continued tipping, he replied 'There are such things as cash limits imposed by the Treasury, and I am certain those cash limits are going to become more exacting than they are today...'. In other words, the Corporation would not always enjoy its present easy access to public funding.

Mr Lintell compared the economic case for the Barrage presented to the Lords Select Committee, with that being considered by the Honourable Members in 1990: 'I think there are a whole series of adjustments which have been made by the Corporation which in the current climate really are incredible. I particularly draw the Committee's attention to the level of private investment which is supposed to be going to be put into the Ferry Road area... 75 per cent

... of the cost of depolluting the Ferry Road area would be borne by the private sector. That, in my experience, is not the way the private sector operates.'[35]

Mark Lintell for the RSPB also described Ferry Road's future in the more rational and sympathetic Living Waterfront project which 'could be phased... while further research is carried out on Ferry Road'.[36]

The Corporation was in an apparently unresolvable dilemma; their plans required the complete removal of the tip for the development to succeed, but removal was so complex and dangerous that its costs were incalculable, and anyway, there was apparently nowhere to move it to. As the Committee Chair said of the Promoters' plans for the tip, 'At the moment, it is a bloody mess...'[37]

Barrage Economics

The debate about the economic case for the scheme ranged well beyond the problems posed by Ferry Road. The latest financial appraisal by KPMG had been published less than two weeks before the Select Committee met. It would provide the petitioners with yet more rich and meaty bones of contention.

As John Popham repeatedly reminded the MPs, the onus was on the promoters to prove their case – their conviction that it was essential if maximum investment was to be attracted to south Cardiff, a case set out in great detail by KPMG. Cross-examined by John Popham, Nigel Mason, their senior management consultant, admitted that it would be impossible to distinguish between investment attracted by the Barrage and investment brought by the PDR, then under construction.

This point was effectively developed some weeks later with typical dynamism and elan by Kate Hunter, Chair of Canton Residents Against the Barrage, when she presented their petition. She produced in evidence a letter from Wayne David, the MEP for South Wales, in which he stated that no European funding would be available for the PDR; it would all have to be paid for by the council tax payers of South Glamorgan. This had been confirmed by no less an authority than the Leader of the County Council, Lord Brooks, in the leaflet, *Budget News*, distributed with everyone's community charge bills, the week before.[38]

Given the difficulty of distinguishing between good transport links, and the Barrage, as attractions for investment in the area, it looked very much as if the tax payers of South Glamorgan could well be heavily subsidising the development project.

If the promoters' argument that the expense of the Barrage would be justified by increased land values, more jobs and homes, and all the other benefits they promised, it followed that somewhere, somehow, someone should be able to produce a balance sheet clearly demonstrating that for the expenditure of a particular amount of public money, a specific amount of private investment had been attracted – the principle of leverage. The presence of a rogue card like the PDR made such a credible balance sheet impossible; no-one would ever be able to say how much had been achieved by the Barrage and how much by the road. Nonetheless, CBDC still insisted on its necessity with all the fervour of a medieval philosopher proclaiming that a pound of feathers weighs less than a pound of lead.

The argument was given a further twist when Mr Popham examined John Bowers on behalf of the RSPB. Dr Bowers was Reader in Applied Economics at Leeds University, specialising in the cost-benefit appraisal of public expenditure projects with implications for the natural environment. He noted that 'The presumption [in the KPMG appraisal] is that Cardiff Bay will divert a lot of employment and investment from other parts of Cardiff and south-east Wales and therefore cannot on any reasonable estimation be treated as benefit for the purposes of an economic appraisal.'

In other words, public investment in Cardiff Bay, including the Barrage, would not create any new jobs; it would simply bring them to Cardiff, instead of some other city. The same applied to land values. He went on, 'The counterpart of higher land values in Cardiff Bay is going to be lower land values or land not being sold in places from which the investment is attracted.' There could be no justification for investing public funds in Cardiff, to build a barrage, if the investment attracted would exist somewhere else in the UK, anyway: no national benefit would be derived from it.[39]

So, even if the Barrage could be shown, on a hypothetical balance sheet, to attract investment and return profits, those profits would be money which, if it hadn't come to Cardiff, would have gone to Liverpool, Belfast or Glasgow. There would be no discernible advantage to the UK economy as a whole, and no justification for such a huge contribution from the UK Treasury to Cardiff Bay.

Popham reminded him that Nigel Mason, for the promoters, had suggested the Treasury discount rate would somehow correct this problem of displacement. (The Treasury discount rate is a mechanism for ensuring an even playing field when comparing likely returns from public investment in different parts of Britain.) Mr Bowers disagreed, 'I think this is simply wrong. The Treasury discount rate is designed to ensure public investment if properly appraised achieves approximately the same return in all cases. That is its purpose. This will only be achieved if the cost benefits are properly measured... If this is not the case, as in this case, where it seems the important benefits are over-estimated, the use of the test rate of discount is not going to correct for this. The implication is that the actual rate of return on the Cardiff Bay scheme is lower than could arguably be achieved by devoting the public funds to some other use.'[40] Not only could the money earmarked for the Barrage be spent profitably elsewhere, it could perhaps be proven to be *more* profitably elsewhere.

The other important argument in the case for the Barrage was the number of jobs it would create – it is very difficult any politician, in opposition or government, to argue against a scheme which is supposed to bring work to a deprived area. However, Jonathan Morris, lead by Kate Hunter, for Canton Residents Against the Barrage, pointed out the flaws in CBDC's job creation scheme. Mr Morris was a lecturer at the Cardiff Business School. He specialised in the Welsh economy and its labour market, and had carried out work for the EEC, the Canadian Department of External Affairs and the WDA. In 1989, he had submitted written evidence to the Commons Welsh Affairs Committee, on inward investment in Wales. He pointed out that there were already 330 small to medium firms in the Bay area, mostly manufacturing companies which were in short supply in South Glamorgan. The county, he added, had a very poor record for the creation of new firms; it was sixth from bottom in UK counties, and second from bottom, among Welsh counties. Consequently it could ill afford to put the future of such companies at risk, but their future was being jeopardised by CBDC's policy of clearance by Compulsory Purchase Order (CPO). He also cited a report by Dr Robert Murray, of Oxford University and Dr Peter Thomas of Cardiff, showing that many firms in the Bay had been badly affected by CPOs, even before relocation.[41]

Mr Morris was sceptical about the job creation claims in the economic appraisal. He quoted the 24,000 jobs to be created in Cardiff Bay itself, and the 8,000 elsewhere in south-east Wales.[42] But, he went on, 'from what evidence has been provided, there has been no real rigorous assessment of demand and no actual concrete examples of firms who will provide that demand for the office, industrial and retail space [planned by CBDC] and certainly not enough to justify these type of claims.'[43]

He was also doubtful about the ability of the local labour market to satisfy the needs of the project. He estimated that there was 6% unemployment in the Cardiff 'travel to work' area, 18,000 registered unemployed in all; it was rare, he pointed out, for unemployment rates to fall by more than 2%, as a result of developments like that in Cardiff Bay: 'I think it is fair to argue that a significant percentage of the unemployed will not be available to fill these jobs'. In other words, CBDC was apparently providing jobs which people from outside Cardiff would have to fill, anyway.[44] CBDC's plan would probably result in extra clerical jobs in Cardiff Bay, but those jobs would not match the skills and experience of the local unemployed. Meanwhile, dozens of small workshops and factories, already providing hundreds of jobs, were being put out of business to make way for those offices.

John Popham's cross examination of Nigel Mason of KPMG, and the evidence of John Bowers for the petitioners, threw serious doubt on the Treasury's awareness of the conclusions of the KPMG appraisal, and how those conclusions had been reached. In response, the Promoters presented witnesses to address these concerns, as they had done before the earlier Select Committee. Of these, Brian Mitchell, head of the Urban Affairs Division at the Welsh Office, and Ron Bone, from the Wildlife Directorate at the Department of the Environment, had already appeared at the Lords Select Committee. They were now joined by Mike Turley of CBDC.

Jimmy Hood was chairing this particular session, as Mr Hicks had commitments elsewhere. He made it clear that the three could not be examined by counsel, but that 'there is a custom that questions may be directed, if so considered by myself. I am prepared to use that discretion...'[45] In other words, the petitioners could put questions to Mr Mitchell and his colleagues, if they observed the pretext that such questions were put, nominally, through the Chair. The subsequent exchanges were possibly rather more frank and substantial than if Mr Hicks had been presiding.

According to Mr Mitchell, their brief was mainly to correct the impression that 'the government had come to a predetermined view on the project before the evidence was presented to Parliament', and to clarify 'the government's response to the Peat Marwick economic appraisal.'[46]

They looked first at the petitioners' criticism that the Barrage received government backing, before its economic feasibility had been sufficiently demonstrated. Mr Mitchell simply gave a general indication of 'a series of discussions' between the Development Corporation and KPMG over the period from March 1987, when Peat Marwick were first given the brief to prepare an appraisal by CBDC, to the publication of the most recent version of that appraisal, three months before.

This was not what the petitioners had been concerned about; they had in mind Nicholas Edwards' linking of the Barrage and the Corporation, ever since his first public announcement of the project,

at the WDA seminar in December 1986, three months before the economic appraisal was commissioned. They were also thinking of the
County Council's proposals for a Development Corporation in south
Cardiff, published another three months previously, in September
1986,

> ... the County Council promotes a private Bill to secure authority
> for the construction of a Cardiff Harbour Mouth Barrage.[47]

There had been consistent, strong, political support for a barrage at
the highest level before the details of the economic case for it had
been considered by any expert in the field, let alone a neutral one.

However, in their examination of Mr Mitchell and his colleagues,
the committee concentrated on the gaps and flaws in the appraisal
itself. Mr Hood asked, 'Mr Turley, what do you think the total cost of
this barrage will be at the end of the day...?' Mr Turley's reply was
hesitant, 'The way the government anticipates the public expenditure
proposals...' Mr Hood broke in, 'You are telling me you are going to
understate [*sic*]...?' Mr Turley continued to avoid an exact reply, and
the Chair began to lose patience, 'I am still waiting on the figure'. He
altered tack slightly, 'What was the rate of inflation you used in your
assessment?'. Mr Turley appeared to be unable to say, and generalisa-
tion seemed to fade into incoherence, 'The assessment that was used
in that particular scenario were the ones used by Peat Marwick as the
Corporation's advisors so it would be a matter for the promoters that
particular figure.'[48] The acting Chair felt strongly that it should also be
a matter for Mr Turley, as a senior employee of the promoters. He
exclaimed, 'You do not know? You are described as an expert on inflation... you do not know the level of inflation used to come out with
this figure?' As CBDC's spokesman apparently struggled to reply, the
Chair seemed to take pity on him, 'We have heard many figures, I am
not trying to embarrass you any further...'. Still without giving any of
the specific figures demanded of him, Mr Turley concluded, '... We
were satisfied... that the economic case was sound and robust.'

Mr Hood echoed, with heavy irony, 'Sound and robust.'[49]

Water Quality

All the arguments put by the petitioners were based on the huge gap
between the superb lakeside development of Nicholas Edwards' imagination, and the likely grimmer reality. None of those arguments
illustrated that gap more graphically than the debate about the state
of the water which would eventually fill the lake.

An undertaking suggested by Lord Moran in the Lords had bound the previous Select Committee to consider the quality of the impounded lake as a priority. He had been particularly concerned about the probability of algal bloom in the near-stagnant water. Algae generally flourish in environments like the Bay, in still, non-saline waters. In warm weather, they expand to cover the surface with a thick, slimy, greenish-brown, or greenish-blue, mat, which, when it decays, gives off a foul smell that could rival the Bay's unreconstructed sewage outfalls – not at all like the bright, sparkling expanse which adorned CBDC's promotional brochures.

As a result of their Lordships' deliberations on these points, they recommended the lake be 'hard edged' to discourage algal growth, and also that the Corporation regularly collect and dispose of any growth in the Bay. However, several petitioners were very doubtful about the effectiveness of these measures.

Paul Bolas, managing director of Consulting and Analytical Scientists, a firm specialising in water and water-related topics, gave evidence for Cardiff Flood Action. He pointed out that, according to the figures supplied by the promoters themselves, it would take two days to clear only 1% of the 400 acres of the lake, in times of high algal growth. Mr Morlais Owens, of the Welsh Region of the National Rivers Authority, appearing for the Promoters, broadly agreed with this estimate, when cross-examined by John Popham.[50] Mr Popham later asked him if there were likely to be times when the rate of algal growth might exceed the capacity of the SLURP units CBDC planned to use for scooping it up (SLURP units are devices originally used to remove surface oil pollution, and had been adapted by Wallace Evans for removing algae from Cardiff Bay). He replied "we do not know if that will occur in practice. I have to say the potential is certainly there.'[51]

The aesthetic appeal of the impounded lake was further diminished by the likelihood of swarms of midges – non-biting midges, as Dr Patrick Armitage of the Institute of Freshwater Ecology pointed out, for the promoters – but midges, nonetheless, and in uncomfortably large numbers.[52] This was, as Mr Sullivan said, when cross-examining Paul Bolas, a relatively common problem around reservoirs. Why, he wondered, would it be so much worse in Cardiff Bay? Mr Bolas replied that the lake in Cardiff Bay would be much shallower than most reservoirs, favouring the survival of midge larvae; in addition, no reservoir was fed by two polluted rivers like the Taff and Ely whose 'nutrients' would provide a constant food supply. He also commented that around the Bay, there would be a higher population to be annoyed by midges, and more 'amenities' to be spoiled, than there were near most reservoirs...[53]

A further major consideration was the survival of local fish in the impounded lake, especially the salmon which were expected to use the fish passes in the Barrage to make their way up the Taff. The promoters accepted that there was likely to be too little dissolved oxygen in its waters to reach the NRA's requirements, because the lake would be so large, shallow and nutrient-rich. Its waters would not only cover mud whose contents would too readily absorb oxygen, but those waters would also remain in the lake for some time, stagnant for as long as sixteen days at a time in summer.

As a solution they intended to install ten Vitox units at strategic points around the Bay; these were machines which pumped liquid oxygen into the surrounding water. Experiments with a single Vitox unit were currently taking place in London's Greenland Dock. Paul Bolas believed that it would be unlikely that the units could be relied on, even if there were as many as twenty, to produce enough oxygen on demand at times of predicted shortfall. He considered it likely there would be periods of illegal shortage, with fatal consequences for the fish population[54]

These problems – algae, midges, low oxygen levels – all resulted from high levels of pollution in the rivers which feeding the lake. They could, it seemed, be solved at a stroke by removing this pollution at source. The most damaging 'nutrients' carried by the Taff and Ely were phosphates. John Popham asked Morlais Owens if the NRA had done any work on phosphate stripping; apparently Welsh Water had a study which indicated that 'something in the order of between 80 and 85 per cent of the nutrients entering the system' would have to be removed, 'to achieve some form of limitation to the growth of algae'. If this stripping took place from the rivers themselves, it would need a mammoth capital outlay of £40 to £60 million, with annual costs of between £1 and £2 million.[57] As John Popham later pointed out, no costs for phosphate stripping were given in the latest economic appraisal.

This point was taken up by a witness for Pontcanna Residents, Dr Peter Randerson, a lecturer in the School of Pure and Applied Biology at Cardiff University. He deduced from the promoters' evidence that they intended to try different methods of phosphate stripping, until they found one that worked. He pointed out 'They do not have to live alongside the consequences; and they can only take this approach because the cost of such an experiment is being borne by the Cardiff Bay Development Corporation. Effectively, they have got a blank cheque...'[56] The promoters, he went on, were fond of referring to their clean-up plans for the Bay as an argument in favour of the Barrage; however, European Directive 518, on Urban Waste

Water, published in January, would require responsible bodies, like the Corporation, to improve the quality of rivers and coastal waters by 1998. So all this work would have to be done anyway, barrage or no barrage.[57]

Dr Randerson was concerned not only about the quality of the water in the Bay, but also its quantity. He feared that there would not be enough water available to meet the many demands to be made upon it in the promoters' plans. These demands included the water needed to operate the remaining docks; the water for the fish pass in the Barrage; the extra supplies of fresh water needed to compensate for loss through the boat locks, and so on. He had studied the river flows of the Bay for over fifteen years, from 1973 to 1989, and concluded that after the Barrage was built, there would be a water shortfall, for at least one month each year, on average.[58] So perhaps the mudflats would reappear like ghosts from the shallows of the lake, to frustrate those who had drowned them.

Just as no-one had ever tried destabilising the fragile water table of a major city, or moving 30 years' worth of waste tipping from a single, saturated site, like Ferry Road, so nobody had ever before tried creating a 'freshwater' lake on the lines proposed by Nicholas Edwards and endorsed by Jack Brooks. As John Popham asked Morlais Owens, 'With two rivers discharging into the lake with pollutants in them – probably low oxygen levels – probably full of phosphates, algae, extensive rubbish tips nearby, storm water flows as sewage, heavy metal pollution, midges and problems with micro-biological quality... are you familiar with a case like that anywhere?' Answer, 'No. Obviously I would have to say I know of no other lake which has been created in such circumstances.'[59] So Cardiff would find itself at the cutting edge of yet another dubious experiment in urban regeneration.

A Living Waterfront, or the Death of an SSSI

Before the Lords, the petitioners had found themselves in the invidious position of having to argue from an apparently negative stance, especially on the Bay's environment. There was a danger they would be seen as favouring of the status quo, a neglected, polluted, waterlogged wasteland, and opposed to CBDC's vision of sparkling blue waters, prosperity and dynamic improvement. The launch of the RSPB's *Living Waterfront* strategy made it easier to emphasise the positive aspects of their campaign. They were offering an alternative development scenario, with the SSSI as the centrepiece, rather than an inconvenience to be disposed of. The preservation of the SSSI also meant that CBDC's plans to provide 'alternative feeding grounds' at Wentloog would be unnecessary.

Much of the conservationist argument in the Lords had been based on the significance of the numbers of wading birds like dunlin and redshank on the mudflats, and Cardiff Bay's relative importance as part of the Severn Estuary Protection Area. In 1990, the petitioners addressed a wider issue, the legality and probity of the case for the SSSI's destruction. They established that –

- the government's own advisers, the Nature Conservancy Council, not only opposed the Bill, but had not even been consulted about its implications

- under current EC law, the barrage could be illegal

- the environmental assessment of the scheme required by UK law had been too narrowly defined, and had been undertaken too late in the planning process.

The Nature Conservancy Council (NCC) had petitioned because of its concern over the destruction of the SSSI. The NCC was financed by a grant-in-aid from the DoE to advise ministers on projects, like the Barrage, which had implications for the natural environment. Dr James Doody, the head of their coastal ecology branch, was examined by Susan Hamilton, agent for the NCC. He referred to a review carried out into the pressures on estuaries in the UK. Of the 115 sites looked at, 54 were the subject of 'land claim proposals', including roads or port developments and 51 marinas were planned – some were the subject of both types of development.[60] He referred to the fact that, at the same time, these estuaries 'had been progressing towards the sea and the sea levels rising... the effect of this is to reduce the intertidal area... which is just the area birds rely on for their food in winter and one of the areas where some of our most important habitats occur.'[61] Cross-examined by Sullivan, he commented, 'Indeed, we have to look at each of these proposals on its merits. Of course, the problem and the point I was trying to make for the Committee, is that there a large number of them.'[62]

So, not only were the dunlin and redshank of Cardiff Bay under threat, the sort of environment which could support them was at risk throughout the UK; the implementation of *The Living Waterfront* would be of national importance, signalling that development and conservation could go hand in hand.

Haydn Williams, the Deputy Director (Wales) for the NCC, was also examined by Susan Hamilton. She established that the Council had had no input into the report to the Committee from the Department and the WO, on the development and the SSSI, although the NCC is financed by a government grant-in-aid, and one of its key roles is to advise ministers on just such matters. He went on, 'Our understanding is that Government reports should normally be neutral and it is difficult to read the report that has been produced and apply the word "neutral" to it.'[63]

In his cross-examination, Boydell followed up this comment, saying 'that [the expectation of neutrality] came as something of a surprise to those of us who have been practising in these rooms for 30 years or so because we can think of scores of departmental reports which were far from neutral. Who gave you that advice, Mr Williams?' The NCC's Deputy Director (Wales) referred him to the DoE/DTI's Private Bill Procedure document, section 4: 'There is a convention that Government should not be seen to take or to inspire action in Parliament on private legislation and the Government's stance is traditionally one of benign neutrality.'[64] As the Government's position on this particular piece of private legislation was clearly one of aggressive enthusiasm, rather than benign neutrality, Mr Boydell did not pursue the matter.

Instead, he referred to the unilateral changes Peter Walker had made to the conservation status of the Bay in the South Glamorgan Structure Plan, in 1988, to ease the Barrage Bill's progress. He went on 'I have a letter in front of me from the Welsh Office of 2nd May, 1989, which says "On 25th May, 1988, the Welsh Office sent to the Nature Conservancy Council South Wales Region copies of the following..." and they include a list of the modifications, including this modification to which I have just referred. The letter goes on to say: "in reply from the Nature Conservancy Council on 8th June 1988 the Nature Conservancy Council stated they would not be objecting to the proposed modifications". ... do you happen to know why you decided not to object to that modification?'

Mr Williams replied 'The point is the SSSI status is still there, regardless of the conservation status in the Structure Plan being extant [*sic*]. Also in November 1987, the then Secretary of State for Wales [Peter Walker] met the Chairman of the NCC, the Chairman of the Welsh Committee of the NCC, the Director of the NCC Wales and Dr Cadwalladr, the regional officer for South Wales, where he went into some depth over his proposals for the Cardiff Bay area.... The Chairman of the NCC pointed out we would have to defend the case.'[65]

The NCC had played scrupulously by the rules; it could make no official objection to changes in the conservation plans of particular local authorities, like South Glamorgan, but it had a duty to advise central government on such issues. When its advice was ignored, or, worse, not even asked, petitioning was the only recourse. National government had thrown away any pretensions to 'benign neutrality', and refused to heed the barking of their own conservation watchdogs. Once more, Mr Boydell did not pursue the point.

Mr Popham's examination of the civil servants from the DoE, WO and CBDC, Messrs Mitchell, Bone and Turley, dealt with the degree of environmental protection to which the Bay was entitled, as an SSSI. In April 1979, the European Community Council had produced directive 79/409/EEC on the conservation of wild birds, including species which over-wintered in Cardiff Bay. Article 2 of the Directive required member states to 'take the requisite measures to maintain the population of the species referred... while taking account of economic and recreational requirements'.

In December 1987, a circular, no.27/87, had been published jointly by the Department of the Environment, the Welsh Office and the Scottish Office, advising local authorities how to apply this directive to proposed developments in their own areas. This circular stated '...authorities must carefully evaluate the balance between ecological, scientific and cultural requirements to ensure the survival and reproduction of... bird species on the one hand, and economic and recreational requirements on the other.' It required authorities to consider '...to what extent could the proposed development be undertaken... in ways which ensure that there is the least possible damage and disturbance to the birds and their habitats.

The promoters claimed that the terms of the Directive, as interpreted in this circular, permitted the destruction of the SSSI, as they believed the economic benefits brought by the Barrage would far outweigh its loss.

The RSPB, on the other hand, considered that the DoE circular took too relaxed a view of the Directive. The conservation groups' petitions were based on the view that the DoE's concept of 'balancing' was contrary to its spirit. Their case was supported by a letter from the European Commission, dated 23rd March, only six days before, which stated clearly that the economic benefits from proposed developments which would affect such sites should outweigh any damage done, 'the Commission does not accept... that in such cases in it is simply a question of equal balancing.'[66]

John Popham pointed out that several challenges to such misinterpretations of Article 2 were currently being considered by the Commission, and asked Brian Mitchell to comment. Mr Mitchell simply replied that he was 'very pleased to see the letter from the Commission.'[67] As a response from an official of the Wildlife Directorate at the Department of the Environment to the possibility that the British government was funding a project which could be illegal under European law, this might be described as inadequate.

Dr David Parker, of Liverpool University's Environmental Assessment Unit (EAU), was cross examined by John Popham, and by David Perry for the NCC, about the report the unit had prepared for CBDC on the consequences of the Barrage. Such assessments were a legal requirement for any major development project, and the SoS for the Environment, Chris Patten, had recently said that 'an environmental assessment that has been prepared after a project has been designed can only be second best if adjustments are made to reduced [*sic*] any damage which might otherwise have been caused.'[68]

Mr Popham's cross-examination revealed that the EAU usually preferred to be involved at a much earlier stage than they had been in the Barrage project; that the EAU's final report was presented to CBDC in November 1989, two years after the first Barrage Bill had been deposited in November 1987, and after the revised Bill, including proposals for 'compensatory' feeding grounds, appeared, in November 1988 – in flagrant disregard of the spirit, if not the letter, of the relevant legislation; that no alternative to a full barrage was included in their brief from the Development Corporation.

It was made very clear that CBDC had commissioned the report as an after-thought, a sop to legality; there was no evidence of any interest whatsoever in alternative projects for the Bay, if the report was unfavourable; moreover, setting such narrow terms of reference, the Corporation had ensured that no such alternatives would be seriously considered. Until the petitioners came up with the Living Waterfront, there was nothing other than a full barrage on offer.

When Mark Lintell of Land Use Consultants was examined by John Popham, he put the fallacy of 'the Barrage, the whole barrage and nothing but the Barrage' in context.

> The full Barrage scheme is flawed for two fundamental reasons...
> [first] those responsible for its conception failed to appreciate the
> true nature of the environment within which it was to be con-
> structed... [they] did not appreciate the effects this scheme would
> have on the environment, until it was too late... [secondly] it is an
> all or nothing scheme. In order to realise the very high develop-
> ment land values on which the whole financial balance of the
> scheme is predicated, the Development Corporation is committed
> from the outset to very high levels of public expenditure. However,
> if the development values identified are not achieved (as seems
> likely in the current model) or the costs escalate (as we predict

> they will) the Corporation has no choice but to press forward at
> increasing cost to the public... it is a scheme with little or no flex-
> ibility.[69]

He shrewdly observed 'What I think has happened is that some very
important people who have power to influence things have confused
the view of the mud with the general appearance of the shoreline,
which I am sure we would all agree is in an appalling condition in
places as a result of the adjoining dereliction, pollution and sewage outfalls. However the solution to the problem is not to get rid of the mud,
and with it the feeding grounds for thousands of beautiful and highly
valued birds and other wildlife, instead it is to tackle the problems of
dereliction and pollution which... characterise the shoreline.'[70]

Perhaps with one in particular of those 'very important people' in
mind, Mr Hood later asked Messrs Turley and Mitchell whether the
Department of the Environment had been consulted over the plans
for alternative feeding grounds. When told that their responsibilities
were devolved to the Welsh Office, and 'the Welsh region of the
National Rivers Authority advises our Secretary of State directly.' Mr
Hood went on, 'The National Rivers Authority chairman is the previous Secretary of State [for Wales] and he is advising the present
Secretary of State?'. Mr Mitchell replied that '... he [Lord
Crickhowell] is taking a totally detached view'. 'I'm sure he is', the former NUM official commented.[71]

Mr Boydell had considered the economics of *The Living Waterfront*
in typically combative fashion on the first day of the Committee. He
briskly dismissed its ability to attract jobs or private investment,

> ... there will be 12,000 fewer jobs and a negative net present
> value. The leverage of private investment to public investment
> would be 4.3 leverage; that is to say, for every public pound, £4.3
> of private.[72]

This was certainly not comparable with the leverage ratio of £7 of
private money for every public pound prophesied for the full barrage
scenario by KPMG in the latest economic appraisal, but given the
dubious nature of CBDC's economic case overall, perhaps the figures
should not have been taken too seriously. But, the promoters found
The Living Waterfront inadequate for their aims of maximising net land
values and attracting investment.

It was left to individual petitioners to make the case most movingly for enhancing, rather than destroying, the Bay as they knew it.
Alison Wilson, who lived on Windsor Esplanade in Butetown, was
concerned that when the Committee had visited the area the Bay had

been covered by the high tide. '… it is an area of mudflats, grasses and tides, with many wading birds. I consider it one of the most beautiful spots in Cardiff. That is partly evidenced by the demand from people wanting to live on Windsor Esplanade. Usually, houses do not get as far as having a For Sale board out up. It is a highly desirable residential area. The desirability of the area is the view and the quietness of the Bay. A year ago, Cardiff City Council Planning Committee issued guidance to all residents on the Esplanade on how to restore original Victorian features in [their] properties. The City Council obviously consider the street to be a valuable area well worth preserving'.[73]

In support of her petition, Susan Plessner, a violinist with the WNO, presented a letter she had had from Gordon Michell, architect and environmental consultant, a former chairman of the Civic Trust, one of the UK's most influential architectural pressure groups, and one-time resident of Windsor Esplanade. He wrote, 'I have many photographs in which I have attempted to capture the beauty of the Bay which is forever changing on account of the rise and ebb of the tides, combined with the changing light. Quite apart from the thousands of birds, which identify it as their natural habitat, the bay has an incredible beauty of its own.'[74]

Alistair Couper, Master Mariner and Professor of Maritime Geography at Cardiff University, criticised CBDC's proposals for their deliberate disregard for the real character of the area,

> We have a large port: it is well-managed, it is busy, it has got many prospects for new trade, westerly orientated trade… The port is important – it is unlike the Docklands area of London, it is a living port, in Cardiff.

He pointed out the contradiction at the heart of the Corporation's plans, in which, 'Cardiff will be recreated "…once more as a superlative maritime city". This will be achieved, as we know, by building a barrier between the sea and the bay… stopping the ebb and flow of the great tides; eliminating the marine bird life; erecting obstacles to fish; destroying a marine site of special scientific interest… it is certainly not a maritime creation – it will put an end to the seascapes which embody the community-held memories of maritime Cardiff.'[75]

Polls, Politicians and Public opinion

CBDC had boasted proudly of its high quality PR campaigns to keep the people of Cardiff informed about the Barrage and the progress of the development as a whole. They believed that leafleting, supplements in local papers, a visitors' centre in the Bay, and an 'information caravan' touring south Cardiff, bore ample witness to their determination to let the people know. The clincher for this argument was the declared support of most County Councillors for the scheme. If their tribunes led, could the people really be far behind?

Many petitioners begged to differ. The Corporation's deficiencies in public relations were not the specific subject of any petitions. However, CBDC insisted that they had the tacit support of most people in the city; it was a major part of their defence against many of their opponents' arguments. It was consequentially viewed as vital that public doubt and uncertainty was presented to the Committee.

County Councillor Peter Perkins of Grangetown was examined by Boydell on local feeling about the Barrage

> 'Now do you, as the ward member, have any view as to what the punter in the local pub is thinking, Councillor Perkins?'
> He answered, '... I have only been asked to go to two meetings of the Grangetown Anti-Barrage campaign. I am [not] always able to go, but the one meeting I attended they managed to get 50 people there. The other meeting was just a committee meeting I attended with Alun Michael. It seems that the people of Grangetown would like this development...'

At this, there were polite, but unmistakable, expressions of dissent from the anti-barrage groups present, and as he dismissed the Councillor at the end of his evidence, the Chair commented wryly, 'Your constituents will give you a rougher time than you have had today!'[76] Later, petitioners from GRAB would prove him correct.

For instance, Christine Dimend, executive officer with an insurance company, who had lived in Grangetown all her life, gave the Committee another perspective on the relations between Councillor Perkins and his ward.

> It was also during this period [the run-up to the May 1989 election] that I realised my county councillor Peter Perkins was also speaking in the other place as Deputy Leader of the South Glamorgan County Council and he was speaking for the Promoters. I was surprised there was nothing in his manifesto about the barrage.

Christine had been very active in the Grangetown anti-barrage candidate's campaign. She stoutly refuted Councillor Perkins' assertions about the popularity of the Barrage in his ward, calculating that he received only 48.8% of the poll, with SDLP and Conservative candidates also expressing concerns about the Barrage. She went on,

> To achieve such a result, over 400 votes for the anti-barrage candidate, against a well-established councillor, with little money, no

party machine and absolutely no experience and very little time, only 4 weeks, you must admit it was a tremendous achievement, particularly the way the vote countrywide swung to Labour.[77]

Jane Davidson, appearing on behalf of Riverside Ward Labour Party's petition, made a dramatic announcement. So great was concern within the local Labour ward parties over the lack of public consultation on the Barrage that,

> Following one of the Committee members' wish to know what the feelings of the average punter in the pub, the Riverside councillors, [Ian Brown, Sue Essex, Jane Hutt and Jane Davidson herself] decided, in an emergency meeting, to commission a professionally independent survey from National Opinion Polls to find out the information. We have not been involved in the setting of the questions and we maintain the independence of the poll and will stand up the result... this is at considerable personal financial liability, because we have no guarantee for the cost, in the region of £4,000, for the poll.[78]

In another of the unprecedented coups which characterised the anti-barrage campaign, local politicians (including MP Rhodri Morgan) paid the cost of the poll themselves, to ensure that the Committee had an accurate view of local feeling on the Barrage. It was a damning condemnation of CBDC's own failure in public relations. The Corporation believed that they had to mould the views of Cardiff residents to ensure support for the scheme. Many Cardiff residents had formed a view on the Barrage, and those views were firmly resistant to moulding...

The NOP poll took place on 1st March, during the Committee's sitting in Cardiff, to achieve maximum exposure in the local media. That day, Mark Drakeford, examined by Peter Davies for Riverside Ward LP, described the background to their decision.

> Both County and City Councils have declined to sponsor or become involved in any sort of test of opinion... It [the NOP poll] will ask people in the area what their views on the construction of the barrage are... [NOP] were clear with us that... they would be responsible for drawing up questions; they would be responsible for organising the conduct of the poll and they would be responsible for the interpretation of the results.

In other words, the poll would be free of any possible bias against the Barrage.[79] Mark had written to Labour colleagues on the County Council asking for their support for the poll. The Chief Whip of the Labour group, Councillor Jarvis of Fairwater, had replied that the poll 'is clearly designed, in co-operation with Cardiff Residents Against the Barrage, [*sic*] to further undermine the explicit policy of the

County Labour Group and of the Council, and the Group may wish to consider the position at the next meeting.' Mark commented, 'I take that to be at least a mild threat to people who do something as innocuous as to ask people what they think.'[80]

He was cross-examined closely by Boydell on the validity of the poll. The promoters' QC was trying to make the point that the 500 people to be polled would be not be sufficiently informed about issues such as 'land reclamation and land values; commercial prospects of attracting inward investment and development; creation of jobs; water quality and groundwater', and other complex issues related to the Barrage. The implication was that if they were not informed about such details, their opinions should count for very little, a pertinent example of the Development Corporation's view of public opinion.[81]

In a typically robust rejection of Mr Boydell's clinical, 'hands off' version of democracy, later that day, Shelagh Llewellyn of Neville Place, Riverside, introduced Dave Burns, to sing 'The Grangetown Gondolier', in support of her petition (see Appendix 3) as fitting evidence in the Land of Song, on St David's Day. So, in a Council chamber bright with daffodils, fortified by Marcia Baskeville's delicious Welsh cakes, the Committee listened to Mr Burns' ditty, while, in the public gallery, swaying to its jaunty rhythm, over 100 Cardiff citizens joined in the chorus with gusto.[82]

On 28th March, Councillor Ian Brown reported the poll results to the Committee. The poll had been taken in the homes of 547 people, in the protected property area defined by the Bill. It had revealed that 86% of those questioned had heard about the Barrage. Of those, 14% thought that it was a good idea, 42% thought it was a bad idea and 43% felt they did not know enough about it to say. So, of those who had an opinion about the scheme, over 80% were against. When those who were in favour were asked why, the most popular reason, for 46%, was that it would bring jobs to the area. The most popular reason for not supporting the Barrage was the fear of flooding, given by 84%.

NOP themselves had extended the scope of the poll with a final question asking whether the person questioned if their home was in the protected property area. Only 39% were sure they were, 21% said they were not, and 40% did not know. In view of the fact that all questioned were in the protected area, this was not a glowing testimonial for CBDC's PR strategy in general, or their information caravan in particular; it certainly did not support their claims to have leafleted the area fully.[83]

Members of the Committee expressed concern over the narrow geographical area of the poll. Giving evidence for the petitioners next day, Kate Hunter was able to put the survey in context. She described two other surveys the anti-barrage campaigners had recently carried out. The first was done by Cardiff FoE, and polled 423 people, 190 living in the protected area, 233 outside. The poll showed similar levels of opposition form both groups, 66% and 67% respectively.

The other poll was carried out beyond Cardiff, on the previous Saturday in Pontypridd market, in Mid Glamorgan. Of the 196 people questioned 16% had not heard about the Barrage. Of those who had, 48% disagreed with the plan, 14% agreed and 38% didn't know; the level of awareness was thus very similar to that revealed by NOP in the affected property area.[84]

The petitioners were also keen to quash the idea that local councillors themselves were unanimous and spontaneous in their support for the scheme. When Councillor John Reynolds, Leader of Cardiff City Council and member of the Cardiff Bay Development Corporation appeared before the committee, Mr Waller asked him about the anti-barrage candidates in the recent County elections. Councillor Reynolds confirmed that while City wards varied from one to four members, while the County ones were single member only. Mr Waller commented, 'So a single issue [anti-barrage] candidate who obtained 400 votes would be doing quite well in my opinion'.

Mr Hood followed with an even more embarrassing inquiry, 'How much does your council get from the sale of land to the project?' After a very evasive response, Mr Hood asked pointedly, 'You sold a piece of land for £8 million?' To which Councillor Reynolds could only answer 'Yes', clearly establishing the City Council's relations with CBDC, and implying the difficulty of maintaining objectivity in assessing the real quality of 'the project'.[85]

On the same theme, Jane Davidson, Labour City Councillor for Riverside, appearing in support of the petition of Riverside Residents Against the Barrage, reminded the Committee that no vote on the Barrage scheme had ever been taken by the City Council as a whole. Councillors who oppose the Barrage, she said 'feel that if a vote had been taken... with the concerns of the City Council in terms of its statutory responsibilities and with the concerns of individual ward councillors about the residents in their areas, there would not have been a vote to actively support the Barrage.'[86]

Jimmy Hood continued to develop his interest in the relative freedom of the various Council votes on the Barrage. He established that the City vote on 25th January, 1989, on whether or not to petition, was whipped. Councillor Davidson went on, 'If I may comment on that, it is very difficult in a matter like this to know how much of your internal party politics you can divulge, but the vote in our Labour group was very close indeed.'[87]

County Councillor Jane Hutt contrasted the votes for Labour candidates who were known to be anti-barrage, with those for councillors who, like Mr Perkins, were known to be in favour.

> We [Labour] increased our majority in Pontcanna, [Mark Drakeford's ward], Riverside South [her own] and Cardiff West, but I think it is worth noting that in the two wards where there were anti-barrage candidates – Butetown and the Marl – the Labour vote reduced between the election in 1985 and the election in 1989.

She also tried to put the many County Council votes in favour of the Barrage, into context. 'It is always hard [for councillors] to take an overall view of the Council as whole, at the other end of the Council boundary. I think it has taken a long time for the evidence to come out. In the early votes, I do not think many councillors were fully aware of the impact of the Barrage. They are not going to read all these reports if they are in a ward at the other side of Cardiff, or in the Vale of Glamorgan... it's very difficult to talk about testing opinion in this way through County Council voting... people are looking after their own patches.' She also pointed out the cross party support for the NOP poll, especially among the Liberal Democrats on the County Council.[88]

Many of the Councillors opposing the Barrage found it put their careers in local politics on 'hold' for some time afterwards; however, one petitioner actually began a political career in that Commons Committee Room. Ben Foday appeared on behalf of the Docks Residents and Tenants Association (DRTA) – its 300 members were drawn from the 6000 residents of the area bordering the old docks, in the heart of CBDC's designated area.

The DRTA's relations with the Development Corporation were very different from those of the other residents' groups appearing before the Committee. From the beginning, CBDC had seen the Docks Residents as The Local People, to be wooed and cajoled to support its plans for the area. There might be disadvantages to living in an area which had to be noisily and dustily redeveloped around you, in which your home was seen as discordant and even inferior, in the light of glamorous strategic plans. But, CBDC had set aside funds for projects to improve the lot of The Local People – new Youth Centres, grants to Community projects, training schemes – which were not available to areas like Riverside or Splott. There were tangible benefits to be negotiated for Butetown and the Docks, and Ben and his fellow residents would have been very foolish not to take advantage of them.

However, as Ben pointed out to the Committee, the CBDC PR machine in the Docks had still operated on the 'Here's our grand plan for the Barrage. Take it or leave it' principle. He went on 'In that grand plan, our houses are but little dots', and described the Corporation as 'bully boys' and 'lager louts'. He later confessed that he had noticed that the Honourable Members had appeared bored by the petitioners appearing before them, and decided, quite successfully, to try and ginger things up a little. The substance of his petition was the unlimited protection given to ABP, compared to the 20-year limitation for private homes, 'I do not think that is fair.'[89]

Ben had been trying to arrange a meeting between CBDC's chair and the DRTA, for some time, without any success, but he managed to buttonhole Mr Inkin as the Select Committee hearing ended that day. This lead to a series of meetings between the DRTA, represented by Ben, and the Corporation. The Corporation's deputy chair, Paddy Kitson, who represented Butetown on the County Council, and was a powerful figure in the South Glamorgan Labour Group. Ben subsequently joined the Labour Party. When Councillor Kitson retired from local politics in 1993, Ben succeeded him as member for Butetown, and joined the board of the Development Corporation, for two years, until his deselection, after local government reorganisation, in the mid-nineties.

The Committee's Verdict, and its Aftermath

The final session of the Committee hearings took place on 25th April, but the MPs did not reconvene to make their recommendations on the future of the Bill until the 15th May. The delay was apparently caused by a clash between the civil servants who had to ensure Parliamentary business was done according to proper procedures, and political managers of both main parties who wanted to get the Bill through.

It transpired that Committee Members were willing to approve the Bill by a sufficient majority, but only on condition that a further year was spent on groundwater research, by Hydrotechnica. The resulting report would be considered by the Secretary of State, who then had to consult the people of Cardiff on the matter. The Hydrotechnica report also, the Committee insisted, had to be reviewed by John Miles. Only if the SoS found the report acceptable, could the Bill proceed. Not only had the Committee rejected the groundwater evidence presented by the Promoters, but in a remarkable break with precedent, had taken the future of the Bill out of the hands of Parliament and placed it with the Welsh Secretary. Even more remarkably, a voice had been given to one of its fiercest critics.

The Clerk to the Committee, insisted that the Bill could not be formally approved until this condition was satisfied: strictly speaking, there should be no further debates or votes on the Bill until the Secretary of State had delivered his final judgement. Senior politicians in the Commons, however, insisted that the Bill be approved at once before the research even began, to ensure it could get through as many stages of the parliamentary process as possible: otherwise, there was a serious risk the measure would run out of time and support.

The Committee had agreed that the petitioners were correct in their view of the inadequacy of the Corporation's work on groundwater. They also made several other recommendations. A complaints administrator would be appointed, at CBDC's expense, to deal with groundwater-related complaints. Householders would be entitled to claim compensation for groundwater-related loss of value to their homes, as an alternative to remedial work. Local properties would enjoy the same protection as that afforded Associated British Ports. Householders outside the 'protected property' line who suffered groundwater damage would be entitled to the same treatment as their neighbours inside the line. Householders within the 'protected property' line could choose whatever reputable damp-testing method they wished, including the BRE's piezometers. Any changes to the Code of Practice on groundwater would have to be agreed with Cardiff Flood Action, and any changes to the plans for replacement feeding grounds at Wentloog with the NCC and the RSPB.

For the petitioners, these changes, though welcome, were not what they really wanted. The majority report failed to even mention water quality, the chaos of Ferry Road*, the flaws in the economic case, or the destruction of the SSSI. The political climate, and the strength of cabinet support for the Bill, meant that no Select Committee considering the Barrage, no matter how strong their reservations on certain aspects of the scheme, would be able to grapple with the very serious consequences of trying to stop such a measure completely.

The petitioners were exhausted – if it took so much work and sacrifice to win so little ground, what, they wondered, would be needed to actually stop the Barrage? But the breathing space afforded by the groundwater research could be exploited, and Norman, Charlie, and Glyn, with their faithful supporters and political friends, immediately set to work on it.

---

* Eventually, much of the tip was sealed: the retail and residential development around the Ely estuary is thus graced with a large, neat, comical mound of concrete and urban waste.

They were able to draw some comfort from the minority report submitted by Jimmy Hood, the lone dissenter. Mr Hood had taken care to consider the Petitioners' arguments in some detail, and spoke of them approvingly. He did not believe the economic case, as presented by the Promoters, justified the £200 million public investment in the Barrage; he was not convinced by the promise of 30,000 jobs; he did not believe the destruction of the SSSI was justified; he felt the problems of midge infestation and poor water quality had not been properly addressed; as for groundwater, he thought the Bill should fall on this point alone.

He spoke with warm approval of the residents' groups who 'did themselves and their neighbours a great service and the standard of their presentation was excellent.' He reserved his highest praise, however, for the councillors who had supported them. This support, he noted, 'was not made easy by the fact that some senior councillors were paid members of the CBDC, where clearly a master and servant relationship clouded the waters... It is not always easy to stand up against bureaucracy and political muscle... There is no doubt in my mind that they were intimidated by threat or innuendo to succumb to the wishes of their other colleagues, and I congratulate them in [*sic*] their decision to stand up for what they genuinely believed in... I hope their colleagues who chose to discipline them for their courage will have time to reflect on their actions'.[90]

After an exchange of the usual courtesies and mutual congratulations, John Popham brought the question of his clients' costs to the Committee's attention. He pointed out that Cardiff Flood Action was not only already in debt, even though all their witnesses had appeared without fee, but also that they would incur further costs in carrying out the responsibilities the Committee had imposed on them, such as consultation over changes to the Code of Practice.

Petitioners against Private Bills were entitled to apply for costs from the promoters if, in the words of Erskine May, they 'have been unreasonably or vexatiously subjected to expense in defending their rights...'[91]

Mr Popham sought to prove they had been; he contended that CBDC and their advisers had been aware of the flaws in the WEP groundwater studies long before the Select Committee met. He cited in particular a newspaper report, which John Miles had produced as part of his evidence, from the *South Wales Echo*, August, 1989. The article referred to flooding in the basement of Mid Glamorgan County Hall, in Cathays Park, which housed the Glamorgan County Archives. The water had apparently come from beneath the floor, because of a rise in the water table. David Crompton, CBDC's

Director of Engineering, had commented that, as the area lay outside the Protected Property Line, 'We are satisfied there will no effect due to the construction of the Barrage'.[92]

The Corporation had known there were dangerously high groundwater levels outside the 'protected property' line, but refused to acknowledge the Barrage would worsen them. Mr Popham contended that this wilful refusal did indeed constitute unreasonable and vexatious behaviour.

After a short adjournment for discussion, the MPs decided to award 40% of the Petitioners' costs to date, and 75% of whatever costs were incurred by fulfilling the responsibilities laid on them by the Committee. The Chair made it plain that, in spite of this award, the Committee did not believe that the 'CBDC have been vexatious in any way.'[93] The Honourable Members forbore any comment on whether they had been unreasonable.

As it was extremely rare for any costs to be awarded to Private Bill Petitioners, the anti-barrage campaigners decided to be content with what they had, for the moment. They had wreaked havoc with the case for the Barrage, and publicly humiliated the Development Corporation. But the scheme was still alive and CBDC did not accept the indignity without protest. It tried to persuade the Committee, that as Hydrotechnica had already done some groundwater work in Cardiff, their report could be ready in less than ten months, for submission in March 1991, rather than taking the full year the MPs required. They were told, politely but very firmly, that a year meant twelve months – four whole seasons of heavy and light rainfall, high and low tides, bright sun and cloudy days: Hydrotechnica had to start work on 1st August 1990, and finish it on 31st July 1991, not a day longer, and not a day less.

So, as the rush of petitioning-induced adrenaline subsided, and the tension relaxed a little, the anti-barrage campaigners prepared to gird their loins for the next round of the fight.

7. A Hybrid Barrage

There is a convention that Government should not be seen to take or to inspire action in Parliament on private legislation and the Government's stance is traditionally one of benign neutrality.
DoE/DTI's Private Bill Procedure document, section 4.

As Hydrotechnica began the groundwater research required by the Select Committee, Norman Robson and his troops began the monitoring of Hydrotechnica. They continued to meet regularly, but fruitlessly, with CBDC and their consultants, often travelling to the Hydrotechnica HQ in Shropshire to do so. Hydrotechnica were to prepare an analysis of the groundwater levels in south Cardiff. The results would indicate where any necessary post-barrage protection measures, whether drainage, pumps or dewatering systems, should be installed.

As the research went on, CFAC felt deepening concern over the of consultants' failure to take account of Cardiff's peculiar geography, and decided to undertake a groundwater survey of their own. Its methods and results were typical of the anti-barrage campaigners – enthusiastic, thorough, inspired and idiosyncratic – one can imagine few other groups having the resource and expertise to carry it out.

It was the brainchild of Kate Hunter, museum curator, and Stan Perkins, retired coal merchant. Stan had long contended that there were wide variations in the dampness of houses in Grangetown, where he had delivered coal for over 40 years – variations not just from street to street, but from house to house. He remembered delivering coal to adjacent houses; in the first, the coal cellar could be an inch deep in water, after heavy rain, while its neighbour was only slightly damp, and the house just beyond would have a bone dry basement. Such variations were frequent, and very striking, especially in terraces of otherwise identical homes.

Kate came from another direction entirely, but arrived at the same point. As a museum curator, with much archaeological experience, she was familiar with the ways in which objects and structures of metal, wood, textile and stone, decayed when submerged for long periods, or buried in waterlogged ground. She was also familiar with the varying degrees of saturation possible in soil over a relatively small area; one part of a site may be consistently muddy, while only a few yards away, the ground will appear to drain quickly, even after heavy

rainfall. She knew there were often sound historical, rather than geological, reasons for such disparity.

At a CFAC meeting, in the July following the Commons Select
Committee, Stan was reporting back on a meeting with
Hydrotechnica at their Wallingford HQ. He was concerned at the
scale of their groundwater research so far and convinced that the
200m square grid system to be used for mapping groundwater levels
would not take into account house-to-house variations. If the results
of such a flawed survey were used as the basis for any property protection scheme in the area, many homes would be left vulnerable.

Hydrotechnica assumed that if groundwater was at a particular
level at one point in a square, it would be at roughly the same level
throughout the whole of that square. Stan was certain that this could
not be so; he knew the height of the water table could vary within each
square, as much as, if not more than, between squares. But he had not
been able to convince the Wallingford engineers this was so. He suggested that CFAC do its own research; key streets would be selected
in Riverside, Pontcanna, Canton and Grangetown, and a house to
house survey of dampness in voids and cellars would be made of
those streets. (Many properties in Grangetown had voids, spaces
beneath the ground floor too small for use as basements, up to five
feet in height, and varying in extent.)

Kate was very interested in the idea, and suggested a possible reason for the variations. Before the Marquis of Bute began to build
there, in the late 1800s, the fields of Canton and Riverside, down to
the marshes beyond Grange Farm, and the Ely estuary, had been frequently flooded at high tide. Local farmers had dug reems, or
drainage channels, to carry the surplus water back to the rivers and
make their land more productive. Less than three generations later,
these fields were developed even more intensively, as the working
class suburbs of Riverside and Grangetown spread over them, reems
and all.

Kate was convinced that these reems, with other natural and manmade water courses, were responsible for the variations. Beneath the
rubble tipped onto the land to support the foundations, the reems
continued to drain rainfall and the raised water tables of high tide into
the nearby rivers. If it could be shown that individual houses with
consistently damp basements were built over the still active drainage
channels, then Hydrotechnica might be persuaded to accept that
Cardiff's groundwater problems needed a very different approach.

Stan designated twenty streets, a total of 1000 homes, for detailed
investigation; he recruited seven CFAC members to carry out house
to house surveys and designed a questionnaire for them to go through

with the occupants. Every evening for four chilly autumn weeks, they knocked on doors, explained, questioned, listened and made notes; hundreds of doors, thousands of questions, bales of notes. Then, when over 600 questionnaires were complete, the responses were marked with painstaking care, house by house, on a huge, specially drawn map – dry, wet or damp, with or without cellars, all punctiliously recorded.

Then Kate made *her* map; based on the 1852 Ordnance Survey of Cardiff, it showed every sizeable reem and surface drain in Riverside, Canton and Grangetown. Drawn to the same scale as Stan's, on transparent paper, it was carefully laid over it. The routes of the drainage channels reflected the sites of the wettest homes like a mirror; Kate's theory was vindicated, Stan's observations were accurate, Hydrotechnica's premise was flawed.

There was much debate in CFAC meetings about what should be done with their findings. Some members wanted to release them as soon as possible, so that Hydrotechnica had a chance to revise their procedures, but the majority did not believe they would do so, voluntarily, and it would be best to keep it all under wraps, until the consultation period on groundwater was announced in a year's time, when the Secretary of State might lend political weight to any such revision. It was decided the report would remain confidential for several months....

There was other unfinished business from the Select Committee; the anti-barrage witnesses had appeared for nothing, but the petitioners still had to pay the fees of their agents, over £1500 for John Popham's services, alone. Although the Committee had made an unprecedented award of costs in their favour, a considerable shortfall remained.

In view of the Committee's acknowledgement of the debt their communities owed to Cardiff Flood Action, they decided to apply for a grant from the City Council, to cover the debts this altruism had incurred. The support they had received from some senior members of the Council, like Sue Essex, gave them some confidence, in spite of the Council Chair's membership of CBDC.

Norman submitted an application, and appeared before the City Finance Subcommittee to support it, in September. The Subcommittee recommended that the Council award the grant in full, and in October 1990, CFAC received a cheque for £3500, towards their expenses. The payment was seen by many as a tacit admission that the anti-barrage petitioners had worked hard to protect Cardiff's interests, when many of their elected representatives had apparently failed to do so.

The Development Corporation did not have to concern themselves with requests for such modest sums. Earlier in the summer,
their first annual report had showed they had spent £1.1 million on
consultants in 1988. Out of a total allocation of £29 million from the
Welsh Office the following year, they had allocated a further £1.68
million.

Autumn brought the end of the parliamentary year, and with it, the
tidying up of unfinished Commons business. Because of the delay
imposed by the Select Committee, the Barrage Bill was subject to
another carry over debate on 17th October, 1990. It was virtually
unheard of for a Private Bill to go through three separate sessions of
Parliament, which was, at that point, the minimum in which the
Barrage Bill could become law. But what concerned many procedu-
ralists in the House was the unfinished state of the Bill itself. CFAC
had produced yet another set of briefing notes for MPs; writing
trenchant summaries of the case against Nicholas Edwards' whim had
become something of a cottage industry in south Cardiff – for the
past three years several spare bedrooms and carless garages in the
area had housed very little else. The resulting leaflet summarised the
parliamentary dilemma neatly,

> Can the Bill be defended if the Commons Select Committee was
> unconvinced by the promoters' technical case to the extent that
> the final decision has been left to the Secretary of State for Wales?

This was a Bill on which, in its present state, Parliament itself
would not have the last word. It was possible to make a good case that
the Barrage Bill did not justify a carry over motion – it was incomplete, until the groundwater research the Select Committee
demanded was finished. But the promoters, and the politicians who
supported them, were becoming increasingly desperate to tidy up the
shambles and get the Barrage built. To achieve this they were ready to
ride roughshod over the most hallowed precedents.

On both sides, the usual suspects were mustered; Ron Davies
spoke up for the SSSI, Rhodri Morgan gave his all to the groundwater fears of his constituents, while Ted Rowlands returned to his
vigorous attack on the economic case, or rather the lack of one,
offered by the promoters, with support from Win Griffiths of
Bridgend. Against them, Alun Michael had the uphill task of justifying the carry over motion, while Ian Grist, the Welsh Office minister
on the case, struggled with his damage limitation brief.

Mr Rowlands homed in enthusiastically on the weakest point of a
very weak case. The latest official figures for the annual running costs
of the Barrage were £1.35 million, he said,[1] more than three times the

figure quoted in the Second Reading debate.[2] When questioned then about how the costs would be met, Mr Michael had replied

> Initially, the corporation will fund the running costs. After its dissolution, it is intended to create a fund from assets to enable the successor body to pay for operating costs.[3]

Now, ten months later, he confirmed that these increased costs could still be met from these legendary assets that the Corporation would bequeath to its successors.[4] Mr Grist was asked to confirm that these assets would be used to repay the Welsh Office investment, but his brief contribution to the debate failed to mention the issue.

However, he announced developments in one of Cardiff Bay's principal growth industries – another groundwater expert had been recruited, this time by the Welsh Office. Mr Roy Stoner of Southampton University's Institute of Irrigation Studies was to act as independent adviser to the SoS, in his assessment of Hydrotechnica's recommendations.[5] Roy Stoner's efforts joined those of Ray Hornby of Wallace Evans, Rowland Edwards of Edwards and Saynor, Glyn Jones of London University and Professor Lloyd of Birmingham. Enough of Baroness White's expert guides had been recruited to get the most reluctant cow up the steepest Alp.

Just as Rhodri Morgan was about to announce the results of the CFAC survey inspired by Stan and Kate, Alun Michael moved that 'the Question be now put' and the House divided. Once again, more than 100 MPs had flocked to the Chamber in the last minutes of the debate, and the carry over motion was passed by 132 votes to 10. The Barrage Bill would set yet another precedent, and take at least three sessions of Parliament to become law. Victory might be eluding its opponents at the moment, but they were getting very good at postponing defeat.

On 15th January 1991, another bill to enable a barrage in south Wales had its First Reading in the Lords. Superficially similar to the Cardiff Bay project, the Usk barrage would also dam a river to create a freshwater lake as a centrepiece for the redevelopment of a derelict inner city area. However, there were many differences. There was no Development Corporation for Newport, and there would be no central government funding for the scheme, all costs would be borne by Gwent County Council and Newport Borough Council. The Taff offered very modest sport for fly fisherman, although salmon were starting to return to the river, but the Usk was an established, flourishing salmon and trout river; the Barrage would need to have a pass to allow migrating fish to get back up river to breed – never tried before on a river of this size and character. Any such threat to the Usk fisheries would affect local tourism, the area's main source of income; many feared that the 2000 jobs promised by the promoters would be outnumbered by bankrupt hoteliers and unemployed gillies, if the salmon failed to negotiate the fish pass. The nature of the proposed barrage was still undecided, whether it would exclude the sea's tides completely or only partially, so there was great uncertainty about its environmental consequences.

Most damaging of all was the opposition of the National Rivers Authority and its Chair that keen fly fisherman Lord Crickhowell. The NRA was concerned about the threat to the salmon fisheries, but, like the Taff, the Usk estuary had several sewer outlets, with disastrous consequences for water quality in the impounded lake behind the Barrage, although Newport had a modest 11, to Cardiff's 381. Anti-barrage campaigners in the Welsh capital awaited developments in the neighbouring borough with interest.

The Cardiff Bay Barrage Bill was next considered by the House at its Report Stage, on 18th February, 1991. The Report Stage, between a Select Committee's report on a bill and its Third Reading, is a way of keeping legislation under review, so MPs could make comments and prepare amendments for the final Third Reading. Rhodri Morgan, Ron Davies and their supporters rallied once more. They carefully rehearsed and updated the case against the Barrage, during the three hour debate, as they had done before and would do in future, but the most telling point, on this occasion, was procedural, rather than environmental or economic.

Rhodri Morgan reminded the House that Hydrotechnica had produced an interim report, on Thursday, 14th April; he confirmed that the Select Committee had required that, in the interests of the petitioners against the Bill, John Miles should see any Hydrotechnica reports, and offer a second opinion on them. He pointed out that John Miles had not been informed that an interim report had been prepared, let alone seen it and formed any opinion about it. The Corporation had wilfully disregarded the Committee's instructions. However, before the Bill's supporters could be invited to respond, Alun Michael, with excellent timing, forced a division, and the debate was over.

Meanwhile, the River Usk Barrage Bill had its Second Reading in the Lords, on 13th March. Its promoters, without any moral or financial support from the Welsh Office and with no high profile political advocates, were struggling hard. The case for Newport's barrage, economically, was no better or worse than that for Cardiff's; it used the same arguments about attracting investment, and developing infrastructure, about trading off environmental loss against material prosperity. Critics of the Usk Bill, like Lord Moran, pointed out the vagueness of the scheme's details, but it was no more vague than the earliest 1987 version of the Cardiff Barrage Bill which had so aroused Norman Robson's interest.

Cardiff Flood Action Committee had a Newport doppelganger, the Barrage Action Group (BAG). BAG was fortunate, did not have to cope with a Gwent equivalent of Lord Brooks or Alun Michael, prepared to invest a substantial political reputation in the scheme. There was no Geoffrey Inkin to present the case for the Barrage as a foregone conclusion, as there was no quango in Newport with a vast PR budget. Above all, Lord Crickhowell, no doubt for his own good reasons, was on their side. All the arguments about dubious economics, rising groundwater and poor water quality which His Lordship thought were so easily soluble for Cardiff, had become mysteriously intractable in Newport. What the Welsh Secretary had started in 1987, the Chair of the NRA wanted to stop in 1991, and Lord Crickhowell usually seemed to get his way.

The Commons Third Reading debate on the Cardiff Bill followed two months later; it began on 16th April, when Rhodri Morgan gave the opening speech. A Third Reading debate gives MPs their last chance to suggest substantial changes to a Bill, before it receives the Royal Assent, and Mr Morgan and the anti-barrage stalwarts intended to take full advantage. They had tabled no less than 300 amendments to the Bill considered by the Select Committee. Under parliamentary convention, the amount of time the House could devote to 'private business' like the Barrage Bill, was strictly limited, so their strategy would be to keep the debate going, if necessary through the night, so the more amendments they asked for, the longer the debate could go on. It was also required that there be at least 100 MPs available to vote to continue the debate on a Private Bill, whenever the relevant division might be called. If the House divided, and less than 100 MPs could answer the Division bell, then the Barrage Bill would fall. If the anti-barrage contingent could talk for long enough, until most of the payroll vote had given up, they could defeat the Bill.

They were also aided by the disarray afflicting the Conservative government. Following the resignation of Margaret Thatcher in November, 1990, and John Major's victory in the consequent election for the Party leadership, there had been a cull of his opponents on the government front benches. As a result, there was considerable disaffection on the Tory backbenches; the Whips might be able to hold such resentment in check on votes about Government legislation, but they certainly could not rely on automatic support for 'private business' like the Barrage.

Perhaps it was anxiety generated by the unreliability of backbench support that led Peter Walker's successor, David Hunt, to take an unusual and very unparliamentary step. On 31st March, he wrote, on official WO stationery, to his Cabinet colleagues, begging for their support.

He told them,

> Because of the conventions on private Bills... it would be inappropriate formally to whip the payroll on this occasion. But given the importance of this Bill to the South Wales area, and the Government's consistent support for it hitherto, I am extremely anxious to prevent the spoiling tactics succeeding. I therefore very much hope that you, your junior Ministers and all your PPSs will do your best to support the Bill, through the night if necessary.[6]

Rhodri Morgan opened the debate by asking the Deputy Speaker, Betty Boothroyd, to rule that the letter be referred to the Committee of Privileges, as a flagrant breach of the rules of the House – the government could not undermine parliament's traditional level playing field on private Bills, even if, over the Barrage, such niceties were already more honoured in the breach than the observance. Her response was strangely inconsistent – there was nothing, she insisted, wrong with 'hon. Members encouraging other hon. Members to attend a debate.'

She seemed to overlook the point of Rhodri Morgan's accusation; there was indeed nothing wrong with asking fellow MPs to attend a debate, but Mr Hunt did not want his fellow ministers to attend the debate, he wanted them and their entourages to vote against the Bill being debated. A cabinet minister might not be formally 'whipping' juniors in his or her department, by asking them to vote in a particular way on a particular bill, but the effect on their future careers of any refusal to do so, could be just as serious. In spite of rumbles of protest from south Wales MPs at this injustice, the long night's trudge through their tabled amendments began.

The usual suspects were joined by Jimmy Hood, the Select Committee member whose minority report had so gladdened anti-barrage protesters. He referred obliquely to CBDC's disregard for the Committee's instructions about the Hydrotechnica reports, and commented '... had we known... that what has happened since would happen, I genuinely doubt whether the three-to-one majority would have favoured the Bill.'[7] As he pointed out, none of the other three committee members were in the House to support the Bill whose passage they had smoothed so controversially.

Most of the amendments, or the few that could be discussed in the time available, dealt with matters already aired at length in earlier debates, like leachate or the effect of European conservation directives, but one of the most far-reaching suggestions was the submission of the Barrage project to the local planning process. There had long been great dissatisfaction with the Private Bills procedure for promoting major public works. Many, inside and outside Parliament, saw it as a way of preventing local participation in such decisions; others saw it as an inappropriate use of Parliament's time, when standard planning enquiries would be more relevant.

After three hours of debate, the first division was called at ten o'clock. Mr Hunt's plea to his ministerial colleagues was granted in abundance; no less than sixteen senior members of the cabinet, several accompanied by a full retinue of junior ministers, filed through the Aye lobby, to support the continuance of the Bill – the highest ever turnout of senior government members in any Barrage debate, thus far.

Undaunted, Rhodri Morgan, Ron Davies and their supporters settled down for a long night's talking. Their performance by this time was like that of a well-established jazz quintet; every player knew the theme, and could play apparently infinite variations with fluency, skill and sympathy for the particular roles of his fellow virtuosi.

As the familiar arguments about algae, Ferry Road, costs and water quality continued into the small hours, the increasingly sleepy spectators in the Public Gallery were impressed by the cogency and logic of their speeches, obviously the result of painstaking preparation and rehearsal. One dominant motif which recurred at least twenty times in their thirteen hour marathon gig was Lord Crickhowell, reprised in various keys – begetter of the Barrage, director of Associated British Ports, and Chair of the National Rivers Authority.

As the night wore on, a comic counterpoint was provided by increasingly emotional contributions from the government benches. At one point, Mr Jeremy Hanley, Minister of State at the Northern Ireland Office, was moved to leave the chamber 'with a gracious gesture, which' Ron Davies hoped, 'will doubtless be recorded for posterity'. Rhodri Morgan took the hint and commemorated the Minister's demonstration in an oblique reference to the Taff and the Ely as the 'two fingers pointing north...' from Cardiff Bay.[8]

When the second division was called, a few minutes before 1a.m., only seven ministers were available to vote, making a total of 97 'Ayes' – three less than the 100 needed to ensure the Bill's survival. However, there were some hours of debate still to go, and its opponents soldiered on. But they had to content themselves with a bout of shadow boxing as their main opponent, Alun Michael, had left the chamber;

by coincidence, the Government whips and the Welsh Secretary decided to take a break at the same time, returning only when Ron Davies forced a division, just after 4 am.

This vote, with 52 'Ayes' and eight 'Noes', made it clear the promoters' support was dwindling fast, as several MPs shared Jeremy Hanley's impatience with the proceedings and it was clear that the Bill was likely to be abandoned. The major burden of sustaining the debate fell to Rhodri Morgan, as he talked, without any significant break, for another two long hours. It was a major *tour de force*, by any standards, after a whole night of argument. At last, just after 7am, the Chairman of the Ways and Means Committee, who was responsible for the conduct of 'private business' in the House intervened, as time had run out; the debate was closed and the Barrage Bill was dead.

There was much rejoicing from the exhausted, anti-barrage campaigners in the public gallery, with a great deal of laughter and some tears of relief, before a concerted rush for the nearest phone to get the good news home to Cardiff, and then to thank and congratulate their valiant MP. Perhaps it was fortunate that their noisy excitement prevented them from hearing much of the debate's coda. Ian Grist waspishly chided the Bill's opponents for their obstructive tactics, and, in a classic Freudian slip, referred to it as ' This public Bill...'[9]; he was briskly corrected by Ted Rowlands. Alas, the correction was valid for only a brief moment; at ten past eight, that same morning, John MacGregor, the Leader of the House, announced that 'the government would be introducing their own Bill to permit the building of the Cardiff Bay Barrage.'

It was clear that in the small hours the government had accepted the Bill would have to be allowed to sink, but not without trace – they would immediately relaunch it, with the full backing of their majority. The new Bill was a Hybrid Bill, brought to Parliament by private sponsors, but with official government support.

The new form differed from its earlier incarnation in several ways, all with much significance for the anti-barrage campaign. Debates on Hybrid Bills could be guillotined at the convenience of party managers; there would be no more night-long talkouts by Rhodri Morgan. Members of Select Committees on Private Bills were chosen arbitrarily, by lot, in the Office of the Chair of the Ways and Means, but MPs considering Hybrid Bills were hand picked by the Chief Whips. Worst of all, whipping of every vote on the Bill would now be official; while the government could command a substantial majority, and had control of the parliamentary timetable, passage into law was inevitable.

The campaign to stop the Barrage had suffered a severe setback, but the all-night drama in the Commons had given the campaigners more publicity than they had ever had before. There were invitations to appear on TV, give radio interviews, write newspaper articles – so many, that CFAC members had to set up a rota to take turns in answering them. When this interest was at its height, it seemed odd for 24 hours to go by, without a mention of the Cardiff Bay Barrage in some national medium or other.

On 13th May, the councillors of Newport and Gwent announced the River Usk Barrage Bill would be withdrawn; instead the scheme would be considered by a public planning enquiry. The prospect of yet another long drawn out barrage battle was obviously not an enticing one. The public enquiry began, in Newport, in May 1993. The inspector heard many of the arguments that had exercised Cardiff Flood Action (raised groundwater, environmental damage, poor economic justification) put by many of the same expert witnesses (John Miles on groundwater, John Bowers on economics, Peter Ferns on wildlife). There was one significant difference, however, in Newport, the force of the anti-barrage case was accepted, and the council withdrew their proposal before the enquiry was complete. Campaigners in Cardiff could only look with envy at the success of their Newport neighbours, and wistfully wonder what they too could have achieved on the more level playing field of a public enquiry.

The impetus of the Cardiff campaign was kept up by changes in the political climate, as well as the new publicity. In the City Council elections in May 1991, Labour won control, with 39 councillors, at least 17 of whom were openly sceptical about the Barrage. At one of the earliest meetings of the Labour group, a substantial majority voted to petition against the new Bill. In the recently deceased Private Bill, the remedial measures on groundwater had been in the body of the Bill itself; however, it appeared that, in its Hybrid form, groundwater protection had been relegated to an accompanying Schedule, which could be changed, even after the Royal Assent, at the pleasure of the Secretary of State.

The City Council decided to petition if the measures were not restored to their original status, so that any change would require further legislation. If carried out, this threat, would make it very difficult for any Select Committee to dismiss criticism of the Bill lightly, or briefly; at the very least, it would take even longer to become law. Many Councillors who, previously, had had no strong feelings about the Barrage, had been very concerned at the government's apparent desperation to get it built by any means, at any cost.

The removal of Paragraph 4, the groundwater measures, from the Bill, caused concern in other, very unexpected quarters. In a statement to the *South Wales Echo*, Alun Michael made an astonishing plea to the Welsh Secretary. The MP for Cardiff South and Penarth was so worried about the disappearance of Paragraph 4 that he asked David Hunt to bring back the Private Bill! He said he was responding to the concerns of his constituents 'who want to know their houses are fully protected... I believe this will be in the best interests of opponents of the Bill for they have won concessions in the Private Bill and this course of action would in no way detract from the spirited opposition which they have put up to the whole idea of [the] Barrage'.[10]

Official government support for the Bill had now put Alun Michael, as a Labour MP and its original sponsor, in an ambiguous position. No member of Her Majesty's Opposition could troop into the Aye lobby in support of Government legislation; Labour MPs were now bound to oppose it in its current form. It was unfortunate for their leader, Neil Kinnock, that he finally stated his unambiguous support for the Bill. This was at the moment of its decease. In an interview with *The Western Mail*, a few days after the marathon 'talk out', when pressed to give his views, he replied, 'If I had been there, I would have voted for the Bill', a clear demonstration of Rhodri Morgan's distance from his party's upper echelons.

Mr Kinnock had not voted in any of the earlier divisions on the Bill; he had carefully refrained from mentioning the Barrage itself in public, while making his support for the '30,000' jobs it would bring quite clear. But now he and Mr Michael would have no choice but to join Rhodri Morgan, Ron Davies and Ted Rowlands in opposition. However, the omission of Paragraph 4 offered a fig leaf for their embarrassment; because David Hunt's Hybrid was not quite the creature Mr Michael had so loyally championed through three years of harrowing debates, he had a practical, as opposed to political, pretext for withdrawing his support. Ironically, the measures whose disappearance he lamented had only been in the original Bill through the efforts of the anti-barrage campaigners he criticised so vehemently only a few weeks before.

Mr Michael was not alone in his *volte-face*; senior members of the County Council found themselves in the same tight spot. Although no elected member would admit it publicly, the dismal performance of the Corporation's groundwater consultants at the last Select Committee had worried them. With the protection measures gone, if groundwater damage occurred after CBDC's demise, the Council could be left holding a large, wet, expensive baby; they wanted those safeguards back, not just for their electors' safety, but for the sake of their own futures.

These cracks in the façade of support for the scheme were very welcome to everyone in the anti- movement. But the campaign had now been going for more than five years; for activists like Norman, Glyn, Stan, Charlie, Kate and Ruth, they had been years of detailed, complex argument, meetings with planners, engineers and politicians, research, letter-writing, recruitment. The case against the Barrage could never be easily summed up in slogans to be shouted at demonstrations, or scrawled on posters; it had demanded scrupulous attention to detail, care and application. This would have been exhausting enough as a full-time commitment; when combined with day jobs and caring for families, it had become almost insupportable, after so long. Now it appeared the struggle would have to be sustained for several more years, with diminishing chances of success.

Cardiff was not the only place where the Barrage Bill's tortuous progress caused concern. For some years there had been growing dissatisfaction nationally with Private Bills procedure for enabling major public works.[11] The parliamentary process was totally inappropriate for assessing large civil engineering schemes, skewed as it was by the need to maintain party loyalties, its scope for meandering, ill-informed debate, and political point-scoring.

For many MPs, the progress of the Cardiff Bay Barrage Bill exemplified all these shortcomings; what should have been a rigorous evaluation of the technical, environmental and economic case for Mr Edwards' dream had become a purely political exercise – he who could cajole, bully or finesse the most votes into the Aye lobby must be right, no matter how poor and unproven his case, no matter how ill-informed his supporters. It was the last straw. In 1991, the Transport and Public Works Bill had its First Reading in the Commons. Its supporters acknowledged the way the Barrage campaign demonstrated the need for more fruitful analysis of such proposals. The Private Bills procedure was to be replaced by public enquiries, where proposals for significant projects could be examined by neutral inspectors, hopefully free of political pressures.

The Transport and Public Works Act of 1992 could be described as Parliament's monument to the anti-barrage campaign; never again would local protesters have to go through that long and expensive charade of Select Committees, or MPs through debate after debate on matters most were ignorant or uninterested. By the time it became law, it was too late for the Cardiff Barrage; that Bill was already too far on its tortuous Parliamentary road to turn back.

Yet in 1991 the fight had not been lost and, if it was to be carried on, there would have to be a re-focussing of energies, a redefinition of aims. In July, Pete Morgan, a university lecturer in Business Administration, arranged an anti-barrage day school, where campaigners could map out future strategy and tactics. One of the movement's strengths had always been its informality and adaptability – Norman had been its founder and inspiration, through his sheer dedication and hard work, but he was the centre of a network, not the apex of a hierarchy. However, his health was showing signs of strain, and a series of hospital visits made it clear that his burden must be lightened. He wanted to step down as Chair, instead he was persuaded to accept a custom-made role as Honorary President; the Chairmanship would be shared out between any members willing to do whatever work was required, whenever it was needed. It says a great deal for the cohesion and fellow-feeling of CFAC members that the organisation not only survived but thrived, with such an informal structure; it didn't depend on the energies and abilities of a few, but on the altruism and commitment of many.

There were some supporters who felt that the Hybrid Bill should mark the end of the campaign to stop the Barrage by conventional, parliamentary means. All that could be done through formal channels had been done, Charlie Burriss argued; now was the time to take to the streets, with mass direct action. But the majority of members felt that there was still a lot of life left in a conventional political campaign; the Labour Opposition was now committed to opposing the new Bill in Parliament, it would take very little persuading for them to oppose the Barrage itself.

This view was endorsed by the fate of the very first Hybrid Bill. As a new bill with government support, it had to be considered, in early June, by the Commons Standing Orders Committee, before being allowed its First Reading. The Committee was dominated by Conservative MPs, who might have been expected to view the measure with sympathy. On the contrary, they savaged it to death, insisting that it was too poorly drafted to be presented to the House. As a result, hundreds of copies produced by the Stationery Office were pulped, at considerable expense, and at considerable embarrassment to Mr Hunt, who had been responsible for its contents. This rejection meant it was unlikely that the new Bill would become law before the next General Election, expected in the early summer of 1992.

Other signs that all was not lost in the political campaign appeared that summer. The groundwater report the Select Committee demanded from Hydrotechnica was due for completion at the end of July. As the Committee had required, John Miles was keeping a watching brief on their progress; he had prepared his own report.

Hydrotechnica's work broadly confirmed the views of Wallace Evans. Their engineers advised that changes in groundwater levels post-barrage would be minimal over most of south Cardiff; in the few areas in Grangetown, where, in an 'extreme case', levels might rise,

'Allowance should be made for simple remedial groundwater drainage works'.[12]

So, alongside compensation for damage, another idea was taking shape – CBDC should be responsible for installing some sort of drainage system in south Cardiff that would take the groundwater raised by the Barrage into the Taff and, ironically, into the impounded lake. This would, in theory, keep the city dry, and reduce the need for remedial measures. Such a project would not appear in the Bill itself, but would be included in formal, legally binding 'directions' from the Welsh Secretary to the CBDC, or its successor body.

The identity and role of this successor body was becoming increasingly significant. CBDC, like all Development Corporations, had a limited life-span, informally set at ten years, but the fight against the Barrage had now dragged on for nearly four years. At a conservative estimate, it would take at least five years to build; CBDC might take responsibility for the finished scheme, and its worrying consequences for only the first five or six years of its life – who would run it after their demise? Who would pay for any groundwater drainage scheme, for maintaining reasonable water quality in the Bay, for keeping the fish passes and the boat locks working, for operating the sluices, that would drain the Bay when river flows threatened?

In June, a meeting was held at the Welsh Office (WO) to discuss Hydrotechnica's work to date. Present were Dr Miles, Roy Stoner, (the WO's groundwater consultant), and several members of CRAB, with senior WO civil servants. John Miles was very critical; his own work, with Kate and Stan's survey, showed that the geology of the area was more complex, and the behaviour of the water table more volatile than the report had assumed. He advised that much more detailed work on the structure of the made ground in Riverside and Grangetown was needed; Hydrotechnica's research to date had been based on too narrow an interpretation of the Select Committee's requirements.

Dr Miles was also deeply concerned at the haphazard collection of data on which the Hydrotechnica assessment was based; important sewer flow readings were available for only a very short period, from February to April 1991, while many of the specially sunk boreholes in the made ground had only provided reliable information for a few days at a time, instead of the consistent twelve months' data the Select Committee had thought necessary.

The Welsh Office tacitly accepted this criticism and agreed that five months more monitoring and investigation take place, on the understanding that CFAC would not make this decision public. No doubt, they had an eye to the evidence petitioners would present to the Select Committees on the new Bill; they did not want any more embarrassing gaps. Mr Stoner would respond to this additional work in a final report to the Secretary of State, in December.

Although the economic case for the Barrage could no longer be aired before any Select Committees, its high costs and uncertain return on investment were becoming a source of grave anxiety to many of its supporters. These anxieties were justified in November 1991, when the Treasury allocated a further £22 million to CBDC, making a total grant of more than £130 million, over the following three years. Rhodri Morgan believed that the government would tighten its grip on public expenditure as the current recession worsened. In such a climate, writing a blank cheque for groundwater damage in south Cardiff could alienate even the most pro-barrage of Treasury ministers.

So, during the hot, dry summer of 1991, the anti-barrage strategy underwent a subtle change. The Bill could not be defeated now by any band of activists, no matter how highly motivated or capable, so CFAC had to work more indirectly. They had to persuade the national Labour Party that plans for the Barrage could and should be abandoned by any future Labour government. They had to use future Select Committees, and any other possible Parliamentary means, to delay the Bill's progress long enough for this persuasion to succeed. They also had to get as many remedial or protection measures written into the Bill as possible, not only to combat the groundwater threat, but also to increase the scheme's costs to a level any government would find unacceptable.

Meanwhile, support for the campaign was increasing. In June, the pro-barrage *South Wales Echo* asked readers throughout Cardiff, whether they were for or against the scheme. In contrast to their earlier polls, there was a small majority against, by 1107 to 1003. However, it was clear that the nearer to Cardiff Bay respondents lived, the more likely they were to vote against – 53% of the votes were cast in Canton, Riverside and Grangetown, with a majority of more than 4 to 1 against the Barrage.

Determined to flaunt their popularity as publicly as possible, CFAC entered a float in the Lord Mayor's parade, in August. Its theme was the threat to the Bay's bird life; over 30 members, with supporters from the RSPB, worked lovingly on it, under Sue Pomeroy's direction, and won enthusiastic applause in their progress through the city to the strains of 'The Grangetown Gondolier'.

The Development Corporation's attempts to woo and amuse the citizens of Cardiff were less successful. One Sunday evening, in late September, they arranged a free open air concert and firework display, publicised as 'Light up the Bay'. It didn't. Most of the fireworks failed to go off and the concert was inaudible. In a fulsome apology in the *Echo*, they blamed the failure on 'severe weather and other factors, including a tidal delay of an hour...'[13] Even CBDC's most loyal supporters were unsympathetic – if they couldn't even understand a tide table, what hope was there that they could manage the fish passes and sluice gates of a barrage?

After this disaster, the Corporation felt it was necessary to rally the troops, to boost morale and demonstrate confidence. To this end, the Prime Minister, John Major, visited the Bay to meet staff at Baltic House and enthuse local residents. However, the attractions of the Bay were not at their best for his visit. CBDC had put up a walkway along the shore, above the mudflats, for the PM to have a better view of the future site of the Barrage. Unfortunately, the workmen building it had, only the previous day, accidentally shattered the main Butetown sewer, which ran just under the line of the walkway. The resulting odour was both vile and penetrating; but there had been no time for concealment, so CBDC's PR staff could only advise the PM and his entourage to breathe as little, and as shallowly, as possible, during this section of their walkabout. The hearts of Mr Major's companions on the trip, Geoffrey Inkin and David Hunt, must have sunk, when Stan Perkins and Les Baxter managed to evade the security cordon at just this point.

Since the days of their first PR efforts with visits, Stan had faithfully shadowed all CBDC's public events, as far as his kidney dialysis sessions, four times a day, permitted. With his charming smile and friendly patience, he would buttonhole every available VIP and leave them in no doubt about the facts of the anti-barrage case. The First Lord of the Treasury was no exception, and received the full force of Stan's sincerity and eloquence. Stan and Les also pointed out that the vile smell from the sewer was only a foretaste of what the entire Bay might be like, post-barrage. Stan was eager for the PM to get its full effect; he advised him to inhale deeply 'and get a whiff of that!' Very much taken aback, Mr Major understandably declined, but agreed to meet Stan later for a tour of the 'Protected Property' area. Sadly, pressing affairs of state intervened, and the tour was never made.

When the Hydrotechnica report appeared, in early October, CFAC members were shocked to discover that Welsh Office had broken their promises about confidentiality. Householders in Grangetown and Riverside had given John Miles details about the dampness of their homes on the strict understanding that the information would never be publicly linked to specific addresses. In spite of this, his research had been quoted in such a way that at least one property had been clearly identified, and its owner was naturally incensed.

The campaigners were also angered by the SoS's decision that public consultation on the Hydrotechnica report would be limited to adverts in local papers, asking people to write to him with their views, rather than the series of public meetings and open debates they had expected. When asked for an explanation, the Welsh Office replied that such an exercise would be too expensive, and take too long.

The Council's own groundwater expert, Professor Lloyd, also took a critical view of Hydrotechnica's work. In a report to the Council that November, he advised that there would be no major problems in most parts of the city, if vulnerable basements could be damp-proofed, as they suggested. However, he conceded that the situation post-impoundment might be more serious in Grangetown, if CBDC did not take preventive action. He implied that, as John Miles had pointed-ed out, Grangetown relied on its sewerage system to drain away excess groundwater. Welsh Water were currently relining and strengthening this system, which would eventually prevent ground-water entering the pipes – alternative methods for dealing with a raised water table in the area would have to be found, if Grangetown was to remain dry.

However, Professor Lloyd disagreed with Dr Miles about the rel-evance of groundwater modelling in made ground. Instead, he advised that the Council should press for a staged impoundment, starting at 4m, so that any changes could be assessed, before full impoundment was complete. He was asked by Councillor John Smith, from Grangetown ward, whether he, Professor Lloyd, would consid-er buying a house in the area, post-barrage; he replied with searing honesty, that he would not, in present conditions. As the meeting closed, councillors prepared to consider the progress of the new Bill, some with much anxiety.

Such exchanges may have given the Secretary of State cause to doubt whether he could rely on Labour councillors' continuing sup-port. There were too many anxious rumblings for his peace of mind. Perhaps it was his desire to keep the CBDC itself in safe and loyal hands that led David Hunt to intervene in the next appointment to its Board. Under CBDC' s terms of reference, local councils would appoint representatives to reflect their own political makeup – Labour councils should appoint Labour councillors, Conservative councils, Conservative councillors. Cardiff City and South Glamorgan author-ities had most seats, and both were now solidly Labour, with all-Labour appointees.

Following the death of Councillor John Reynolds, Leader of the

City Council, there was a vacancy to be filled on the Board. The City Council informed Mr Hunt that they intended to send Geoff Mungham, Chair of their Finance Committee, lecturer and journalist, in his place. Councillor Mungham had maintained a careful neutrality about the Barrage; he had observed the party whip in Council votes, but had remained silent in debates. It might have been due to this failure to express any reassuring enthusiasm for the scheme that the Secretary of State took the unprecedented step of overruling his appointment. Instead, he brought in Councillor Jeff Sainsbury, Leader of the Council's small Conservative group and a very public supporter of the Barrage. Whatever Mr Hunt's real motives may have been, the message he sent was, at best, of a great desire for reassurance and, at worst, of a forceful 'Do what I wish, or I will appoint someone else, who will.'

CBDC were determined to improve their damaged public image, and they launched their own national advertising campaign, in November. Posters appeared on more than 200 hoardings, throughout southern England and south-east Wales – the most prominent immediately over the departure board at Paddington Station. However, as their main purpose was to publicise the regeneration of south Cardiff outside the city, it was remarkable how many appeared within the city itself – where surely no extra publicity was required? Cynics thought that their appearance had been timed to coincide with the new Bill, to rouse some fresh local enthusiasm for the scheme.

The posters each carried two pictures: one, labelled 'Dormant' was apparently a photo of Cardiff Bay in its present state, dirty and derelict; the other, labelled 'Vibrant' showed an imaginary post-barrage Bay, lively, colourful and clean. Glyn Paul, as a professional photographer with a lifetime's knowledge of Cardiff Docks, inspected the pictures with great care and interest. He came to the firm conclusion that many of the 'Dormant' photos were not taken in Cardiff Bay at all, but further down the coast, near the Rumney estuary; others were out-of-date, featuring parts of the area which had already been regenerated, well before the Development Corporation had even been set up. He lodged a formal complaint about such flagrant misrepresentation with the Advertising Standards Authority.

Since the ASA was rather slow in reaching a decision on the matter, Charlie Burriss, ever the keen street fighter, persuaded Norman and Hilary Robinson to join him in a little direct action against one of the 'Dormant/Vibrant' posters, on a roundabout near South Glamorgan County Hall. So, late one October evening, the police were informed by a passer-by that three vandals, slightly above the usual age for such mischief, were defacing an advertisement hoarding

near Council property. Officers of the law appeared at the scene, and
one constable politely held the ladder on which Hilary was perched,
paintbrush in hand, as she descended, while his colleague loaded
Norman's bicycle into the boot of their patrol car and gave all three a
lift home, Charlie still clutching his can of black gloss. What exactly
they intended to write, or draw, on that poster has remained a mys-
tery to this day. But, in the fullness of time, the ASA upheld Glyn's
complaint, and all the posters, defaced or not, were withdrawn.

In early November, the second version of the Hybrid Bill was published, suitably redrafted. But the clauses on groundwater damage
protection were still tucked away in Schedule 7, so that 'The Secretary
of State may by regulations... amend any provision of that schedule.'[14]
There was a very real fear that if the cost of remedial works escalat-
ed, the SoS would be able to save money, by unilaterally restricting
them.

The Private Bill had also included the setting up of the Cardiff Bay
Advisory Committee, to advise CBDC on the management of the
'inland bay' and its amenities. Various bodies would be represented,
including, for instance, the local councils, with seven members
between them, the Royal Yachting Association, with three, one each
from the NRA and ABP, and six from CFAC. Although the new Bill
referred to the Advisory Committee, its membership was now left
completely at CBDC's discretion. It would be only natural for them
to appoint members would who offer little resistance to their plans –
further cause for concern for those as yet undecided about their good
intentions for Cardiff.

To comply with recently adopted EC policies, the new bill was
accompanied by a fresh environmental assessment, from the same
team at Liverpool University that compiled the original, in 1988.
There were few changes – the risks of midge infestation, algal bloom
and poor water quality were still noted, with their possible remedies.
Although the term implies independence and rigour, such 'environmental assessments' were actually presented to government by the
companies that commissioned them, not the academics who prepared
them. There were no regulations or guidelines to prevent them being
carefully edited by bodies like the Development Corporation before
submission to government officials, so that any unfavourable facts
could be left out. The law required an environmental assessment to be
done; it did not require it to be comprehensive or objective.

By coincidence, Professor Chris Baines, one of the moving spirits
behind the RSPB's Living Waterfront scheme for the Bay, gave the
Landscape Institute's annual address at the Royal Institute of British
Architects, only a few days later. His perspective was much wider

than that of his Liverpool colleagues and his views were unavailable for editing. The address was devoted to his contempt for what he called 'instant landscaping', where natural environments with potential to flourish, like Cardiff Bay, were destroyed, in misguided attempts to tidy away what ought to be preserved. He had special scorn for the Cardiff Bay Development Corporation, 'run by the kind of people who can't cope with the fact that the tides go up and down', spending £200 million on a 'large cesspit surrounded by bistros and devoid of all the wading birds who are currently clearing up the pollution'.[15]

Professor Baines' opinion of the environmental credentials of the Corporation and its supporters in the Welsh Office was justified by a joint announcement by the WO and the Department of the Environment late in the afternoon of Friday 1st November. In those politically twilit hours, when the week's parliamentary business was complete, and minimal publicity guaranteed, they declared that Cardiff Bay would be excluded from the British government's designation of the Severn Estuary as a Special Protection Area.

The European Commission's Wild Birds Directive 79/409 required all member states to designate unique and valuable habitats as Special Protection Areas (SPAs). Under Article 2 of the Directive, wherever there was irreconcilable conflict between any proposals to develop SPAs and their conservation, 'ecological needs' had to take priority. As an SSSI, and a significant part of the Severn Estuary conservation area, Cardiff Bay should have been automatically entitled to this protection. Peter Walker had stripped it of its SSSI status, and now David Hunt removed the last vestiges of its possible protection by the EC. The Directive itself was quite unambiguous; there could be no 'balancing' of commercial and environmental interests, no compensation for lost habitats: the feeding grounds of Cardiff Bay could not be drowned under an impounded lake, the Barrage could not be built.

To exclude Cardiff Bay from the Severn Estuary SPA was ridiculous; its over-wintering birds supplied many of the Estuary's rarest species. But the only way the British government could avoid infringing the Directive and get the Barrage built, was to pretend that the Bay was not worth preserving, and its bird life insignificant, in contradiction of the advice of its own watchdog, the scientifically independent and rigorous Nature Conservancy Council.

The RSPB were firmly committed to fighting this decision, in Europe, although they knew such battles were long and complex, and the Barrage could be complete before a judgement emerged. However, they were heartened by the result of a case brought against the German government. Leybucht Bay had been, like Cardiff Bay, a

protected site, threatened with development; opponents had successfully brought a case to the European court and prevented its
destruction, in February 1991.

In spite of such desperate measures as the unprecedented conversion of a failed Private Bill into a Hybrid, bound to succeed, and the
declaration that a unique conservation area did not deserve conservation, the Barrage was not proving the magnet for developers that its
supporters had planned. No companies of any size had relocated to
the Bay from inside or outside the UK since CBDC's birth in1987; the
only economically significant employers were those, like Allied Steel
and Wire, who had been there all the time.

The Corporation and the Welsh Office were increasingly desperate to find some justification for their claims that the project was
essential for the commercial regeneration of the docklands.
Government support for the Bill meant they could no longer use the
delays caused by the opposition to the Private measure as an excuse
for companies' underwhelming enthusiasm for relocation there.

Moreover, the Conservative government was tightening the limits
on public spending as recession deepened: Treasury support could
not possibly continue at the present level without some visible return
on investment. Even worse, CBDC had launched its development
sites onto a buyers' market; all the other development corporations in
the UK had set out to attract employers and builders at just the same
time – in Sheffield and Teeside, Liverpool and Bristol, new business-
friendly environments were being promoted to the same dwindling
number of potential customers. Most of these other development corporations did not have the costly albatross of a barrage slung round
their necks, to push up costs, prices and rents. So, in such a climate,
it was inevitable that rumours should start to circulate among local
businesses, about the tempting 'special terms' available from the
Corporation for any companies ready to be enticed to Cardiff Bay.

It was against this background that, in autumn 1991, the Welsh
Health Common Services Agency (WHCSA) made the surprise
announcement that it would be moving to a purpose built office development in Cardiff Bay. The WHCSA was the body responsible for the
procurement and supply of equipment, furniture and other resources
for all NHS institutions in Wales, employing about 800 people. It had
long been planned that it would move from its original, inadequate
accommodation, split between Wrexham and Rookwood hospital in
Cardiff. The expected destination was Merthyr Tydfil, where office
space was cheap enough, at less than £10 per sq ft., to satisfy the
Treasury's stringent financial requirements, and where unemployment
was high enough for such an influx of jobs to be welcomed.

The head of the WHCSA was a former brigadier, Peter Crawley, who had spent much of his military career in the same regiment as Geoffrey Inkin, Chair of the Development Corporation. Kim Howells, MP for Pontypridd, commented at some length on this coincidence in the debate on the Second Reading of the new Barrage Bill. He also pointed out that, as it didn't really matter where in Wales the WHCSA was based, choosing Cardiff Bay with rents at £14.50 per sq ft, rather than Merthyr, where rents were 30% lower, needed some justifying.[16] He had been told by the WHCSA that they had made their decision on the advice of a property consultant. It appeared that this property consultant was none other than Grosvenor Waterside, the recently created subsidiary of Associated British Ports, who were, in turn, the owners of the land on which the offices were to be built, and major beneficiaries of any financial advantage brought by the development of Cardiff Bay. There was no response from the government benches.

By 25th November, 1991, the Second Reading debate, Alun Michael had had time to adjust to the new terms of engagement; Barry Jones, the Shadow Welsh Secretary, and other Welsh MPs, had tabled a 'reasoned amendment' to the Bill, asking for the debate to be postponed, because the public consultation period on the Hydrotechnica report required by the earlier Select Committee was not yet finished. The Bill was now part of a strict timetable of government legislation, and its four hour slot was completely devoted to discussion of the amendment, rehearsing yet again the arguments put forward during previous debates on the Private Bill. When the division was called, it was defeated by 278 votes to 130; the Bill was deemed to have been given a Second Reading, and 'committed to a Select Committee'.

Meanwhile, Roy Stoner had produced his recommendations for the Welsh Secretary, based on Hydrotechnica's research. He, like Professor Lloyd, suggested that prevention was better than cure, as far as raised groundwater was concerned; he outlined three possible measures: pumping sewers, where these would be the main drainage course for groundwater; special drainage systems, where sewers were inadequate for the extra flow; and, where neither of these measures were sufficient, remedial work on damaged homes.

Although comment on costs was not part of Mr Stoner's brief, it was clear that none of these measures would be cheap; the costs of the Barrage continued to stack up, and there was growing anxiety among County and City councillors about who would be paying for it. Mr Michael's earlier suggestions about sinking funds and trusts seemed both vague and optimistic compared with the hard facts of funding a civil engineering project on this scale. On 20th January, 1992, David Hunt announced in the Commons that he had asked CBDC to carry out tests on the feasibility of the dewatering systems suggested in the Stoner Report, nearly a year and a half after the Commons Select Committee on the Private Bill had first asked for such research.

The virtuoso performances of the CFAC witnesses, especially John Miles, before the previous SC in 1990 had had a significant effect on public opinion, as the unofficial *South Wales Echo* poll showed. In the run-up to its successor on the new Hybrid Bill, the campaigners thought another authoritative test of residents' views was needed. With all the expenses of another parliamentary appearance looming, they had no money to spare for another NOP, but the provisions of the Local Government Act of 1978 offered an attractive alternative. It stated that if a majority of residents at a public meeting attended by more than 15 electors voted to hold a poll on a matter of local concern, the relevant local authority was bound to arrange and finance such a poll.

So, in December 1991, a public meeting was held in Pontcanna, attended by over 100 electors, most of whom duly voted to hold a poll about the Barrage, just before the next Select Committee was to meet. Naturally, Cardiff City Council was unwilling to incur the considerable expense of arranging a full-scale election in the area – with the full panoply of returning officers, polling clerks, polling stations, poll cards, notices of election, etc. So, to PRAB's disappointment, they had to be content with minimal arrangements; there were no polling cards, no notices of election and polling hours were only from 4pm to 8pm, instead of the usual 14 hours. Undaunted, Pontcanna Residents Against the Barrage arranged their own publicity: a packed meeting in a local church hall, addressed by Rhodri Morgan; a fun run by fitter members along the 'Protected Property Line'; door-to-door leafleting of more than 6000 homes.

On the 16th January, a damp, drizzly evening, one in seven of Pontcanna voters turned out to give what the *Echo* described as 'an overwhelming 93 per cent NO to the controversial project'. Of the 1376 votes cast, only 83 supported the Barrage.' Inevitably, the 14% turnout was criticised by a CBDC spokesman, 'Such a narrowly based poll cannot accurately represent public opinion.' But, as Geoff Waites, Chair of Pontcanna Residents Against the Barrage later pointed out to the Select Committee, that turnout was higher than for some local government polls, especially as voting had been so restricted.[17]

The Committee first convened on 21st January 1992; as the Bill under consideration was a Hybrid Bill, seven MPs were sitting. Once more, the committee included Mr Michael Welsh. The Chair, a

Conservative, was Sir Nicholas Bonsor, Baronet. Sir Nicholas represented Upminster, and seemed the very model of a Knight of the Shires, with his affection for hunting, and his country seat at Liscombe Park, Bedfordshire; he later became Minister of State at the Foreign Office, in the twilight of the Major administration. He was a punctilious Chair, very concerned that petitioners should appreciate they were enjoying a privilege in appearing before him and his colleagues.

The proceedings of all parliamentary committees generate immense quantities of paperwork, evidence, reports, statements, maps, plans. As the necessary heaps of files began to accumulate around this one, and Sir Nicholas' patrician demeanour firmly set the tone of the proceedings, it seemed as if an eighteenth century magistrate had decided to conduct the business of the Bench in his muniment room.

The MPs would consider over 80 petitions from nearly 100 petitioners. The cost of petitioning had recently risen from £2 to £20, so to reduce expense, several groups of neighbours had submitted joint petitions. As there could be no more consideration of the principle of the Bill, there would be no longer be any opportunity for petitioners' agents to make introductory presentations, or concluding summaries, to the Committee. Only counsel for the promoters, led by the formidable Jeremy Sullivan, would make opening and closing addresses; the petitioners' case had to be made point-by-point, with the promoters responding, if they wished, petitioner by petitioner.

In this new format, Kevin Standring acted as agent for the residents' petitions, with those of Taff Housing Association and the local Labour ward parties, while John Popham appeared for the RSPB, Cardiff Flood Action, and Cardiff Friends of the Earth. Mr Sullivan was attended by a large and well-equipped team of junior barristers and clerks, Kevin and John Popham had the quick wits and physical agility of the ever-adaptable Francis Maxey.

The petitions and evidence heard by this Select Committee were much more subdued than those presented to its predecessors. Under the limited requirements of a Hybrid Bill, there could be no more bravura performances by the Great and Good of merchant banking and property development on CBDC's behalf; there could be no more thorough demolition of the case for the Barrage by articulate and well-briefed campaigners. Instead, the Bill had to be considered piece by piece.

It was difficult to bring the spirited vigour of earlier sessions to careful dissection of the wording of paragraph 4, subsection (ii) (a) of the new Bill, or an exact definition of the duties of a groundwater complaints administrator, but the petitioners did their best. Kate

Hunter for Canton Residents outlined the health risks for asthmatics from increased dampness, post-barrage; Pete Morgan graphically described the products of the many unofficial sewage outlets along the Taff, which he saw embellishing its banks on his morning runs; Dave Burns sang 'The Grangetown Gondolier' again.

But it was Glyn Paul who succeeded in silencing, for a moment at least, the promoter's Counsel, Jeremy Sullivan. In his opening remarks, Sullivan had referred to the possibility that in the gardens of Grangetown, 'the roses might welcome a rise in groundwater'. In reply, Glyn quoted his own gardening books, which insisted 'a well-drained soil is essential for successful rose growing', before presenting the baffled QC with what he thought might be 'the last rose of Grangetown'.[18]

The most significant difference between this and the earlier Select Committees was that one of the local councils was now petitioning against the Bill. Nicholas Bonsor and his colleagues were confronted with the unprecedented situation of the leader of one public body, Councillor John Smith – Chair of the City Council – objecting to a measure proposed by another public body, CBDC, of which he was also a member. Councillor Smith, and the Council's agent, George Bartlett, pointed out that the Bill as redrafted by Mr Hunt no longer included those provisions which had protected their interests, especially in issues like land drainage (dealing with changes in groundwater) and public health (dealing with the quality of the water in the impounded bay).

Two recent pieces of legislation, the Land Drainage Act of 1991, and the European Urban Waste Water Directive, adopted as official UK government policy in early 1992, made clear that these responsibilities rested squarely on district councils, like Cardiff City. So, it was amazing that the Welsh Secretary and his advisers should have pressed on with the Bill without clarifying them, vis-à-vis the Barrage. It was even more amazing that such a glaring omission could not have been remedied by amicable discussion between the parties concerned.

It was clear that the change in the political colour of the Council, and the Welsh Office's apparent support for the Corporation's shabby treatment of them over the Ferry Road tip, had reduced the relations between the City Council and the Bill's sponsors new low. This was precisely the sort of conflict which Lords Crickhowell and Brooks had intended to pre-empt by giving local councillors seats on the Development Board.

Mr Sullivan for Promoters asserted that, under the Land Drainage Act of 1991, the City Council had responsibility for dealing with saturation flooding, that is flooding caused by surface groundwater. The

City Council's own lawyers, although enjoying lower fees then the planning QC, begged to differ. The Committee Chair, after discussion with his colleagues, agreed with them, and suggested that the matter be resolved by the interested parties. Astoundingly, there was no suggestion from the MPs for an amendment to the Bill to clarify the matter.

The omission was surprising, because this is the function of Select Committees – to ensure that Bills give the minimum opportunity for future contention and uncertainty. Opponents of the Bill believed the subject was left unresolved in order to speed it through Parliament; the admission that the City Council was not responsible for the potentially expensive task of dealing with saturation flooding, would have meant that CBDC and its successors might be liable, with all the legal and cost implications that implied, including the redrafting and resubmission of the Barrage Bill.

The government's business managers could not tolerate such a prospect; it would not have been surprising if the Committee had been persuaded to tidy the matter away as quietly as possible. Indeed, Gwilym Jones, as Parliamentary Under Secretary at the WO, supported Sir Nicholas' decision when questioned about the Bill by the Welsh Grand Committee, a few months later.

In the event, it took several months, because the NRA, the WO, the Development Corporation and the City Council were plunged into inconclusive discussions about the NRA's requirements for drainage, flood defence and fisheries monitoring, and who would carry them out.

Evidence from John Miles and Professor Rushton dominated the proceedings. As petitions now had to refer specifically to clauses in the Bill, or its schedules, groundwater issues assumed even greater prominence than they had at earlier Committee hearings. Dr Miles confirmed that the Hydrotechnica report cleared up many of the uncertainties of the original Wallace Evans research. But it was flawed in one crucial respect – it still failed to give enough information about the made ground in Grangetown; of the 120 boreholes sunk to assess groundwater conditions, only ten were in made ground. Of the ten Grangetown boreholes, three gave readings which showed that the current level of the water table was already higher than Wallace Evans had predicted it would be post-barrage.

He also confirmed that Hydrotechnica's work endorsed the view that he, Professor Rushton and Brian Connorton had given to the previous Select Committee; sewers were important for maintaining the water balance in the underground strata of south Cardiff, especially Grangetown. Hydrotechnica estimated that 80% of groundwater was removed by sewers; however, an independent study he had done with Professor Rushton indicated that the proportion was rather smaller, at 40%.[19] But, as he later pointed out, their over-estimate of the amount of water entering the sewers lead to an under-estimate of groundwater levels in the made ground, which Hydrotechnica estimated at 1m, as opposed to Miles' and Rushton's 0.3m.[20]

Dr Miles also shared Stan Perkins' low opinion of the 200m grid system they had used – the wide variations in the nature of the made ground, the role of sewers in draining that ground, and many other variables made the task of predicting water table behaviour post-barrage far more difficult to predict than Hydrotechnica's report suggested. The more detailed small scale studies that he had made with Professor Rushton, indicated that certain areas would have problems much more serious than predicted by Hydrotechnica. Dr Miles was very critical of Mr Stoner's acceptance of Hydrotechnica's methods and results; he tried to convince the Committee that the remedial measures Stoner recommended to the Welsh Office would be inadequate.

As a result of Hydrotechnica's work, Mr Stoner had suggested additional drainage measures would be needed, including dewatering wells, to pump high groundwater back into the Taff and the Bay. In his evidence, Professor Rushton showed that such wells would be inadequate for dealing with such serious problems. He believed 'extensive field drains using... no dig sort of technology' would be required, and that the cost of such work would be considerably more than the £400,000 Mr Stoner estimated.[21]

One of the most powerful arguments against dewatering wells, the Professor believed, was their short term viability; such schemes were used in small scale projects, for short periods – five years at most.[22] In south Cardiff, they might have to operate for a hundred years.[23] Anxious local politicians began to fear that any cheque a successor body wrote for installing and sustaining them would not be large – it would just be blank.

Several councillors petitioned, but this time Jane Davidson, Sue Essex and Mark Drakeford were joined by colleagues from the Plasnewydd area, in Central Cardiff, further from the Bay than Canton or Riverside. Hydrotechnica's original May 1990 report had implied that this area would be vulnerable to raised groundwater levels post-barrage, but further reports failed to define or remedy the likely risks. Councillors Julie Morgan and Ann Cox asked that their constituents be given the same protection as the residents of Grangetown. Councillor Cox told the Committee that the City Council had asked CBDC, before Christmas, to sink more boreholes in her ward. CBDC replied that it could not justify the extra expense; that sort of cost-cutting didn't inspire confidence.[24]

Councillor Ian Brown was one of several petitioners to try, unsuccessfully, to widen the debate once more to include the economic fallacies on which the scheme was based. However, he managed to make one good point. In the heyday of Cardiff docks, with the steel works going three shifts every day, and ships crowding the port, between 8000 and 10,000 people worked in the area; where were the jobs for 30,000 promised by CBDC to come from, in a less labour-intensive era? Not only was there no reply, but there was not even a comment from the promoters' counsel.[25]

However, Mr Sullivan allowed himself a brief burst of outrage at the petitioners' strategy of trying to delay the Bill, by asking for yet more research and reports, when 'whatever study is done it is not going to satisfy these petitioners unless it concludes... that there will be no barrage'. He accused them of 'steadily increasing the administrative complexity and cost of the Barrage' by asking for 'pre-emptive works, Victorian buildings [sic]... further street cleansing...'.[26] At the back of the Committee Room, CRAB members nodded in agreement; their little ration of democracy had apparently been used up in April 1991, and now they had to resort to less conventional manoeuvres, even if Mr Sullivan disapproved.

The new Bill included details of the 'replacement' feeding grounds CBDC still had to provide at Wentloog. For the RSPB and other conservation groups, Peter Ferns gave evidence about the inadequacy of their proposals. The site was too small and offered too little nutrition for the fraction of Cardiff Bay's dunlin and redshank which might find their way to it.

His criticisms were so damning that, in their final report, the MPs advised that all mention of Wentloog be excised from the Bill – it would have cost £400,000 to set up, and about £600 per bird in annual running costs. Where critical naturalists had hoped a parliamentary scalpel might be delicately wielded by the MPs on the feeding ground proposals, they received a wholesale bludgeoning. The proposed alternatives would be too expensive, so when the Bill returned to the Commons there would be no provision for alternative feeding grounds at all.

In response to Cardiff Flood Action's petition, gardens and public spaces like parks would have the same protection against groundwater as houses. The City Council, indemnified by CBDC, would be responsible for drainage measures although it was left unclear what exactly they should be. The role of the groundwater complaints administrator was more clearly defined. There were slight changes to limitations on claims for remedial work, but the Bill remained substantially the same. As one Pontcanna resident commented after Sir Nicholas read out the Committee's final verdict, 'Blessed are those who expect nothing, for they shall not be disappointed'.

While the Committee was sitting, a General Election was called for 9th April. The Conservative majority fell to twenty seats, and the Major administration began its steep descent into disrepute and sleaze. Labour's third successive defeat led to the resignation of the pro-barrage Neil Kinnock; he was replaced by John Smith, whose Scottish constituency distanced him from the Barrage controversy. Unlike Kinnock, Smith was happy to leave Labour response to the Bill in the hands of Welsh MPs. Both Ron Davies and Rhodri Morgan became frontbench spokesmen on Welsh Affairs, with Alun Michael supporting the new Shadow Home Secretary, Tony Blair.

The CFAC campaigners now had much credibility, as well as a formidable case. Burdened by the mounting costs of their agent's fees, Cardiff Flood Action Committee made another appeal for help – this time to the County Council. The former promoters of the Barrage were now ready to pay the expenses of the campaign against it. A discrete donation of £4000 from the Chief Executive's office was made, in acknowledgement of the work done by Norman, Stan and Glyn in monitoring the groundwater monitors.

The high profile of the anti-barrage campaigners bore fruit in other ways. For some months, they had been seeking an interview with David Hunt, to discuss issues which could no longer be aired before Select Committees, such as the economic case for the Barrage, the viability of *The Living Waterfront* scheme, property blight and the inadequate groundwater investigations.

Eventually, Glyn, Stan, Charlie and Ruth were invited to meet him on 9th June, at the Welsh Office. David Hunt had been Secretary of State for nearly two years. A solicitor from the Wirral, he was renowned for his perpetual smile and emollient manner, which had won him the nickname 'Dai Delighted.' Both were much in evidence that day.

In the Tory leadership election, he had 'voted for Michael Heseltine in the morning and in the afternoon announced that John Major [the victor] would be this century's greatest Prime Minister'[27]. Such well-honed survival skills stood him in good stead as he was given an abrasive run down on the most pertinent points of the anti-barrage case. When Charlie took him to task over the 'jiggling of procedures' in Parliament, he replied that these things were organised by the 'party machine in the Commons' and nothing to do with him; he added 'these were the points I was hoping you would get off your chests', as if he was helping them with a little anger management therapy.

It was clear that Mr Hunt had no intention of departing from his standard WO brief; he insisted on replying in writing to all but the blandest of their questions (and this particular quartet wasn't very good at being bland). It was a letdown; they had come expecting a dynamic discussion, and ended up throwing stones down a well, listening in vain for a responsive echo about subsidence, economics or accountability. His written replies were models of Panglossian self-satisfaction; all was for the best, and he remained 'confident that the Barrage would be built'.

Later that day, in pursuit of Hunt's aim, Gwilym Jones opened a debate on the new government's amendments to Commons Standing Orders for the Welsh Grand Committee (WGC), which was due to consider the Barrage Bill in a few weeks. This apparently modest suggestion was yet another sign of increasing government desperation to get the Bill passed as quickly as possible, even if it meant the 'jiggling with procedures' Mr Hunt was so ready to distance himself from.

Under Commons Standing Order no. 36, the WGC was entitled to examine and propose amendments to any legislation specifically affecting Wales; all 36 Welsh MPs were eligible for membership, and any Welsh MP who had expressed an interest in the Bill under consideration was automatically entitled to a seat. As far as the Barrage was concerned, this meant that all those feisty South Wales members who had spoken so vehemently against the Bill would be on the Committee, proposing long and time-consuming amendments to their hearts' content. The General Election had reduced the number of Welsh Tory MPs to an impotent four, and Lib Dems or Plaid members included were unlikely to be a restraining influence on their Labour colleagues.

To save time and government face, Mr Jones proposed that the WGC on the Barrage Bill should be reduced to twenty members, only twelve of whom would be from Welsh constituencies. So, eight English or Scottish MPs would water down Welsh enthusiasm, to make sure discussion on a matter about which they were not concerned was kept as brief as possible. The Welsh Grand Committee would be Welsh in name only.

The proposal was not well-received. There was outrage that most Welsh MPs would be unable to consider such a contentious Bill. Mr Jones suggested there were precedents – WGC Standing Orders had been altered in this way at least five times in the past 25 years. Paul Murphy of Torfaen was quick to point out that those Bills had been non-contentious, enjoying all-party support, or had been Labour government legislation at a time when the vast majority of Welsh MPs were Labour, anyway.[28] It would be the first time in its 85 year existence that the full WGC had been denied its right to discuss such a hotly debated, controversial Welsh issue. As Alex Carlile, MP for Montgomery, said '...tonight there has been an important constitutional departure for Wales, and with it, a diminution of the constitutional rights of the Welsh people'.[29]

An elected Assembly for Wales was then official Labour policy, so opposition MPs were eager to point out the contrast between this commitment, and the Conservative government's willingness to destroy what small opportunities existed for Welsh MPs to consider Welsh issues.

The amendment was passed by 191 votes to 86.

On 30th June, the Barrage Bill was trimmed yet again, to suit government convenience. David Hunt announced that any provision of alternative feeding grounds would be omitted from the Bill; apparently, CBDC and the Land Authority for Wales, both chaired by Sir Geoffrey Inkin, had commissioned a feasibility study of possible sites on the Gwent Levels. As the power to set up such a substitute reserve was available under existing legislation, it would not be included in the next draft of the Bill.

Their report was published in February, 1993, and recommended the creation of a freshwater wetland habitat at Redwick, near the Llanwern steelworks, and the neighbouring saltwater lagoons at Goldcliffe. The RSPB made clear that its willingness to advise on this project was without prejudice to its continuing opposition to the Barrage, or to its complaint to the European Court about the destruction of the Cardiff Bay SSSI.

In the Commons debate on the Report Stage, four months later, the government made a clumsy attempt to placate environmentalists, and compensate for the Bay's exclusion from the SPA, by tabling an amendment, inserting a commitment to 'developing flora and fauna'. Elliot Morley, MP for Scunthorpe and a keen RSPB supporter commented, 'It is rather like running a motorway through a nature reserve and then offering to put a bird table at a service station...'[30]

The First Reading of the Hybrid Bill in the Lords followed on 28th October. Government eagerness to get the Bill onto the statute book as led to a Second Reading debate on 16th November. During the debate, all the arguments about dewatering wells, destruction of an SSSI, the quality of the economic case and the future of fishing on the Taff were aired by Lord Moran, and dismissed by Lords Callaghan and Crickhowell. After due process, the Bill was referred to its fourth and last Select Committee.

Concern over the cost of the Barrage continued to grow, and not only on the Opposition benches. On 1st Feb 1993 in an Oral Answer,

David Hunt had outlined the Welsh Office capital programme for 1993-94; between them, the Butetown Link, as the PDR was now known, and the Barrage accounted for £279 million. When this massive investment in the development of south Cardiff alone, was compared with a total spend on the Welsh NHS of £138 million, or £130 million on housing, or £31 million on WDA land reclamation schemes for the whole of Wales, it was easy to understand the resentment which fuelled the opposition to the Barrage Bill from Valleys MPs.

On 17th February 1993, the members of the final Select Committee on the Barrage Bill assembled at the House of Lords. It was fitting that one of the presiding spirits at this ultimate confrontation should be Lord Allenby of Meggido, the Israeli town known to St John the Divine as Armageddon, site of the last battle on earth, between the forces of good and the powers of evil. Viscount Allenby's colleagues were Lords Addington and Holderness, with the former Labour Home Secretary, Lord Merlyn-Rees. The committee was chaired by Lord Brabazon of Tara.

Their Lordships conducted their business in a more relaxed and sympathetic atmosphere than Sir Nicholas and his fellow MPs, the year before. Where Sir Nicholas had not hesitated to rebuke petitioners who adopted too familiar a tone, Lord Merlyn-Rees, a proud new grandfather, actually offered to soothe one fractious anti-barrage baby, whose wails threatened to drown his mother's statement to their lordships.

Perhaps it was fortunate the peers were minded to be tolerant; the petitioners were certainly not minded to obey parliamentary conventions as scrupulously as in they had in the earlier, more optimistic days of their campaign. They knew that there was no more help for them in the parliamentary process; the government had already broken several precedents in its desperation to get the Bill this far, including the conversion of a private bill to a public one and the rewriting of the Standing Orders of the House to neuter the Welsh Grand Committee. The only route left to prevent the start of construction was an appeal to the European Commission, a frail and untried strategy. Once building began, the only chance of preventing completion was an anti-barrage Labour government, but the next General Election was over four years away. In any event, the 93 petitions to this Select Committee would have little affect; Nicholas Edwards' dream would come true, one way or another.

However, Norman did enjoy an unexpected moment of optimism when, as he returned to his seat on the public benches after giving evidence, he saw Lord Merlyn-Rees nodding and smiling at him, with encouraging approval. But any hopes for His Lordship's support in overturning the Bill were soon dashed, when he realised the nods and smiles were for Lord Jack Brooks, sitting just behind him.

In these circumstances, a more fragmented, less spirited group would have gritted its collective teeth, and gone through the motions, one last time. CFAC members were made of sterner stuff; they played their parts with rigour and style. Many of the issues they raised had already been heard by the Commons Committee, like protection for gardens and open spaces, or a clearer definition of the role of the Groundwater Complaints Administrator – heard and set aside, or ignored. But, the petitioners had no compunction about bringing them up yet again – much to the irritation of Jeremy Sullivan. In his opening remarks, the promoter's Counsel complained, 'that, really, whatever improvements are made, they [the petitioners] will never be satisfied, and it will be a matter for the Committee to decide whether, after all this lengthy and detailed consideration, the remaining detailed complaints are reasonable or, as we would suggest in a number of cases at least, are a disguised attempt to frustrate the Bill by hedging it about with a mass of restrictions...'[31]. As a summary of the anti-barrage strategy, in the face of a draconian and unresponsive political process, this was completely accurate.

To their credit, their lordships listened to these anarchic wreckers with unfailing patience and courtesy; no word of criticism was suffered either, when they listened to anxious pensioners from the 2-up-2-down terraces of Grangetown, or the worried parents of asthmatic children, concerned about damp homes getting damper, or representatives of Riverside's Asian community, who just wanted to be told what CBDC was planning for their neighbourhood, in a language they could understand.

Lord Brabazon acknowledged the combative persistence of the campaigners, in his closing remarks on Day 8 of the Committee, their last day in Cardiff. He thanked their agent, Kevin Standring, and his assistant 'who have marshalled and organised the appearances of the petitioners here in Cardiff... I can imagine it has not been a particularly easy job as we have noted the individuality of many of the petitioners. We have noted with great respect the individuality of the petitioners and we would like to thank you for the work you have done down here...'[32] A close observer of the anti-barrage campaign would have no difficulty translating 'individuality' as 'sheer bloody-mindedness'.

Of these persistently recidivist petitioners, Kate Hunter rose to the challenge of Mr Sullivan's disapproval with the most spirit,

I would remind him that it is our constitutional and legal right to

fight proposals which are clearly going to adversely affect our
interests...[we] have been prepared all along to argue before you
in the face of very uneven odds. It would become him more to
accept it is our right to do so.'[33]

She went on to revisit the Barrage-related health problems she had
discussed before the previous Select Committee. Her concerns about
child health, in particular, had greater immediacy now, as she and her
husband, Francis Maxey, were to become parents themselves; the formal adoption of their foster children, Jamal (4) and Soraya (2), was
expected soon. Soraya had remained in Cardiff with Francis, but
Jamal sat quietly in the Lords committee room, drawing big red
London buses with his new felt tip pens. He watched in fascination,
as his mother outlined the results of a research project in Glasgow, co-
ordinated by Sonia Hunt, an advisor to the WHO, on the effects of
damp and mouldy homes on public health. As a result of her work,
Glasgow Council had made the improvement of damp housing stock
a priority. Because of the acknowledged risk of increased dampness
from the Barrage, Dr Hunt had recommended that health surveys
should be carried out in south Cardiff, pre- and post-barrage, on the
same lines as the groundwater surveys, to assess its impact, especially on the very young and the very old. Kate asked that a requirement
for this be written into the Bill.

Although the economic arguments against the Barrage could no
longer be rehearsed officially, Charlie Burriss had no compunction
about reminding the peers of the real cost of the 70 or 80 dewatering
wells that would be needed to stop south Cardiff decaying from its
current slightly damp state, to what he believed would be a post-barrage morass. A cool £14 million, the Welsh Office had reported, and
Mr Sullivan saw no need to contradict him.[34]

Glyn Paul, striding in to bat for Grangetown again, thwacked the
promoters' bowling to the boundary with his usual savagery. He took
Mr Sullivan to task for an earlier assertion that the Stoner Report to
the Welsh Secretary had laid 'to rest the fears of Petitioners on
groundwater'. The Committee were reminded that earlier Wallace
Evans and Hydrotechnica reports implied 1650 homes would need
remedial work, post-barrage. But the supposedly soothing Stoner
Report had actually raised that figure to 5695, almost every house in
Grangetown![35]

He was scathing about attempts by their groundwater experts to
forecast the water table's behaviour post-barrage, especially as
Hydrotechnica freely admitted that 'without building the Barrage they
cannot simulate post-barrage conditions'.[36] There were major anxieties

over the impounded Bay's capacity to absorb high river flows. The promoters insisted that when the Taff flooded next, and torrential rain from the Beacons surged down the river, the sluice gates would be opened to let the water out into the Bristol Channel. But what if, asked Glyn, there was already a high tide in the Channel? The highest sea tides would cover the top of the sluice gates, and no water could escape for several hours. Who would take responsibility for the resulting damage? The petitioners had asked the Development Corporation, who said it would be the National Rivers Authority, still under the guardianship of Lord Crickhowell; but the NRA insisted that CBDC would have to take charge...[37]. He respectfully urged that this vital point be clarified definitively.

Stan Perkins, in his evidence, pointed out a significant advance for the anti-barrage campaigners. A few weeks before the Committee met, the Development Corporation had at last been persuaded to include Hydrotechnica's 'Extreme Case Run 77', in their groundwater predictions – this was that worst case scenario of flooding due to a 'once in 100 years' combination of high river flows, high rainfall and high tides in the Channel, which had already afflicted Cardiff three times in living memory. Until now, the promoters insisted on basing all their calculations on less damaging 'probable' scenarios, which could have been prepared for much more cheaply.[38] But Stan was scathing about the fate of the boreholes the Corporation's consultants had sunk in the made ground of Grangetown, to get the data for those calculations. His frequent and thorough inspections showed that of the 28 sunk in 1991, only 20 were working properly, two years later; the others were vandalised or blocked, and gave no readings. Of those 20, four were filled to the brim with water; the water table at these points could rise no further without flooding. These shortcomings did not inspire confidence in CBDC's commitment to the whole process of groundwater monitoring. Stan's apprehension would later be fully justified.

The RSPB did not appear before this last Select Committee. The Countryside Council for Wales (CCW) had agreed to accept ownership of the 'replacement' feeding grounds planned by the Welsh Office at Redwick on the Usk estuary: once created and vested in CCW, the reserve could not be abandoned. So, in view of this serious commitment by central government, RSPB withdrew their petition against the Bill. However, they made it very clear that they still opposed the Barrage as destroyer of an SSSI.

Their Lordships presented their final report to Parliament, on the 16th March, 1993. Their recommendations largely restored the Hybrid Bill to the condition of the Private one, two years before, with a few modest additions; gardens could be included in remedial works, for instance; any 'directions' given by the Secretary of State to CBDC, about dewatering wells should be binding on whatever successor took over their role; CFAC would have to be content with only one place on the Cardiff Bay Advisory Committee, instead of the six in the Private Bill. Like Alice, the anti-barrage campaigners had had to run very hard to remain on exactly the same spot.

However, in considering the Bill, Their Lordships had been concerned over the terms of Clause 22, which dealt with the contentious issue of who was responsible for any saturation flooding in Cardiff under the Land Drainage Act, which the previous Committee had left so vague. The peers were not satisfied that Clause 22 assigned those responsibilities correctly; they believed the City Council's lawyers had been right – Cardiff would not have to carry this particular can. As the Bill was now substantially different from that approved by the Lower House at the Second Reading debate, it had to be considered by the Parliamentary Examiners, a step which needed Commons debate and approval.

As a display of dazzling ineptitude by the government this would be hard to surpass, as Rhodri Morgan pointed out with some emphasis in the Commons debate on 17th May. He included Geoffrey Inkin among the targets for his scorn. In a recent interview on Radio 2, the CBDC Chair had referred to the 'exhausted opposition' to the Barrage: a strange description of the record 93 private individuals who had recently petitioned the Commons Select Committee. He had gone on to say that tenders for building the Barrage would be invited shortly, so confident was he that the Bill would become law. The Cardiff West MP took a poor view of this optimism:

> That is an unwise remark for any promoter of a private or Hybrid bill to make. People should never presume about this House... If Damon Runyon had drafted 'Erskine May' it would be, 'It ain't over till the gracious lady signs'.[39]

The House of Commons was not the only political institution it would be unwise to presume about; the loyalty of electors to their ward councillors should never be taken for granted either, as Lord Brooks found to his cost. He had stepped down from the Leadership of the County Council in 1992, and had been spending more time in the House of Lords. Whether or not this led His Lordship to neglect the interests of the people of Tremorfa who had elected him is a matter for debate. Certainly Margaret Cook, secretary of the Tremorfa Ward Labour Party, received much support when she left the party to stand against him as an unofficial Labour candidate in the County

Council elections in May, 1993. To the great surprise of everyone in Cardiff, at least outside Tremorfa, she won, and Lord Brooks was forced to end nearly 30 years in local government. However, two weeks later, his successor as Leader, Councillor Russell Goodway, announced that Lord Brooks would remain a Council representative on the CBDC board, and its Deputy Chair, at a salary of £18,454 per annum for a two-day week.

On a wider stage, the RSPB's plans to bring action over the Barrage before the European Court of Justice were boosted by the Court's judgement, delivered on 2nd August, in the Santona Marshes case. Santona, in Spain, was an even more exact match for Cardiff Bay than Leybucht. Leybucht had actually been part of a designated Special Protection Area, under the wild birds directive. The complaint against the Spanish government had been that they, like the Welsh Office and the DoE, had failed to designate the area as a SPA to start with, and had then failed to protect it from destructive development. The European case against the Barrage was shaping up nicely.

When Lord Prys-Davies raised this point in the Lords debate on the Committee's recommendations, on 13th October, Lord St Davids, for the government, brushed aside the suggestion that the ruling had any implications for the Barrage. He also dismissed the spirited arguments of Lord Moran and Baroness White over CBDC's ability to meet the water quality standards of the EC's Urban Waste Water directive. Both Lord Moran and Baroness White had studied their briefs well, and updated their case since they had first spoken against the Barrage in the Upper House, five years before. But the juggernaut rolled irresistibly on to its Third Reading, on 28th October, and then, if things had gone according to plan, the Royal Assent.

But things did not go according to plan. It appeared that the Major government and its business managers had not yet plumbed the depths of incompetence over the Barrage Bill. On 3rd November, instead of being despatched for the Royal Assent, the Barrage Bill was back in the Commons. On the advice of the Examiners, their Lordships had amended the notorious Clause 22 to apportion responsibility for saturation flooding more clearly.

This altered the Bill substantially enough for Commons agreement to be needed before it could get onto the statute book – another totally unprecedented move. The Hybrid procedure had been designed specifically to allow interested parties to petition about any provision in such bills; here the government was significantly changing an important clause, too late for petitioning. Still worse, Tony Newton, the Leader of the House, introduced a guillotine motion, so debate was severely limited.

Rhodri Morgan still seized the chance to discuss amendments that the usual suspects had tabled alongside those from the Lords, such as charging ABP for use of the Barrage locks. He suggested that these were justified by ABP's profits from public investment in the area, pointing out that the company had recently received a grant of £2.5 million from CBDC 'under its urban investment powers'.[40]

Alun Michael tried to make his usual point about the Barrage's importance for attracting firms to the area, citing the Dutch company NCM's move there as proof. This was an singularly poor example of the project's pulling power. NCM had taken over the work of the Export Credit Guarantees Department, privatised in 1990. The ECGD had been based in the Crown Buildings, owned by the Welsh Office, at Cathays Park. But, under a covenant of the Bute estate, the Buildings could only house government departments. As a private company, NCM had to look elsewhere; how convenient it was that office space should be so readily available from a source, CBDC, to which the Welsh Office had always been so helpful and supportive. As the company's president, Harry Groen, confessed in an interview in *The Western Mail*, in May 1994, as soon as he had been given a helicopter tour of the Bay, and expressed an interest in locating there 'Financial support from the development corporation and the Welsh Office then came into play...'

Once the serious points had been made in the debate, the boys in the band gathered for one last riff. Ron, Kim, Ted and Allan played it again with energy and verve, while Paul Flynn recited Tennyson, provided an amazing coda on the conservation needs of black and brown rats, and finished with a brief tour of the midge-infested lakes of Iceland.

The harsh realities of Parliamentary life were soon re-asserted by another intervention from the Leader of the House. Tony Newton announced that as the House of Lords had also referred the British Railway Bill back to the Commons for urgent review, that night; the Barrage debate would have to finish immediately. Another piece of ineptly drafted government legislation had been thrown back by the Upper House, as the burnt-out Conservative administration tried to rush it prematurely into law. Under protest from the Opposition benches, but without further debate, the Barrage Bill moved on, to receive the Royal Assent on 5th November, 1993, just a few days before its sixth birthday. Conceived on the back of a Welsh Office envelope, burdened with defects only the most besotted parent could ignore, it seemed fitting that the Barrage Act should go out into the world at last, amid such chaos and confusion.

As an ironic postscript, two official reports were published within days of the new Act. Both cast serious doubts on the Barrage project's ability to deliver the prosperity its begetters had promised. The first was a South Glamorgan County Council report on local unemployment. Unemployment in Butetown had, after five years of CBDC investment, risen to 28.7%. Ben Foday, now councillor for the area, had tried to persuade CBDC that local people were given priority for any future vacancies. A spokesman replied that 'The Bay can't guarantee that local people will be given priority in the job market'. Why then had Alun Michael pleaded so hard for the Barrage as salvation for his jobless constituents?[41]

The following day, property consultants DTZ reported that because of the continuing recession, 'As land values fell along with the demand for CBDC sites, the corporation's liabilities have risen sharply.'[42] Critics of the economic case for the Barrage had long argued that it relied too heavily on a consistent and unprecedented rise in land values; their fears were being realised.

8. Fighting On

Any coward will fight a battle he is sure of winning, but give me
the man, sir, who will fight when he is sure of losing!

George Eliot – Janet's repentance from *Scenes of clerical life*

The Fast Track from Hammersmith

Like every high drama, the Barrage campaign had some interesting
sub-plots – like the progress of the Peripheral Distributor Road,
(PDR). Since the 1985 South Glamorgan (Taff Crossing) Bill, all
plans for the development of south Cardiff had been based on two
major civil engineering projects; a road linking south Cardiff to the
M4, and a barrage in the Bay. As far as South Glamorgan County
Council and the Development Corporation were concerned, they
were complementary; a barrage was necessary to make the area
attractive to investors, and the road link was necessary, as Geoffrey
Inkin said, to bring those investors, 'joining the M4 at Hammersmith
and not leaving it until they reach Cardiff Bay.'[1]

The Highways Department of the County Council had planned
the PDR for several years before the Development Corporation was
thought of. However, although Council and Corporation were united
in support for the project in principle, it became clear soon after
CBDC was formed that they differed over important practical details.
The route originally planned by the County's engineers cut a swathe
through Butetown, dividing the community in two and displacing a
primary school. As a result, it had needed a great of diplomacy and
hard talking to placate angry local opponents.

However, CBDC were also worried at the prospect of a busy four
lane highway in a residential area, not out of concern for the welfare
of those already living there, but because they saw it as a threat to the
rise in land values which was the whole reason for their existence. Not
only would the noise and smell of fast traffic be unappealing to developers, the road itself would eat up tracts of land which were the most
potentially lucrative in their domain. So, in 1988, the Corporation
demanded that the PDR's route through Butetown should go underground, through a 'cut and cover' tunnel, that would keep it out of
sight.

In early 1989, it was estimated that this change would double the
cost of the road, to over £100 million; the Council was naturally
unwilling to pay the entire increase, and it was expected that an EC

development grant would make up the shortfall. However, after the European elections in June that year, there was a sea change in policy at Brussels; grants for road building would only be given to projects which offered demonstrable benefits for entire regions, so the PDR no longer qualified; the money would have to come from elsewhere. The Welsh Office eventually agreed to pay half the cost, but more than a year later, when work was due to begin on cutting the tunnel, CBDC and South Glamorgan were still haggling about who should make up the rest. Eventually, the County Council accepted responsibility for capital construction costs.

Anti-barrage campaigners saw the WO contribution as yet more Dangeld levied on tax payers, to subsidise Nicholas Edwards' expensive whim. Without the need to raise property values to justify the Barrage, there would have been no need for the tunnel, and no need for further Welsh Office funding. As a protest, in September 1990, they handed over a giant 'invoice' for the WO's £21 million contribution, to the Corporation at their new offices in Baltic House.

But the vexed question of running costs remained unanswered when CBDC's Chief Executive, Barry Lane, announced his retirement for May 1992. The continuing uncertainty over the PDR, the slow progress of the Barrage Bill, the chaotic plans for the Ferry Road tip, the snail-like pace of the redevelopment itself (after four years, CBDC had persuaded just one new employer into Cardiff Bay, a Volvo garage, employing about 70 people) and the Corporation's trail of PR disasters, begun by Mr Lane himself, all meant their reputation was at a very low ebb. Even those who were not opposed to the Barrage, who had believed the early promises about jobs and high returns on public investment, felt there might be some truth in the canard that CBDC had become 'Can't Build, Don't Care.'

Coincidently, South Glamorgan's Chief Executive, Michael Boyce, was due to retire at about the same time, and there was some hope that a fresh approach by their successors would decide once and for all who would pay to maintain the PDR and its tunnel; in October 1992, the annual costs of lighting, ventilating and safety measures, (including pumping) were estimated at £1.4 million.

There was much surprise, in late May, when CBDC announced that Michael Boyce, so recently retired from the County Council, was to be their new CEO. Surprise was quickly followed by disquiet, when it was realised that Mr Boyce still had access to his substantial local government pension, as well as the even more substantial salary offered by CBDC, and a chauffeur-driven car. In an attempt to allay such disquiet, he made it known that CBDC had actually been looking for a candidate with considerable experience in the private sector, and therefore his many years in local government were irrelevant to his appointment; his embarkation on a completely new career thus apparently justified him keeping pension and salary.[2]

Even more interesting, the negotiations about PDR running costs had been at a particularly delicate stage when Mr Boyce made his dramatic transfer of loyalties. Many councillors and senior officers were under the impression that CBDC had at last agreed to pay much of the PDR's annual cost. But, very soon after their most senior legal officer had cleared his desk and moved across Bute Street to Baltic House, it appeared that they were, in part, mistaken. While it was true that discussions had reached that conclusion, no formal agreement had apparently been committed to paper – it seemed still possible that the Corporation could evade any financial responsibility in the matter.

In October and November further talks were arranged between the Council, the Corporation and the ever-helpful Welsh Office. Eventually, early in 1994, yet more money was found from the latter's elastic resources to subsidise Cardiff's future. It was most fortunate for the Development Corporation that Nicholas Edwards had been so successful in tightening the WO's control of local authority spending in the early 1980s.[3]

On 23rd March 1995, the Cardiff Bay section of the PDR was ceremoniously declared open by Neil and Glenys Kinnock.

Cashing in the Policies

Some months before the Barrage Bill was given the Royal Assent, Geoffrey Inkin was knighted, and a few days after, Cardiff Flood Action threw a party. These events were only distantly connected. Sir Geoffrey's knighthood celebrated his years of well paid public service to the Land Authority for Wales and the Cardiff Bay Development Corporation. CFAC's party celebrated its survival, through many battles with the Corporation, and its undiminished zeal for other battles to come. It also marked a rebirth; CFAC had always presented itself as a chameleon organisation; sometimes it spoke as the representative of all those who had suffered as a result of the 1979 floods, and sometimes it spoke as the umbrella body for all the anti-barrage residents' groups. The 1993 Act and its Code of Practice defined a future role for it, representing those groups on the Cardiff Bay Advisory Committee, the forum for those parties immediately affected by the impounded lake, and the Barrage itself. As an umbrella body, the Cardiff Flood Action had been referred to before the various Select Committees as Cardiff Residents' Against the Barrage (CRAB) and it was decided to make this its official designation.

Although Rhodri Morgan had fought on in the Commons until the last possible moment before the Gracious Lady signed, Norman, Glyn, Stan, Ruth and the others had known for some months that the Barrage Act was inevitable. But the Barrage itself was not a foregone conclusion. The Act was an enabling measure only; it meant that a barrage *could* be built, not that it *must* be built.

As noted some months before the final Commons debates on the Bill, Geoffrey Inkin had announced the invitation to tender for building the Barrage had been advertised in the Official Journal of the European Community, as all contracts of such size had to be. Given that it would take about four years to build[4], the six-year delay in realising Lord Crickhowell's dream meant an early start was vital in the light of the corporation's expected lifespan[5].

Even if construction began immediately, it was very unlikely to be completed in the Corporation's lifetime. However, much preparatory work would be needed before construction could begin; the Barrage with its sluice gates, shipping locks and fish pass would be a complex structure, and its location at the mouth of the Bay would pose problems for the most experienced civil engineers, as the sea floor at this point varied from firm bedrock on one side, to deep and shifting sand at the other. Providing adequate foundations for a structure of this size would be a difficult task. So, although work on the Barrage itself would not start for over a year, the bulldozers, dredgers and piledrivers were on site within weeks of the Royal Assent.

Although their failure to stop the Bill becoming law might be viewed as a defeat for the campaign, CRAB took some consolation from the many changes made to the final Act. In the very first Bill to be considered by either House, dated November 1987, the only bodies protected from any problems caused by the Barrage were British Gas and Associated British Ports; groundwater and the scheme's other consequences for the ordinary people of Cardiff had not even been mentioned. CRAB's dialogues with CBDC, the County Council and the Welsh Office, and especially their petitions to all four Select Committees had changed the final provisions beyond all recognition. With the undertakings required from CBDC by the Lords Select Committee it looked as if CRAB had achieved a substantial insurance policy for their fellow citizens.

There was provision for property surveys by contractors appointed by CBDC to assess possible increase in dampness, one before and one after the Barrage was impounded. However, the illogical 'Protected Property Line' still divided streets and neighbourhoods, in Canton and Pontcanna, with its different provisions for the homes on either side.

CBDC was required to send letters to all occupiers of property in Cardiff and Penarth, at least 28 days before construction began, informing them of their rights to surveys, and when the surveys were likely to begin. The Lords Committee provided that the anti-barrage groups were to be included in all decisions about the content and wording of these notices.

In the surveys, occupiers could opt for the Building Research Establishment's (BRE) recommended method for measuring damp, piezometers. The BRE was the UK's leading independent authority on civil and domestic construction: the piezometers it endorsed were more expensive than any alternative, but gave more reliable and consistent readings.

CBDC had also to monitor dampness in 26 homes, in the Protected Property Area, on a monthly basis for twelve months before and twelve months after impoundment. This was intended to give produce an overall view of how groundwater behaved in local homes, through all the seasons and over all the tides.

The bore holes already provided throughout what CRAB still insisted was the Endangered Property Area, would be increased to 62, to be monitored continuously for groundwater changes. An Independent Groundwater Complaints Administrator (IGCA) would be appointed to settle any disputes between residents and CBDC on groundwater protection.

CRAB had a solitary seat on the Cardiff Bay Advisory Committee, formed to discuss matters relating to the use of the impounded lake and the Bay with CBDC on behalf of interested groups. Other bodies represented included the local councils, ABP, the Cardiff Yacht Club, the Countryside Council for Wales, Welsh Water, the NRA and Camper & Nicholson, the operators of Penarth's Portway Marina.

Following the expert evidence on likely groundwater changes by John Miles and Kenneth Rushton, CBDC had agreed to install a dewatering system in the areas of south Cardiff most at risk. It consisted of 75 wells, each of which housed a pump which operated automatically when sensors detected a significant rise in groundwater. The water would be returned into the Taff.

CBDC were also committed to diverting fifteen raw sewage outfalls in the Bay. This would have to be done whether or not the Barrage was built, to satisfy the requirements of the EC directive on waste water treatment in towns which would come into force in 1997. However, there was no attempt to address the equally serious problem of pollution from the hundreds of unofficial outlets, further up the Taff and Ely, in spite of Peter Randerson's well-documented evidence to two Select Committees.

Over the next seven years, each of these insurance policies were unilaterally cancelled, cashed in or watered down beyond recognition by the Development Corporation, except for the waste water directive, which was clear-cut, and non-negotiable, unlike those other EC directives on habitat, which gave the wading birds of Cardiff Bay so little protection.

This process began immediately after the Bill became law. A CRAB subcommittee had worked for months with the Corporation's Chief Engineer, David Crompton, their legal team and the WO on the content of the 'notice of commencement of construction' letters. At the last minute, Michael Boyce, stepped in, throwing out their careful drafts and appointing Quadrant, a PR company, to prepare the letters. He made it clear there would be no further discussion with CRAB on the matter.

An angry Glyn Paul wrote to Lord Brabazon, as the Chair of the Lords Select Committee, pointing out this flouting of their lordships' requirements. The notices went out, nonetheless. Stan found many people outside the Protected Property Line had apparently been misled over their rights to a survey; the new notices did not make it clear that part-occupiers (e.g. tenants of flats) were entitled to surveys.

The date quoted on the notices for the start of construction was 21st March, 1994. But, that day came and went without any sign of construction beginning. Doubtless, the Corporation and the UK government were waiting until some accommodation had been reached with the EC's Environment Commission, over the exclusion of Cardiff Bay from the Severn Estuary SPA. But whatever the reason for their lack of punctuality, CBDC should have done the whole exercise again, to meet the requirements of the Act.

Rhodri Morgan took advice from the Private Bills Office about this failure to comply with the Select Committee's instructions. As a result, the MP wrote to the Chair of the Lords' Committee Office, the Upper House equivalent of the Commons Ways and Means Committee, Lord Ampthill.

His Lordship replied that the Lords' Committee Office was not responsible for the supervision of Hybrid bills, and, most disturbingly, he could not advise CRAB who was. It appeared there was no one empowered to resolve the dispute over notices, or indeed any other failures by CBDC to comply with the Barrage Act. Apparently the only parliamentary course available was to ask a sympathetic peer to table a motion on the matter, giving a very faint chance of a debate in the Lords. Stan contacted several members of the Upper House, all were sympathetic, but the Barrage was now old news politically, and their lordships had many, more rewarding causes to advance.

On 1st June 1994 Marie Lee, recently appointed IGCA, was asked to deal with her first complaint, from Stan, about the notices. Ms Lee would spend two days a week in Cardiff, handling any complaints. She was appointed by the Corporation, and her salary was paid by the Welsh Office. At their first meeting with her, CRAB were amazed to discover that neither her employer nor her paymaster had told her that her appointment was solely due to anti-barrage petitioning. She seemed unaware of the high profile anti-barrage campaign, or the strength of local feeling against the scheme.

The IGCA forwarded Stan's complaint to CBDC, who had at last agreed to send out further notices about start of construction, but this concession would still not give people the twelve months in which to request pre-impoundment surveys, which Schedule 7 of the Act required.

It was also becoming clear that Marie Lee at the IGCA had a rather idiosyncratic view of her role; she continued to respond to any complaints about CBDC's actions, by sending it to the Corporation for comment, and then forwarded those comments to the complainant. She seemed to think this was an adequate response; CRAB found it disappointing, and lacking in rigour.

Even greater disappointment was to follow; from October 1995, the anti-barrage groups received a series of letters from Michael Boyce. As the Corporation's CEO was bound to do under Schedule 7 of the Act, he was consulting them about proposed changes to the Code of Practice, which set out the fine detail of the groundwater surveys and monitoring. These changes varied in scope from restrictions on the survey methods householders could ask for, to a redefinition of at what point the Barrage would be finally impounded. This last change was to be a matter of bitter contention between the Corporation and CRAB for several years.

It could be argued that it was in CBDC's interest for any formal definition of impoundment to be as late in the construction process as possible. The later impoundment was deemed to be complete, the less chance there would be of a detectable rise in groundwater, during the post-impoundment surveys. CRAB considered that impoundment would not be complete until the last rock, or sack of concrete, was dumped in the last gap in the wall from Penarth Head to the Alexandra Dock. CBDC thought it would be complete when water in the bay reached a constant level, although what that level would be, and what exactly 'constant' meant, was never clarified. Apparently, impoundment would take place whenever CBDC decided it had taken place.

The consultation process appeared an empty sham. Schedule 7

required consultation, it did not require the Corporation to take any notice of the consulted, or give any reason for rejecting their views. However, there was still a lively hope that a Labour government (a General Election was due in 1997) would not complete the Barrage. After John Smith's death in 1994, his successor Tony Blair had made the vociferously anti-barrage Ron Davies shadow Welsh Secretary; Ron had publicly committed himself to stopping the Barrage, if at all possible, when he reached Cathays Park.

The consultation process might prevent CRAB having much influence on CBDC, but slow responses from the anti-barrage groups could take valuable time, and every week's delay brought the possibility of an anti-barrage government nearer.

As there was apparently no political remedy for CBDC's behaviour; the only legal option was a judicial review. This procedure would possibly take a long time, years rather than months; by the time a review was complete, the Barrage would be built, and anyway the procedure was certainly too expensive for CRAB and its members. The only course left was the one used so often in the past, making a persistent and well-informed nuisance of themselves.

CRAB was invited to send a representative to the first meeting of the Cardiff Bay Advisory Committee, on 5th October, 1994. Christine Dimend agreed to attend, with a watching brief, as there was no expectation that any CRAB member so heavily outnumbered could make any impact. Fortunately, the City Councillor on the Committee was the combative and well-informed Sue Essex. From the beginning she emphasised that the Advisory Committee would have to get expert technical advice if it were to fulfil its responsibilities to local people. However, the rigours of Local Government Reorganisation (LGR) meant that she did not stay on CBAC for long. The Committee's impact on the Corporations' activities remained minimal.

CRAB's worst fears were confirmed with the first pre-impoundment surveys in May 1996. The surveys were brief and limited; the contractors stayed only 30 minutes in each property, whether they were looking at a mansion in Cathedral Road, or a terraced house in Riverside.

CBDC unilaterally withdrew residents' right to the BRE piezometers, possibly on the grounds of cost. Les Baxter, of Adamsdown Residents Against the Barrage, and Norman, who had successfully petitioned the Lords' for precisely this right, complained to the Corporation. They were told that the BRE was now acting as a consultant to CBDC and would advise the Corporation 'on cases where it [the BRE test] is suitable.'[6] It appeared that, contrary to the specific directions of the Lords Select Committee of 1993, the test was only to be available if CBDC's consultants wished it to be.

The Code of Practice specifically stated that contractors should inspect voids – those gaps beneath the ground floors of many houses in Grangetown and Riverside, too small for use as cellars, where raised groundwater was often visible, at high tide, or after heavy rain. When householders invited the surveyors to look at their voids, they were told the contractors had no remit to lift floorboards or move fittings, both essential if voids were to be visible, let alone inspected.

The Corporation had also completely overlooked the requirement for continuous monitoring of 26 properties for twelve months either side of impoundment, in spite of frequent reminders from Glyn Paul, until it was too late. Detailed monitoring began only a few months before impoundment and the resulting measurements were useless for any post-barrage comparisons.

It appeared that the dewatering system, as originally planned, would cost £14 million, as Charlie Burriss had told the Select Committee in 1993. But, in 1997, when the Barrage was nearing completion, CBDC decided to substitute a smaller system of horizontal drains and pumps, at a lower cost of £6 million. This substitution, with less than two years of life left for the Corporation, and with increasing criticism of its excessive spending, looked like a dangerous last-ditch attempt to cut costs.

As for the impounded lake itself, CBDC had commissioned a report on water quality from consultants L & R Leisure, in 1994. Their confidential assessment was leaked to the *Echo*, nearly two years later. It said, 'major improvement in water quality is not likely to be achievable due to the excessive expense of dealing with the whole river catchment area'.[7] The report concluded that swimming in the Bay could not be permitted, and 'there would be a question mark over sports like canoeing and water-skiing' which needed full immersion. The report vindicated CRAB's arguments about the dubious condition of the 'freshwater' lake, which CBDC's publicity material still portrayed as a very unlikely shade of bright, clean blue. Such backhanded compliments were little compensation for the continuing erosion of quality and quantity of CRAB's hard won insurance for their fellow citizens.

CBDC's Successors – Who's Waiting in the Wings?

Meanwhile, the question of which body, public or private, would take on CBDC's responsibilities for the Barrage and its associated works after its legal demise, was becoming increasingly urgent. Given the slow pace of development in the Bay, and especially the delays in starting the Barrage, the Corporation's lifespan would probably be extended by two years, but this still meant a suitable successor would have to be in place by 1999. Officially, CBDC's powers would revert to the Welsh Office, and the SoS would in turn invest those powers in another body. In the case of other Development Corporations, these powers had been returned to the relevant local councils, and it was assumed that this would happen in Cardiff. However, Welsh local government was undergoing a root-and-branch restructuring, the most comprehensive for over twenty years.

Under the Local Government Wales Act of 1994, Wales' 8 counties and 37 districts would be slimmed down to 22 unitary authorities, from May 1996. There would no longer be a two tier system, with the confusing allocation of responsibility between two authorities for the same area; each County, or County Borough, would have just one local Council. Shadow unitary authorities would be elected in May 1995, to understudy their predecessors for a year, before the old structures were finally dismantled.

As expected, there was a substantial Labour majority on the new, restructured Cardiff Council. Whoever was elected to lead the Council Labour Group would also be the Leader of the Council itself – the largest and richest in Wales. There were two candidates, Sue Essex, Chair of the former City of Cardiff, supporter and ally of Rhodri Morgan, professional town planner, staunch opponent of the Barrage, and Russell Goodway, once Jack Brooks' colleague, his successor as Leader of the County Council, an ally of Alun Michael and a member of the CBDC board.

The election was called, as such elections have to be, at very short notice. By an unfortunate oversight, several announcements of the meeting were posted too late, and many councillors did not receive them until the morning after the election. By an equally unfortunate coincidence, most, if not all, of these belated notices were addressed to former City Councillors. Councillor Goodway was elected Leader of the Group, and the Council, by an substantial majority of those fortunate enough to be present.

Whatever other qualities the new Council had, any Welsh SoS could be confident most of its senior members would be firmly pro-barrage. However, other constitutional developments raised a question mark over the future role of the Welsh Office itself. An elected assembly for Wales had been official Labour party policy since the 1992 General Election campaign. When the strongly pro-devolution John Smith had succeeded Neil Kinnock as Labour leader, it had become a cornerstone of the party's proposed constitutional reforms.

However, exactly what powers the Assembly would have, its composition and structure were still being hotly debated in the Party only months before Labour won the General Election in June 1997.

But, even those anti-barrage members who were keen supporters of a Welsh Assembly did not see it as relevant to their campaign – Ron Davies was practically certain to be Welsh SoS in a Labour government, and he was firmly committed to halting the Barrage if at all possible. All their hopes were built on the expectation that, long before an Assembly of any kind was even elected, the Barrage would be no more. Those hopes were to be cruelly disappointed.

The Cardiff Bay Opera House – A Fiasco in Several Acts

When he announced his plans for the Development Corporation and the Barrage in December 1986, Nicholas Edwards outlined another scheme for the Bay, a much-needed performing arts centre for Cardiff. Edwards was a keen music lover and supporter of the Welsh National Opera (WNO).

Unlike his hopes for the Barrage, this dream was shared by many others in the city. For decades, anyone who had anything to do with dance or musical theatre in Wales, had been daunted by a lack of any suitable venue in the capital. Even the world-class WNO had struggled in inadequate quarters at the New Theatre since its beginnings 50 years earlier. So, many arts organisations in Wales were delighted to realise an SoS was prepared to do something about Cardiff's cultural deficit. But this dream was even slower to become reality than the Barrage: funding a barrage was difficult enough, funding an arts centre as well was beyond even the Welsh Office's resources.

But, in 1995, Mr Edwards, now Lord Crickhowell, spearheaded a bid to the Millennium Commission, by the recently formed Cardiff Bay Opera House Trust to fund an opera house in the Bay. The site would be made available by ABP's Grosvenor Waterside: this was a generous gesture in support of a cause so near to the heart of one of their directors, or a way of pushing the flagging Bay development further upmarket, or possibly both.

The project had become an opera house, rather than a centre for the performing arts in general, in an unfortunate renaming by Peter Walker during his time as SoS. The WNO would have use of the building for twelve weeks each year, and its special requirements would heavily influence the building's design, but most of the time it would be used for other art forms – musicals, plays, modern dance. However, the renaming would lay the project open to damning charges of 'elitism', which played an important part in its demise.

The failure of the Opera House bid is an interesting contrast to Lord Crickhowell's earlier success in attracting support for the Barrage. This time, local councillors saw no political advantage in this 'elitist' project. Lord Brooks was involved in the work of the Trust, but he no longer carried weight in the new council, and his successor, Russell Goodway, was a supporter of the Welsh Rugby Union's rival bid for Millennium funding for a new stadium at the Arms Park. The *South Wales Echo* had backed the Barrage to the hilt in the crucial early days of the scheme; they gave no such support to the Opera House.

The Millennium Commission required strong public backing for any successful bid, which the Opera House Trust failed to demonstrate. Even more damagingly, the Commission also required a sound business plan, and the Trust's was dismissed as inadequate. Doubtless, the Trust's plan was no weaker than the one for the disastrous Greenwich Dome, but the Dome had friends in Cabinet, and by 1995 Lord Crickhowell was no longer playing in that league.

Ironically, it was left to the decidedly anti-operatic Rhodri Morgan, and his fellow Assembly members, to deliver a centre for the performing arts in Cardiff Bay, another ten years later – but that is another story.

The Barrage in Europe

One of the best hopes for stopping the Barrage before construction began in earnest, was the case the RSPB were bringing against the UK government in the European Court of Justice. It was about Lappel Bank, an area of mudflats in the Medway Estuary. Like Cardiff Bay, it had been earmarked for development as an extension to the nearby port of Sheerness; like Cardiff Bay, it was part of a designated Special Protection Area (SPA) under the EC wild birds directive; like Cardiff Bay, the UK government had deliberately excluded it from the SPA so development could go ahead, contravening both the letter and the spirit of the directive. The mudflats and the feeding grounds they supported were destroyed and by early 1994 had vanished under a cargo and car park.

The timing of the judgement on Lappel Bank would be crucial for Cardiff Bay. Were the Court to decide against the UK government, the Barrage would be illegal under European law. If such a judgement were made before the £200 million contract to build it had been signed, even if the government tried to brazen it out and carry on, no major construction company would take the risk of involvement in an unlawful project. If the contract had been signed, but construction had not begun, then the Barrage could still not be built, and the successful company would require heavy compensation. For CBDC it was essential that the contract was let, and construction irrevocably underway before judgement was handed down.

The Welsh Office and CBDC could do little to speed up the tendering process, which was governed by strict EC regulations that, unlike the wild birds directive, were not open to debate or misinterpretation; the contract to build could not be signed for at least a year.

So, their best hope was to look for help elsewhere in the EC. Neither CBDC nor the Welsh Office could negotiate directly in Brussels; when dealing with something like the wild birds directive, they had to work through the Department of the Environment, where John Gummer was Secretary of State. But, in 1992, the Commission had begun proceedings against the UK government for 'insufficient designation of Special Protection Areas', because of complaints from several conservation groups.

They had been particularly interested in Cardiff Bay, and in December 1993, representatives of the European Commissioner for the Environment, Iannis Paleokrassas, visited the Bay. They spoke to WO and DoE officials, as well as members of FoE and the RSPB. The Commissioner had further, more detailed discussions with Mr Gummer, himself.

A few months later, in early 1994, the *Guardian* published details of a leaked letter from Mr Gummer to his colleague John MacGregor, Secretary of State at the Department of Transport, saying that the government was certain to lose the Lappel Bank case[8]; the Barrage was in desperate need of yet another rescue operation. The success of that rescue operation hinged on a significant difference between the destruction of the mudflats at Lappel Bank, and the planned destruction of the mudflats of Cardiff Bay. In response to the petition by the Nature Conservancy Council against the 1988 Barrage Bill, CBDC had proposed 'alternative feeding grounds' on mudflats in the Rhymney estuary – the unlucky birds of the Medway had not been offered any such second chances. Although that particular site had proved unsuitable, the principal of creating substitute feeding grounds had lived on, for the Corporation and its supporters in the Welsh Office to use as a bargaining counter in European negotiations over the Barrage's legality.

So, an accommodation was duly reached, which Mr Paleokrassas described in a letter to Ken Collins MEP, on 15th July, 1994. He pointed out that the wild birds directive made it plain that only safety issues, such as flood prevention schemes, could override a government's duty to preserve SPAs, like the Severn Estuary, including Cardiff Bay. However, he went on, the new habitats directive,

92/43/EEC, with effect from June 1994 [only days before the date of his letter] allowed the destruction of SPAs for 'overriding socio-economic reasons', and he believed the plans for Cardiff Bay's regeneration provided those reasons. He confirmed the Barrage was acceptable, if the plans for compensatory feeding grounds and for the care of the remaining Severn Estuary SPA were improved.

But, with unusual foresight, CBDC had already sent out the notices of start of construction to local residents. The notices had given the date as 25th May 1994, although the new habitats directive which Paleokrassas apparently believed made the Barrage legal, would not take effect for another month.

In spite of these irregularities, Mr Paleokrassas' view would provide just enough cover for John Redwood, who had succeeded David Hunt at the Welsh Office in May 1993, to authorise any contracts for the Barrage. It was possible for the WO to argue that the Commissioner's words would grant the UK government immunity from possible EC prosecution about Cardiff Bay, under the wild birds directive. The contracts to build the Barrage were finally let, in June 1995, just a year before the final judgement in the Lappel Bank case.

The conservation groups who had made the original complaint were very concerned about this sequence of events. As a result, Rhodri Morgan met two members of the legal staff of the EC's Environment Directorate, in September 1995. They made it clear that Commissioner Paleokrassas had neither sought nor been given any legal advice on his convenient accommodation of Mr Gummer and Her Majesty's government.[9] So the UK government had accepted his statement as having the force of law when, as Rhodri Morgan said, 'It was simply a bargain struck behind closed doors, the terms and text of which we were never allowed to see.'[10]

In contrast, the terms of the decision of the European Court of Justice on Lappel Bank were clear, authoritative and fully available for public scrutiny. In June 1996, the Court ruled that under the new habitats directive, governments could allow socio-economic arguments for development to over-ride the *preservation* of designated SPAs. However, they could definitely not allow socio-economic arguments to influence the *decision* to designate, or not designate, an area as an SPA in the first place, and that was just what the UK government had done at Lappel Bank, and Cardiff Bay. As Mr Gummer had predicted, the UK government lost its case.

However the new Welsh Secretary, William Hague, insisted on the primacy of Mr Paleokrassas' view; replying to Rhodri Morgan, in the Commons, on 18th July, 1996, he said, 'The European Court of Justice's judgement on Lappel Bank does not... have any implications for the Cardiff Bay Barrage.' However, even Commissioner Paleokrassas' blessing for the destruction of the feeding grounds was conditional; the UK government had to provide alternative sites for the birds displaced by the drowning of the Bay.

It was proposed that the new feeding grounds would be at Goldcliff and Uskmouth in the Usk estuary. In December 1996, a coalition of local and international conservation groups, including the Worldwide Fund for Nature (WFN) published a report highly critical of CBDC's plans; the new sites were too far from the Bay to be of any use to the hundreds of shelduck and redshank, or the thousands of dunlin, who over-wintered there, and they would certainly not reproduce conditions of lost feeding grounds. As Carol Hatton, the WFN's planning officer, commented 'We are losing tidal mudflats and they are giving us wet grassland'.[11] Certainly wet grassland would provide an acceptable habitat for a number of bird species, but it was unlikely to support dunlin, redshank or shelduck, the very species the Severn Estuary SPA was designated to protect.

It would be necessary to sacrifice several hundred acres of productive agricultural land for the creation of the alternative feeding grounds. So, compulsory purchase orders (CPOs) were served on the three families who farmed there by the Land Authority for Wales, on behalf of CBDC. LAW, the body responsible for the purchase of development land in Wales, was still chaired by Sir Geoffrey Inkin, who was also still Chair of the Development Corporation. It must have made negotiations between the two bodies efficient and speedy.

Naturally the farmers contested the CPOs, at the public enquiry on the proposed reserve. Their solicitor pointed out that their land and livelihood was threatened only because of the Cardiff Bay Barrage, and arguments against the scheme were rehearsed, yet again, with feeling. To ensure the grassland of the new reserve was wet enough, much of the acquired land would be flooded, by the products of a nearby sewage treatment works. Sir Geoffrey insisted that this 'would be subject to tertiary treatment'[12]. D.K. Blayney, representing the farmers, replied '…readers will decide for themselves whether they would feel reassured by the knowledge that the waters lapping their gardens is [*sic*] not raw, but treated sewage.'[13] To no avail, the appeal was dismissed; in October 1999, the land was bought, and preparation of the new nature reserve began.

The transformation of the Barrage Bill into a Hybrid had meant that the Select Committee appearances of environmental and conservation groups like FoE and the RSPB had been limited to protests about the inadequacy of the alternative feeding grounds. So, although they were very active on the European stage in the months before the

Bill became law, their local campaigns became rather muted. Once the Act was passed, however, FoE in particular were keen to play a more conspicuous role in the anti-barrage campaign. Peter Boyce, chair of Cardiff FoE resuscitated the AntiBarrage Consortium, (ABC) from the campaign's earliest days, before it had become almost exclusively focussed on the battle in parliament.

ABC's role was to maximise public support in Cardiff for the possibility that the Barrage could still be stopped. They were joined not only by the residents' groups, but by activists of Earth First!, who practised peaceful but physical opposition to destructive environmental projects. They were especially expert at the inexpert navigation of their tiny canoes or dinghies into the path of the dredgers excavating the foundations of the Barrage. On one occasion a handful of Earth Firsters even found their way into CBDC's Baltic House HQ, and draped anti-barrage banners from the portico.

Meanwhile, FoE and their CRAB allies contented themselves with more conventional projects – arranging petitions, marches and demonstrations. In 1994, a petition with over 3000 signatures supporting FoE's concern about Commissioner Paleokrassas' readiness to exonerate the UK government was handed over at the EC's Welsh headquarter; in July that year, Rhodri Morgan addressed over 500 marchers at an anti-barrage demonstration outside Baltic House, where he pledged that the fight would continue.

Between 1994 and 1997, FoE and the WFN had lodged a series of complaints with the European Commission over Cardiff Bay's exclusion from the Severn Estuary SPA, in the light of the precedent established in the Lappel Bank case. In 1997, the Commission agreed to consider the matter; it was possible that the UK government would incur heavy fines if the complaint was upheld. A final judgement was still awaited when Labour won the General Election in May 1997, and the anti-barrage Ron Davies became Secretary of State for Wales.

Shovelling Cash to Sustain Success?

In the early eighties, a Cardiff councillor, when told about the resources available to the Merseyside Development Corporation, had exclaimed, 'I want that sort of cash for Cardiff, even if I end up shovelling it into the Taff myself!' Over the next ten years, shovelling cash, if not into the Taff, then into Cardiff Bay, was a high priority for the Welsh Office.

The money from Cathays Park was intended as a public sprat to catch bigger private mackerel; as Peter Boydell had told the Commons Select Committee in 1990, every pound of public money was intended to attract £7 of private investment – that is, with the Barrage. The RSPB's competing Living Waterfront scheme was estimated to raise only £4.3 of private money for each public pound would come to a barrage-less bay.

Alas, six years later, in 1996, the figures did not stack up like that. As the Corporation neared the end of its life, John Redwood, exasperated by the rising costs of the Barrage, and building delays, set a deadline for its completion – 31st March, 1999. It would have to be finished before the Corporation itself was wound up. He also asked for a public consultation document, summing up CBDC's activities so far, and inviting suggestions about how the development be continue after its demise.

This paper, 'Sustaining Success', did not make reassuring reading for CBDC supporters. One of its most damning statistics was the low leverage of public to private investment; the £1.4 billion private investment to date represented a leverage rate of only 1:3.8, about half the 1:7 promised in KPMG's economic appraisals, on a public investment of £437 million.[14] Not only had the Corporation failed to meet its own barrage-dependent targets, it hadn't even met those of the RSPB's without-barrage scenario of 1:4.3. Of course, the RSPB employed few merchant bankers, or property developers, which may have detracted from the rigour of their analysis...

It would have been very difficult indeed to spend such large sums in an area of 2700 acres, without creating significant numbers of jobs. Moreover, the Barrage's power to enhance job creation for his constituents had been one of Alun Michael's main arguments in its favour, repeated in every Commons debate on the scheme. 'Sustaining Success' quoted 7845 permanent jobs created in the Bay area, by 1996, with a forecast of a possible total of 15,273 by 2000. Even this optimistic prophecy was just half the total promised by the Barrage Bill's promoters. To make matters worse, in the undeveloped Bay, in 1987, as Llewelyn Davis Planning had pointed out,

> ... there are nearly 1000 enterprises, employing 15,000 people.[15]

More than a third of the 'new' jobs, both actual and forecast, apparently were in the industrial sector, based around the former steelworks site in Tremorfa, where the Barrage would have no significant impact on development or job creation.

KPMG had commented in 1989,

> It should be emphasised that we have continued to exclude any land east of the Bute Dock. Although LDP [Llewelyn Davies Planning] have projected considerable industrial development of

this area, they do not see it as being dependent on the barrage. We have therefore excluded it from the evaluation, as it does not impact on the economic costs and benefits of the Barrage.[16]

But the most damning indictment of all for the Barrage as investment/job magnet were the unemployment figures for the area. In 1986, of all UK Parliamentary constituencies, only seventeen had higher levels of unemployment than Cardiff South and Penarth. In 1995, after most of that £437 million had come its way, only two other constituencies in Britain had higher unemployment than Mr Michael's. Who then, was filling those new jobs in the Bay? The sad truth was, as John Bowers had prophesied to the Commons Committee in 1990, that most had come with people already in them.

This surely was not what Mr Michael envisaged in the first Commons debate on the Barrage Bill, in 1989:

> Unemployment in south Glamorgan is still above the Welsh average. Much of that unemployment is concentrated in my constituency... the barrage is the key to the redevelopment that will bring the jobs that are so vital to the area. These jobs will help my constituency, but the impact will be felt throughout the region.[17]

Any realistic calculation of the net job creation achievements of the Barrage had to take into account the fate of the 350 firms trading in Cardiff Bay in 1987, which had been served with compulsory purchase orders by the Development Corporation. Between them, they had employed about seven thousand people. According to a report by Cardiff and Vale Enterprises[18], by 1995, 107 of these firms had ceased trading and 124 had moved outside the Bay area. If the jobs lost in this way had also been included in the figures quoted in 'Sustaining Success', the net gain overall would have been much less.

CBDC had to be seen to attract investors from outside the UK, in the face of heavy competition from similar developments in Europe and the States; the Barrage was seen as Cardiff's unique selling point, it would bring developers who would otherwise have gone to Baltimore, Hong Kong or Canary Wharf. But unfortunately, foreign investors were reluctant to come, barrage or no barrage. CBDC's excited press releases about the few firms that did come, in the early 90s, seemed rather sad, like a over-hyped restaurant, which could only offer baked beans and iceberg lettuce.

A Volvo dealership and a branch of Harry Ramsden's had been greeted warmly in the local press, and gave a multinational gloss to the project – at least the cars were Swedish – but other incomers were decidedly parochial. An article in a *South Wales Echo* business supplement listed several, in May 1992; Thyme Design had moved a few miles from Llandaff North, the other side of the city centre; Milsom Kane came from Windsor Place, a brisk 40 minutes walk from the Bay; the NUT moved its regional HQ three miles, from Whitchurch to Mount Stuart Square, for example. Only one of the companies mentioned had come from outside Cardiff. In 1995, AXA Insurance moved half a mile from the city centre to the Bay, bringing 250 employees, 'increasing to 300, after the transfer'.[19]

It all made a sad contrast with that earlier *Echo* article, written in the first optimistic flush of CBDC's creation, which had enthused

> Major firms, many of them from overseas, are queuing up to invest in Cardiff Bay... As well as inquiries from scores of British companies, approaches have been made by Japanese, Saudi Arabian, Canadian, German and Norwegian businesses...[20]

Six years later, as we have seen, there were only two major foreign investors in the Bay. Nippon Electric Glass, of Japan, had built a TV glass factory in partnership with Schott Glaswerke, a German company. Even this could not be claimed as a vindication of the Barrage's power to attract investment; in a letter to FoE Cardiff, their vice president confirmed that the project had little to do with their decision to come to the Bay.[21] The other foreign incomer, Dutch-owned NCM, had simply moved to the Bay, when it took over the privatised Export Credit Guarantees Department, and had to leave its former offices in Cathays Park. Here too, the charms of the Barrage had not been exactly magnetic; CBDC had given NCM a grant of £2.5 million – what for? Were £450 million of publicly funded infrastructure and the prospect of a 'freshwater' lake not enough?[22] It rather looks as if they weren't, and after several years of regeneration, CBDC were getting rather desperate for anyone to come to the Bay and justify the massive public investment in their plans – Volvo dealers and Harry Ramsden weren't quite enough.

Until 1995, the major home-grown employer in the Bay, except for the County Council, was the Welsh Health Common Services Agency (WHCSA), whose 800 employees had been based in Crickhowell House since 1991. In another fit of generosity, CBDC gave the WHCSA a grant, as well – £480,000, which must have been some help with one of the highest commercial rents in Wales – £14.5 per sq ft.[23]

However, when the ultra-dry John Redwood succeeded David Hunt at the Welsh Office in 1993, he drew up plans for WHCSA's privatisation. The Agency was broken up; the resulting smaller, private bodies found the rents in the Bay far too expensive, and by then the grant must have been running low. By 1996, nearly all had moved out, and most of the offices in Crickhowell House were empty, although under the WHCSA's 25-year lease, the Welsh Office was still paying the landlords, Grosvenor Waterside, £1.5 million a year in rent.

Even the site on which Crickhowell House was built had aroused fierce controversy. It was one of two parcels of land in the Bay, together-er worth about £50 million, belonging to Associated British Ports, which in 1989 had been declared exempt from the compulsory pur-chase orders CBDC was entitled to serve on other less privileged landowners in the area. As a result, ABP was able to maximise profits from rising land values in the Bay.

The presence of a large, new, empty office block in the Bay would have been embarrassment enough for the Corporation; when that office block was a flagship development, named after their founder himself, it was a deep public humiliation. John Redwood was not sym-pathetic; indeed, of all the five Tory SoS who had to deal with CBDC, he was the most sceptical and the least supportive.

After a meeting with the Corporation board at Baltic House, he was typically caustic

> The Bay has had its toys, in the shape of the barrage, the PDR, the WHCSA.... It is now time for the Bay to go out into the world and sell itself, to bring in the private sector involvement which will make the development even more successful.[24]

It was in just this spirit that Redwood had taken the unprecedent-ed step of returning an 'unspent' £112 million from the Welsh Office budget to the Treasury. He was not interested in building a political reputation on job creation, or providing social housing; the Welsh Office was an opportunity to demonstrate his commitment to the unfettered operation of market forces. He disliked quangos as much as he disliked the use of public money to featherbed private invest-ment, and Cardiff Bay included both. CBDC had been given clear notice that the Welsh Office purse strings were no longer at their dis-posal. However, Redwood's stay in Cathays Park was brief; his unsuccessful challenge to John Major for the Conservative leadership in 1995 meant a return to the back benches. It was left to his succes-sor, William Hague, to attempt to control the soaring costs of barrage construction.

The Barrage had been designed by Will Alsopp, for Sir Alexander Gill and Partnership, and was being built by the Balfour Beatty and Costain consortium. It would be 1.1km long, 100m wide and 10m high, curving across the estuary in an S shape, with four shipping locks, five sluice gates and a fish pass.

When work had begun on 24th May 1994, the cost of the scheme, including associated works like the replacement feeding grounds, was officially estimated to be £154 million. In less than two years, by March 1996, the final estimate had soared to £191 million. It was the prospect of such ever-escalating costs, and their effect on the budget for the rest of Wales, which had inspired the opposition of MPs outside Cardiff like Ron Davies and Kim Howells.

In November 1995, the Welsh Local Government Association, representing all the new Welsh local authorities, including Russell Goodway for Cardiff, had met with William Hague. They were looking for an additional £29 million from the Welsh Office, to fend off a rise in council tax. When Mr Hague refused, they wanted to know why he didn't cut the CBDC budget for 1995-96, then set at £57.5 million.[25] The Corporation's budget remained intact, but the suggestion bore some fruit when, in February 1996, Hague announced that Barrage costs would be capped at the current 'final' estimate of £191 million. As a result, the Corporation had to cut costs – there would be four not five locks, the programme for diversion of sewers and sewage treatment would be reduced, and a planned fishing pier on the seaward side of the Barrage would not be built.[26]

Such a prompt and sweeping response to rather modest restraint reflected growing concern that CBDC's approaching demise might leave more liabilities than assets, in every sense.

9. A Conversation about Bird Watching

Before I resigned I almost ceased to exist as a person. I was Secretary of State for Wales and the pressure was on my time from first thing in the morning to last thing at night. I enjoyed it enormously, but every conversation you have is about defending government policy or listening to what people have to say or explaining what you are going to do next. Never a conversation about bird watching...

Ron Davies, quoted in Paul Flynn, *Dragons Led by Poodles*, Politico's, 1999 (p28)

As the European case against the Barrage dragged slowly on, its opponents continued to hope that a Labour government, with that keen ornithologist Ron Davies in the Welsh Office, would stop it at last. He still firmly opposed the scheme, even after the contracts to build were let, and construction had begun. All the anti-barrage campaigners in CRAB, FoE, RSPB or the WFN knew that he was their last real chance of dismantling or decommissioning it; a judgement against the UK government in Europe would be a propaganda coup, but by the time it was pronounced the Barrage might have been in operation for years, and the SSSI would have been lost for ever. Ron in office in Cathays Park was a much sounder bet.

There was some relief when one of his first decisions as SoS was to hold a 'major review' of the Barrage project. This relief was followed by surprise and great disappointment when he announced, on 11th July, that construction would continue. Campaigners were gravely disillusioned, and astonished that the review had only been an internal one, conducted solely within the Welsh Office, with no briefings, evidence or contributions from any outsiders. They had serious doubts about the adequacy of the process, and feared it was simply a face-saving exercise for a politician who was looking for escape from a difficult commitment. They wanted full details of the review, its methods and its results. Some of the more aggressive, or idealistic, wanted blood as well.

The following day, the Director of FoE UK, Charles Secrett, arranged a press conference in Cardiff, at the Angel Hotel. All the anti-barrage groups were there; Sue Essex and Rhodri Morgan spoke, with support from Norman, Charlie and Peter Ferns. They all expressed their disillusion in the strongest terms, and called on Davies to think again. Then Rhodri Morgan led a march to Cathays Park. In the bright summer sunshine, Ron Davies came out onto the Welsh Office steps to meet the demonstrators; he promised Rhodri he would arrange a formal meeting with all the interested groups, to give full details of his reasons for not abandoning the Barrage.

That meeting eventually took place more than five months later, on the 1st December, 1997. A small committee room in Cathays Park was crowded with people from most of the major conservation pressure groups in Wales. They represented enough bird watchers to keep Mr Davies chatting for months – Friends of the Earth, the Royal Society for the Protection of Birds, the Worldwide Fund for Nature, the Marine Conservation Society, Taff Ely Wildlife Coalition, as well as local naturalist groups and Cardiff Residents Against the Barrage. Rhodri and Julie Morgan attended; Julie had defeated Gwilym Jones in the General Election, and was now MP for Cardiff North. Sue Essex, formerly Leader of Cardiff City Council, was there as a member of the new City and County Council of Cardiff.

It is rare for a Minister of the Crown to give up almost two hours of his time for a detailed justification of a particular policy to members of the public who oppose that policy. That this should be so, says a great deal about the wretched quality of our democracy: that Ron Davies should reluctantly provide such a unique opportunity, throws interesting light on his apparent political priorities at that moment.

Ron Davies was now a prominent member of Tony Blair's first cabinet – a cabinet from which Rhodri Morgan, an able and committed Shadow Spokesman, had been excluded because the Prime Minister judged him too old for office (although this judgement was set aside for the Deputy Prime Minister, who was two years older). Discerning onlookers believed his exclusion was a punishment for some even more unspeakable political vice, like having a mind of his own, being wittier than the Leader or representing a constituency with a lot of socialists in it, who liked him. Ron Davies, in contrast, was seen as a doggedly loyal party man – energetic and fiery, but lacking inspiration and charisma.

The most important task for the new SoS had been to arrange the referendum on devolution promised in the Labour manifesto. This was an awesome burden in itself, but he also had to deliver the result of that referendum. The new government had identified itself irrevocably with the principle of decentralized government for Wales and Scotland: for this project to be rejected by the voters of either would be a total humiliation. But every Welsh Labour MP knew that defeat was definitely possible: their constituents had always been much more ambivalent about inserting an extra tier into government than their leaders on the front bench. The timetable was tight – the referendum was held in September, just four months after the Labour victory – and the pressure on the SoS had been immense. To deliver the result Downing Street wanted, Ron had needed Rhodri's support in selling devolution to a sceptical electorate. Rhodri was popular throughout Wales, not just within the Labour party: he was also a fluent and entertaining Welsh speaker – Ron had only just started learning the language. If Rhodri had not put his popularity and reputation at the SoS's disposal in the campaign, uncertainty could have become defeat. As a pillar of the Welsh Labour movement, Rhodri had certainly worked to bring out the 'yes' vote, and any neutral bystander would have assumed Ron was therefore in his debt.

While the granting of this unique audience in Cathays Park might not be the result of formal bargaining or negotiation between the politicians, it was possibly a reflection of their roles on a larger stage, Ron needed loyal support not only in the recent devolution referendum, but also in the Assembly elections to come; Rhodri wanted a meeting to drag the distasteful details of the Barrage 'review' by the WO into the light of day – both got what they wanted.

The SoS was accompanied by four senior civil servants; it was interesting to speculate whether any of them had attended that momentous briefing session in the same building, thirteen years before, when Nicholas Edwards' civil servants had told him what a good thing a barrage in Cardiff Bay would be, and what role they might have played in the recent internal review.

Ron Davies appeared surprised by the number of groups represented, but briskly went on to define the purpose of the meeting. He would give details of the enquiry into the future of the Barrage, explain the reasons for his decision that the project should go ahead, and answer questions from the groups represented. He apologised for the delay in calling the meeting, originally planned for July, but he wanted to see the Inspector's report on the planning enquiry into proposed alternative feeding grounds on the Gwent Levels, before further discussion.

He did not explain how the results of that enquiry could make any difference to a justification of his declared aim of completing the Barrage: if the Barrage was built, replacement feeding grounds would have to be provided, if not on the Gwent Levels, then elsewhere. If the Gwent Levels were deemed unsuitable as a replacement, then a substitute would have to be found elsewhere: the issue was not relevant to the Barrage review.

Instead, he passed quickly on to emphasize that the Barrage would not have been started, if he had been SoS when the original decision was taken. The question confronting him on taking office in May had been, could the contracts with the construction consortium, Balfour Beatty Costain, be cancelled? After lengthy discussions, he had decided that there were no grounds for him to intervene.

At this point, Julie Morgan commented that she was concerned about the apparent speed and secrecy of the reappraisal – for such a complex issue, less than seven weeks seemed rapid. The SoS replied that he would have preferred the process to be more open – but given the nature of the project, speed was vital. In view of the money spent, he added, it was 'better value for money' for the Barrage to go ahead – intervention was not an option.

Throughout the meeting, Ron Davies was to use the word 'intervention' frequently, when referring to his influence on the Barrage project, as if he saw the scheme as naturally rolling on, under its own volition: any action on his part would almost be an intrusion into an autonomous process, instead of an appropriate expression of government responsibility.

He gave out copies of a more detailed statement of his reasons for not cancelling, which he then 'talked through'(See Appendix 1). The first concern he raised was the £30 million that would be needed to pay off contractors and demolish the structure. The relevance of this argument was not disputed, at least in principle, by anyone present: some compensation would have to be paid, the debatable points were how much, and how far these costs would be outweighed by the savings to be made in future by cancelling.

His second point was rather more contentious: investors in Cardiff Bay had legitimate expectations of the Barrage, so there was a possibility they might take legal action if it did not materialise. There were two major flaws in this argument. First, investors had taken up development options before the environmental impact assessment of the Barrage was complete: what if a properly rigorous impact assessment had concluded that the project posed, for instance, insuperable public health problems, would the WO still have insisted it go ahead, because it would be too expensive to compensate those developers for their lost investment? The underlying principle, that 'injured' companies should be automatically entitled to compensation in such a situation, appeared morally and legally untenable.

The second flaw was that the economic justification for the Barrage, that land values in the Bay would rise by x% if it was built and only x minus y% if it wasn't, was impossible to prove or disprove; even the most optimistic supporter would see it as an expectation, not a certainty. Dealing in land is, like any other speculation, uncertain and risky: the idea that governments should be expected to compensate such entrepreneurs for loss of possible profits is an interesting

precursor of the PFI win/win scenario, for the Private bit of the
Initiative, anyway. No sale of land in the Bay had been accompanied
by a cast-iron assurance that specific profits were guaranteed. To a
neutral observer, the SoS was under no obligation to behave as if such
guarantees existed.

His final argument was that the European Commission had decided in February that year not to take action against the British
government over its unlawful exclusion of Cardiff Bay from the
Severn Estuary's designation as a SPA and Ramsar site. He apparently accepted that the exclusion had been made specifically to allow
the building of the Barrage, and was justified by the government's
contention that the economic development of south Cardiff depended on the Barrage – the view he had campaigned against so forcefully
only a few years before.

This statement drew a withering response from Carol Hatton, for
the WFN. She quoted extensively from the European Court's judgement. She reminded the SoS the exclusion itself was not unlawful, it
was the failure to designate the Bay in the first place that made the
Barrage illegal.

Rhodri Morgan pointed out that the SoS was assuming the EU
Environment Commission had accepted the Gwent Levels as a site
for alternative feeding grounds. On the contrary, they only accepted
that the UK government viewed the Levels as a possible alternative:
there were no grounds for assuming the Commission agreed with that
view.

Julian Rosser of FoE produced a letter to FoE Wales from the
office of the EU Commissioner for the Environment, dated October
1997. It clearly stated that the economic arguments put forward by
the UK government to justify excluding the Bay from the designation
of the Severn Estuary as a possible SPA under the EC Habitats
Directive, were unacceptable. As far as the European Environment
Commission was concerned, a decision about the appropriate
response to the British Government's action had not yet been made –
the SoS had no justification for believing his administration was in the
clear, so far.

This apparently came as a complete surprise to Mr Davies, who,
after a brief *sotto voce* consultation with the civil servants, declared
that this contradicted the advice the WO lawyers had given him on the
matter. It appeared that no relevant correspondence had reached the
WO, or, at least, the SoS' desk. He asked for a copy of the letter, 'for
further consideration.' During this exchange, Mr Davies seemed to
become more flustered than a minister with a reputation for formida-
bly thick-skinned toughness should allow himself to be. It was clear

that, when the meeting ended, full and detailed explanations would be required from the civil servants sitting beside him; someone, somewhere, would have to account for the wrongfooting of the Welsh Secretary.

He was still more flustered when Rhodri Morgan reminded him that when the contracts for building the Barrage were signed with the Balfour Beatty Costain consortium, in 1994, the Lappel Bank case was still being considered by the European Court of Justice. He pointed out that, legally, CBDC should therefore have waited for the judgement before letting the contracts, for if the exclusion of the Bay was declared to be unlawful, the Barrage could not be built. This should have been a major consideration when the new SoS was deciding whether or not building should continue: if he was seriously looking for a get-out clause, this would have been perfect.

Ron Davies tried to defend his decision by insisting that as incoming SoS, he had no right to know what policy advice had been given to his predecessors in the period immediately before the letting of the contract. Such a restricted interpretation of election handover convention could only be justified if he and his advisers were desperately looking for excuses for not 'intervening'. This was an issue the anti-barrage campaigners wanted to examine much more closely, but time was limited, and there were other important matters to discuss. Rhodri Morgan suggested that he would write to the Welsh Secretary, setting out in full the flaws in this argument, as he saw them. This letter, and any response from the WO, would be circulated to all present. With obvious relief, the SoS agreed.

It is worth quoting here the relevant bit of Rhodri's subsequent letter, dated 12th December 1997 (for the letter in full, see Appendix 2).

> Let us say, for example, that there were in fact two views about how much account should be taken of the expected loss of the Lappel Bank case. Let us say that some civil servants took the view that in the anticipation of the loss of the Lappel Bank case, it was unwise to proceed until the case was concluded. Other civil servants may have been more gung ho and may have advised the Minister that 'we will be able to get away with it' (or words to that effect).
>
> You were the anticipated incoming Secretary of State. You were known to be less gung ho on the Barrage than your predecessor Secretaries of State. The civil service 'faction' which I am hypothesising here would have been much more likely to win the day as regards postponing letting the contract until after the Lappel Bank was finished if you had been the Secretary of State; that would surely justify you having some indication of the totality of the advice given to the then Secretary of State. There must surely have been some discussion of your known position as the Shadow

Secretary of State in the advice to the then Secretary of State. As
the contract was bound to run over into the post-election period
by a year or two, your arrival and its effect on the lawfulness and
regularity/propriety must have been thought about. You must surely have the right to know...

With the civil servants still shifting uneasily in their seats, and the
SoS obtrusively glancing at his watch, the debate passed on to other
topics.

CRAB members asked if the costs of maintaining the Barrage, the
groundwater measures and the necessary environmental protection
measures had been calculated, and, if so what they were. Ron Davies
replied that they had been set at about £60 million. In an aside, he
mentioned the possibility of a PFI being set up to meet such costs.

Peter Ferns asked whether the Barrage would be left open if no
successor body were willing to take on the costs? The SoS refused to
reply. We may assume that to acknowledge publicly that the financial
burdens might be too heavy to attract a successor body, would damage the commercial future of the project irreparably, and the SoS was
already identifying himself closely with its commercial survival – a
PFI, for instance, would be essential, to prevent the entire cost being
found from public resources.

Rhodri Morgan commented acidly on the figure of 9100 'permanent jobs created' in the SoS' statement, by 31st March 1997
(Appendix 1). Job creation was one of main aims of a barrage-centred
development: when questioned, the SoS admitted that the figures
referred to all jobs 'created' in the area covered by CBDC, not to jobs
which were specifically due to the presence of the Barrage.

Rhodri asked whether employees of the NEG factory were included in the total. When told that they had been, he commented 'Isn't that
rather naughty?' NEG had built their factory in the Bay because they
needed access to the open sea, which they still had, via the Queen
Alexandra Dock. They had certainly not been attracted to the area
because of the Barrage: if anything, it would have been a disincentive.
Significantly, they were still the largest employers in the area, with a
workforce of over 700. If this was the only sort of evidence supporters of the Barrage could produce to justify their case, it showed how
threadbare it really was. In fact, it would be impossible for CBDC or
the WO to prove that a particular employer had come to the Bay
because of the Barrage, and would not have come if it remained
incomplete – at the start of the project, they could have set whatever
unrealistic employment targets they wished, without fear of contradiction. For the SoS to attempt to justify his inaction with these
unsupportable statistics might seem an admission of abject failure.

Before the meeting began Ron Davies could not have expected to receive a particularly warm reception. He may have anticipated sharing a few of the grittier facts of economic life with some rather over-idealistic conservationists and anguished residents; he did not expect to have those facts briskly and thoroughly shown up for the fictions they were. His interrogators seemed better briefed, better informed and more committed to their cause than he was, and everyone present knew it. It was not a situation that the most equable of career politicians would have welcomed; for someone as abrasive and combative as Ron Davies, it was intolerable.

As the meeting drew to a close he wondered aloud why, if anti-barrage groups were so keen to debate their case in public, none of had asked for a public enquiry yet – no such request had apparently reached him. Peter Ferns produced a letter he had written to him as Shadow SoS, on behalf of TEEWC, in April, asking for just such an enquiry. The SoS burst out 'I can't be expected to read everything I get, can I?' and the meeting was over.

For most anti-barrage activists, this meeting marked the end of their long campaign. Changing Ron Davies' mind about the results of his review had been their last hope, and now that was finally dashed. The sense of an ending was intensified later that same month when Stan Perkins lost his valiant battle against kidney failure. With no hope of victory and without Stan's cheerful resilience and endless optimism, there seemed only the prospect of a gently fading coda. However, it was to be a most interesting and eventful coda.

10. From Bay of Tigers to 'A Pleasant Setting for Eating Ice-cream'

This kind of reclamation can create a pleasant setting for eating an ice-cream. It cannot make a city feel like a city'.
Jonathan Jones, 'The regeneration game' in the *Guardian*,
16th October, 2000

Since the regeneration of Cardiff docks began, the Barrage and the redevelopment had been yoked together only by a politician's caprice. The business of the anti-barrage campaign had been to separate them, to demonstrate that development could succeed without a barrage. The arguments put to Ron Davies at that WO meeting in December 1997 were sadly the last time a senior politician and his advisers would have to try to justify their connection.

Lord Crickhowell saw the struggle to build his barrage as a steeple chase.[1] But what this particular sporting event had always lacked was a judicious, impartial referee. In the council chambers of local government, on the floor of the House of Commons, even in the editorials of the *South Wales Echo*, every round of this competition was loaded heavily in favour of the scheme's sponsors. There had been no public body with the objectivity, power and resources to hold the Barrage and its pretensions to strict account, until, ironically, it was almost complete, when the Environment Agency for Wales took a critical look, in 1999.

After that, the next time the cost of building and running the scheme would be looked at in public, and in detail, would be by the Auditor General for Wales (AGW), reporting to the newly elected National Assembly (NAW), which had to meet those costs from its own limited resources. By the time Sir John Bourn produced the first of those reports, the concrete of the Barrage had set hard, and there no longer seemed any point in arguing that regeneration could have succeeded perfectly well, and much more cheaply, without it. But, the story of the anti-barrage campaign was a long and honourable one, and it deserves the dignity of a proper conclusion.

Water Quality and the Environment Agency

For all the energy and commitment of its supporters, CRAB could do little to force CBDC to deal with algal bloom or midge infestation, or even improve the quality of groundwater monitoring, but fortunately for Cardiff, the Environment Agency for Wales (EAW) could. The EAW was the only organisation to challenge CBDC effectively, and force it comply with at least some of the terms of the Act. In 1996 the Agency had succeeded the defunct National Rivers Authority, formerly chaired by Lord Crickhowell, and inherited its powers, which included ensuring the Corporation would 'operate the Barrage in accordance with any reasonable direction... to prevent or alleviate flooding'.[2]

Dave Andrews was the EAW Project Manager for the Barrage. As the date of complete impoundment drew closer, he and his colleagues kept up a sceptical vigilance. During the summer of 1999, blue-green algae appeared in the waters of the Bute East Dock; its likely effects had been graphically described by Peter Randerson in his evidence to the Commons Select Committee in 1990, when he warned that it would infest the Bay post-Barrage. EAW officials echoed his concern. They knew 'it could severely upset or even kill animals who drank it in large quantities'[3] Dave Andrews was even more specific '...This algal bloom... provides a good indication of what we expect to happen under similar conditions in the Cardiff Bay lake.'[4] CBDC were being given clear notice that the Agency took their responsibilities under the Act seriously.

But blue-green algae was not the greatest threat to the Bay; EAW had to be satisfied flood protection and other systems were working properly before they could give CBDC a license to operate the Barrage. For more than six months before the last gap in the wall across the Bay was filled in November 1999, the Agency had been worried about the inadequacy of the system used to control the sluice gates, especially in times of high river flows. So, the Barrage was operated under a series of temporary licences, while the Corporation's engineers tried again and again to get the system to work. After all the years of plans and promises and all the millions of pounds, the Barrage was still considered a safety hazard.

The Corporation were given several warnings that even the temporary licence would be withdrawn unless things improved. They did not improve and on Friday 3rd December, EAW ordered CBDC to stop operating the Barrage, open the sluices, and drain the Bay. They remained officially in ignorance of the order for some hours, as the notice of withdrawal was delivered to Baltic House late in the afternoon, when senior management had already left their desks for the weekend. When they did find out, they refused to accept it; in public, they would only admit that the computerised flood protection system had 'some teething problems'.[5]

But in a radio interview for BBC Radio Wales' 'Good Morning, Wales' the next Monday the EAW's legal officer, Anthony Wear, used rather more robust language. He referred to 'an accumulation of problems going on over the last months, especially in key systems in how [*sic*] the Barrage will be operate, have been shown not to be working as they should be.' In particular, the sluice gates were 'operating in a random manner... not operating according to their design.' He complained that these 'fundamental systems' have been shown to be seriously deficient, so there were 'serious risks... possibly to flooding and to other aspects of the environment'.

It was an extraordinary situation: the EAW could not have taken such a decision lightly. Their officers must have been convinced, as Charlie, Norman and Glyn had feared all along, that CBDC were incapable of operating the flood control systems properly. CRAB's worst fears about the Corporation's readiness to put expediency before safety were confirmed. They would accept their legal responsibilities only under heavy duress. It was most fortunate that the Environment Agency were willing to apply that duress. CBDC appealed against the decision, but to no avail – the sluices had to be opened, and the Bay drained whenever Mr Andrews and his colleagues required, until it could be proved that the system could operate to their satisfaction.

At an extraordinary meeting between Michael Boyce, for CBDC, and Roger Thomas, the EAW's Regional Manager, the Corporation was forced to concede a temporary lowering of the level of the impounded lake from 4.5m to 4m – just what Cardiff City Council had petitioned for, and been refused, by the Lords Select Committee in 1992 – and the sluice gates had to be manned 24 hours a day, for as long as the Agency demanded.[6]

For a public body with CBDC's assets, power and pretensions, it was a bitter humiliation; for CRAB, with no assets, power or pretensions, it was a vindication, although far too late, of their view of the Corporation's competence and altruism. If the Environment Agency's thorough examination of the flood prevention system had been applied by other bodies to other aspects of the scheme, who knows what would have emerged...

As if the problems with the sluice gates were not enough, in April 2000 another report from the Environment Agency raised concerns about the reliability of the fish pass, intended to allow migrating fish, especially trout and salmon, to move from the sea upriver. Under an agreement with the Agency, the Cardiff Harbour Authority would have to compensate them for every fish that doesn't get through the pass compared with pre-barrage figures.

CHA were reportedly having to catch returning salmon in the Bristol Channel, and put them in the Taff estuary, on the other side of the Barrage in an attempt to keep fish stocks in the river at pre-impoundment levels.

But it was not only salmon that were at risk,

> In Cardiff Bay, saltwater marine life is reported to be dying out in the Penarth Marina and sea anglers have reported the worst winter cod season in 17 years. Well known flyfisher Cliff Harvey, of Cilfynydd near Pontypridd, said that anglers fear the bay will become a stagnant pond. 'Marvellous as the barrage fish systems are, they are no good if the salmon can't detect the smell of the home river. The fish can't do that with all this transition work going on. It could take years for the fish to come back and for what? A yuppie waterfront in Cardiff Bay.[8]

But while the fish remained rather baffled, the tests on the operation of the Barrage itself continued until March 2001, when a licence to impound was granted at last, and the sluice gates finally closed, sealing Cardiff off from the sea tides that were its life blood and its history.

The Assembly and the Barrage

On 19th September 1997, the referendum on devolution which had so preoccupied Ron Davies, brought forth a very narrow 'Yes' vote, on a 50% turnout. At a meeting of his constituency party, later that same month, Rhodri Morgan announced that he intended to stand for election to the Leadership of the Labour Group in the Assembly-to-be – the first candidate to do so.

Ron Davies declared his own candidacy later that autumn. So in the small, but far from cosy, world of Welsh politics, the Barrage campaign's troops began to muster once more. The more influential members of the Welsh Labour Party (WLP) Executive, who knew a dangerously good thing when they saw one, were worried by the prospect of a Rhodri Morgan victory. Ron Davies would, it was felt, be a much safer pair of hands, with the right friends at Westminster and Milbank. Rhodri's friends tended to be grassroots Labour supporters who just believed he was the best person available to look after their interests.

To neutralise this democratic advantage, the WLP Executive decided to set aside the tried and tested OMOV, (One Member One Vote) system, in favour of an electoral college. This meant that the leaders of several of the largest unions were able to cast votes on behalf of their members, without the inconvenience and expense of a

ballot, and so give Ron Davies, for whom their votes were cast, a substantial advantage – more a matter of One Union Leader, Several
Thousand Votes.

Most constituency parties did stick with OMOV, but a few
arranged equally interesting variations on a democratic theme.
Cardiff South and Penarth CLP, for instance, held a special meeting,
where, after a show of hands under the watchful eye of Lord Brooks,
Ron Davies won by a narrow margin. However, as the CLP's
Standing Orders required, he was put forward as the candidate having the support of the whole CLP.

But Ron was not to enjoy his victory for long. Following his walk
on Clapham Common a few days later, he resigned as SoS Wales.
Tony Blair appointed Alun Michael to replace him, within hours.
After some hesitation, Ron was also persuaded to resign as Leader of
the Welsh Labour Group in the still-unformed Assembly. The Welsh
Office was in the Prime Minister's gift, but the Labour Group
Leadership was not, or not directly, at least. Another election would
be needed. However, while Ron had been prepared to fill both roles,
Alun Michael apparently had a very different agenda. He had just
been made a Privy Councillor; he had played a minimal role in the
devolution campaign. It was clear that he was planning a career in
Westminster not Wales, and there was probably only one man who
could persuade him to change course – the Prime Minister. Tony Blair
was apparently unwilling to risk the Welsh leadership falling into
unsafe hands. Alun had been seen as the quintessence of safety and
reliability for delivering a pet project of the powerful with little popular support, like the Barrage. Now he had to reprise that role, in the
campaign to keep the Welsh Assembly firmly under Downing Street's
thumb.

There was a suggestion, probably from Number 10, that Alun be
allowed a free run, unopposed, with Rhodri joining him on the ticket.
The MP for Cardiff West's response was typical,

> The answer is very simple. It comes in folding ballot papers. It's
> called democracy and it's reached Wales, but only in patches.[9]

As soon as Mr Michael had made a demeaning scuttle for one of
the few remaining chances of an Assembly seat, Welsh Labour's electoral college cast its mystic runes again, after going through all the
many interesting declensions of the verb 'to vote', and he was elected
leader by a fragile majority.

When the new National Assembly for Wales convened for the first
time in June 1999, a number of seasoned anti-barrage campaigners

took their seats; Jenny Randerson for the Lib Dems, Sue Essex, Jane Davidson, Jane Hutt and Rhodri Morgan for Labour, while Mark Drakeford became one of Rhodri's political advisers.

The Assembly now had to choose which body or bodies would run the Barrage and the impounded lake when CBDC's legal life ended, in March, 2000. It was readily agreed that the Welsh Development Agency (WDA) as the principal development authority in Wales would be responsible for completing the regeneration that remained, and the Countryside Council for Wales (CCW) would run the replacement feeding grounds on the Gwent Wetlands, as the Barrage Act required. But what of the Barrage itself, with all its ongoing expenses and 'attendant works'?

In 1998, CBDC had put the contract to run the Barrage out to tender. The most favourable bid was from Thames Water, but, to the consternation of Assembly members, its estimate far exceeded the financial limits set by the Corporation. It was clear that the Barrage would require large regular subsidies, if it was to be run as the terms of the Act demanded.

In contrast, Teeside had been the only other Development Corporation to include a barrage in its plans. It was a much smaller scheme than Cardiff's, specifically designed to create a major inter-national centre in the north east for water sports like kayaking, canoeing and white water rafting. The Teeside UDC was wound up in 1997, its assets realised and the resulting £17.6 million was made over, as a one-off payment to British Waterways, who would run the Barrage, entirely funded by revenue from sporting events.

Certainly there were differences in scale – the Teeside barrage was much smaller than Cardiff Bay's – but there were also differences in costs, planning and execution. The Teeside barrage was planned to be self-supporting; the Cardiff Bay Barrage would have to be sustained for the foreseeable future by the Assembly out of its limited resources. Assembly Members were anxious to discover how the wealth sup-posedly generated by the Barrage could be fed back to fund such subsidies, as natural justice required. Natural justice was rather less vocal in its demands than some politicians, like Alison Halford and Llew Smith, whose constituents lived too far from Cardiff to benefit from the legendary advantages brought by the Barrage.

> If the people of Cardiff want that pond maintained, then either they should pay for it, or the property companies that have made so much money out of selling land down there should foot the bill.[10]

However, just when Thames Water's thought-provoking bid was

being considered, NAW officials were discussing quite different aspects of the handover with Cardiff Council. During these discussions, it emerged that the Council were prepared to undercut Thames Water's offer; they would deliver the necessary services, while making savings of £3 million for the Assembly over the next three years.

The speed and firmness of the agreement between the Assembly and the County Council were an interesting contrast to earlier negotiations between the two bodies. For instance, the discussions between Ron Davies, the Assembly's would-be leader from the Valleys, and Russell Goodway, for the Council, about the use of Cardiff's handsome, spacious, empty City Hall as a home for the Assembly. The simplicity and logic of this arrangement were widely accepted, yet that ancient Cardiff/Valleys enmity reared its ugly head, as it had over the Barrage. This, combined with the Welsh Labour Party's apparently insatiable need to tear its own flesh, led to an irretrievable breakdown. So, the Assembly moved temporarily into meagre, bland accommodation at Crickhowell House. However, Russell and Alun, with their common background in the smoke-filled rooms of Cardiff local government, reached an understanding over the Barrage with much less fuss.

After a very short period of intensive negotiation in late August and early September 1999, it was announced that Cardiff County Council would maintain and run the Barrage after March 31st 2000, only six months away. The Council would set up a whole new department, the Cardiff Harbour Authority (CHA), specifically to deal with the Barrage, the water quality in the impounded lake and groundwater protection. Assembly funds for managing the Bay would be passed directly to the CHA, ring fenced from all other Council expenditure.

As the Auditor General for Wales commented in a report to the NAW in June 2001,

> To put this in perspective, a 1997 National Audit Office report on the wind up of the Leeds and Bristol Urban Development Corporation [*sic*] recognised the need for decisions on successor bodies to be made at least two years before the wind up date.[11]

Because of this ludicrous time scale, there was a desperate scramble to set up the new Harbour Authority by March 2000. But then, this was quite natural; the whole story of the Barrage so far had been one of desperate scrambles, alternating with periods of serene, thoughtless optimism.

But before the handover could take place, Alun Michael resigned, on February 9th 2000, when it seemed inevitable that he would lose a vote of no confidence on his handling of the Assembly's bid for

Objective One funding from Europe. The Labour Group choose Rhodri as Acting First Secretary and Alun returned to Westminster with much relief – he had prudently retained his Commons seat for Cardiff South and Penarth.

In July 2000, Sir John Bourn, the Auditor General for Wales, revealed the full extent of the Assembly's commitment to the Barrage. Cardiff County Council had been allocated £21.4 million to run the Barrage, for 2001-2002. That amount would be reduced to £19 million in 2002-2003. Sir John added that it was important that the Assembly 'develops ways of controlling costs and ensuring continuing value for money.' A sentiment which AMs whose constituents had no chance of benefiting from this largesse echoed with some vehemence.

The Auditor General said 'the final cost of the Barrage has yet to be known, but is estimated at £220 million, including £7 million worth of measures to maintain water quality', an overrun of £30 million on John Redwood's cap of £191 million, set in 1996. In particular, the cost of the Gwent Levels reserve had risen from £5.7 million in 1995, to £10.4 million.[12]

The report also highlighted that costs were affected by the need to deal with 'unforeseen ground conditions in the construction of the Barrage.' These conditions had not been picked up by earlier surveys. Sir John said CBDC 'took a risk' in reducing its provision in the early stages of the project for inflation and contingencies.

These sums might seem insignificant outgoings from a total Assembly budget of £11 billion. But when the unavoidable costs of running Wales, its schools, its roads, its hospitals, were deducted, the Barrage was taking a huge bite of the remaining disposable budget – the money AMs could actually expect to make decisions about using, the sort of projects which would make a difference to their constituents' lives, distinguish Wales from the rest of the UK and justify the Assembly's existence. Neither the Barrage nor the Cardiff Harbour Authority were popular at Crickhowell House.

The Assembly's own Audit Committee, chaired by Janet Davies, Plaid Cymru AM for Llanelli, produced its own report on the Barrage in February 2001. As part of their investigation, they reprised the Commons SC on the Barrage Bill, more than ten years before, when they tried to assess the benefits of the Barrage, and weigh them against its costs. In pursuit of this aim they took evidence from Michael Boyce, former Chief Executive of the Development Corporation.

He told them that 'the cost of the Barrage had almost been repaid by a single inward investment in the Bay of £200 million by Nippon Electric Glass Company Limited. The company had looked at locations all over Europe for this investment and it had chosen Cardiff because it was the Cardiff Bay product that made the difference. And at the heart of the Cardiff Bay product was the Barrage...'[13]

Whether NEG's directors had seen the Barrage as the heart of 'the Cardiff Bay product', or whether Mr Boyce had put this spin on their decision was unclear. What was clear was that more than four years before, in the confrontation between Ron Davies and the anti-barrage groups, at Cathays Park, NEG had been also cited as an example of the Barrage's unique pulling power, for wealth and job creation. An argument which Rhodri Morgan had effectively demolished. Moreover, the factory was in that part of the Bay, where according to CBDC's own consultants, regeneration would not be dependent on Mr Edwards' Barrage. No evidence was produced then to support NEG's legendary dependence on the scheme, and none was produced by Mr Boyce. It was rather sad that one factory employing 700 people should have to bear the whole burden of justifying the £220 million Barrage's existence; it was a major tragedy for Wales and Cardiff that it was incapable of doing so.

It was very clear to most AMs that a project like the Barrage, the costs of which were spread evenly throughout Wales while its benefits accrued only to the capital, would never be undertaken again. If a Welsh Assembly had existed in 1987, it would never have been begun. As things were, the NAW had no alternative but to shoulder the burden of Mr Edwards' whim; the Barrage could not be dismantled, it would have to be coped with.

Groundwater

By April 1998, 22,600 properties in south Cardiff had been surveyed out of the 23,000 at risk; the planned dewatering system for Grangetown, Riverside and Adamsdown received Welsh Office approval the following November. The 62 test boreholes for monitoring changes in south Cardiff's water table had been sunk, and damp-detecting equipment installed in 20 or so sample properties – as the Corporation had promised.

In its final months, CBDC continued to adjust the Code of Practice. The legal date of impoundment quoted in the Code was the point at which a constant water level was maintained in the Bay. This had to be adjusted to cope with the uncomfortable reality that the Bay had actually been impounded and then disimpounded several times, in just over a year, as the Environment Agency demanded, causing the water level to rise and fall. This process made a nonsense of the whole business of pre- and post-impoundment surveys. The surveys had been intended to provide a benchmark for measuring likely damage to property from raised groundwater – any increase in dampness between the two surveys might be assumed to be a result of the Barrage, and repairs provided accordingly. The apparently arbitrary choice of November 1999 as the date of impoundment meant that effectively, the bench had been chopped up and used as firewood.

CRAB members continued to meet with Corporation staff and their successors in the new Cardiff Harbour Authority; they fiercely contested constant weakening of the Code. Glyn Paul and Kate Hunter in particular fought a spirited battle, but mostly in vain; there were no weapons left, no neutral arbitrators: the Barrage, as the responsibility of a Harbour Authority, fell outside the jurisdiction of both the Parliamentary and the local government Ombudsman. The Independent Groundwater Administrator's rulings in favour of the Corporation or, later, the CHA could be challenged only by ruinously expensive judicial review.

However, there was one faint reminder of CRAB's former glory days when it had successfully pricked so many of the Corporation's pretensions. Kate became so exasperated by lack of assurance over monitoring of groundwater flow in the bore holes, that she asked to visit the monitoring centre, based in Pontypridd. It was sited so far from Cardiff, because Hyder, the company who ran it, also managed the local sewage pumping station, and the same staff and equipment could be used for both.

So, in December 1999, Kate Hunter set off for Pontypridd. She was accompanied by Kate Hansford, equally articulate, well-informed and, when occasion demanded, forceful. They made a daunting duo. Their first impressions of the monitoring arrangements were not reassuring. They expected gleaming banks of computer screens, displaying constantly changing columns of figures, intently watched by teams of technicians in white coats. After al this was the system designed to save south Cardiff from inundation.

Instead, they were shown a small PC in a cupboard, by a rather nervous young man in a suit. As a museum curator, Kate Hunter was quite familiar with the sort of software used at Pontypridd; humidity and temperature have to be measured carefully for maintaining collections of fragile artefacts. She asked to see the system in action, as the PC was apparently switched off. It was linked to six monitoring stations along the Taff and each was dialled once an hour (there seemed to be no warning system if any of the stations did not respond) and the volume of water flowing through the station was measured. If it was above a certain level, an engineer would be despatched to Cardiff, to see what was amiss.

The attendant technician duly dialled up a sample station, and received a satisfactory response. The ever-sceptical Kate Hansford, however, wanted further confirmation, and asked for a random reading, from a station she had chosen. The results showed a pressure of water equivalent to the Taff in full spate, passing through a pipe some 10cm in diameter. Given the current combination of low tide and dry weather, this was not only catastrophic, but impossible, and Mrs Hansford permitted herself a quiet giggle of satisfaction. On her return to Cardiff, she wrote to the former councillor for South Riverside, Jane Davidson, now the AM for Pontypridd. Given that Ms Davidson had cut her political teeth, in her early days on the Council, trying to achieve just such a warning system for her ward, she was concerned to hear of this arrangement, and suggested she accompany them on a second visit.

All three returned, in March 2000. This time they were greeted, not by a lone technician, but by a bevy of managers, anxious to please, and ready with a reassuring demonstration of their system's reliability and veracity. Ms Davidson watched in judicious silence, wearing a elegant black leather outfit, which might have been specifically chosen to command maximum respect from all beholders. She made it clear she would be keeping a very close eye on the station's future performance.

Soon afterwards the monitoring system became the responsibility of the Harbour Authority, and was moved to Cardiff, where visits are not encouraged. Professor John Lloyd, formerly the City Council's groundwater consultant, took over supervision of the pumping and monitoring systems. Official reports confirm that no significant changes in groundwater have yet taken place; the drainage system is apparently keeping the water table in place, and with that achievement CRAB has to be content, for the time being.

Flying to Gwent

The alternative feeding grounds on the Gwent Levels were completed in March 2000. Their cost had leapt from the original £5.7 million, in 1997, to over £10 million, another large tab to be picked up by the Assembly. The new wetland reserve was not intended to provide alternative feeding grounds for the wading birds of Cardiff Bay; their habitat was too delicately balanced to be easily replicated. Instead it simply added to the acreage of land within the Severn Estuary SPA available to any bird species that could nest or feed there.

A few of the dunlin, redshank and shelduck found their way to the mudflats of the Rumney estuary, but the site is too small to be a permanent substitute for the thousands of birds that enlivened the Bay.

The only birds there now, are the ducks, swans and cormorants that can live and thrive anywhere there is freshwater and food provided for them; the delicate wading birds that made it unique have gone forever.

In June 2000, the Environment Directorate of the Europe Commission, quietly closed its file of complaints about Cardiff Bay from FoE and the Worldwide Fund for Nature. The Barrage was built, nothing could bring the SSSI back now; there were other SPAs under threat that could still be saved, regrettably there was no more time to waste on one which could never be resurrected – environmentalists, like mourners, must know when to direct their energies towards the living, not the dead.

Renaissance in Cardiff Bay – A World Class Waterfront?

Just as the Assembly had passed the responsibility for running the Barrage to the new Harbour Authority, so the Welsh Development Agency (WDA) took on CBDC's unfinished development projects.

It was extraordinary that at the time of its demise, in March 2000, after thirteen years and £500 million, both the Corporation's key projects were unfinished – the Barrage and Bute Avenue, the wide boulevard which was to connect the waterfront with the City Centre, half a mile away.

The Harbour Authority had to see the Barrage through the difficult final months of Environment Agency supervision, and the frequent draining of the Bay. But Bute Avenue was barely begun – the Public Private Partnership needed to built it would cost over £100 million, to which the Corporation's remaining assets could make only a tiny contribution. The City would soon be reunited with its waterfront, but the Development Corporation would have had very little to do with the scheme.

At least, their housing target was within reach; over 4000 houses and flats had been built and a quarter of them were indeed social housing. But the developments on Lloyd George Avenue, and Windsor Quay seem strangely lifeless, there are no meeting places, no social space, no libraries, no clinics; the two schools are in old Butetown, and people who pay £200k for a two bedroom flat don't use community centres. It's a place where people go home to sleep – they do their living elsewhere. Moreover, the city's needs had moved on; there had been 5000 people on Cardiff's homeless register in 1987; in 2001 the Council's housing department reported that this had risen to over 8000 needing somewhere just to sleep.

In spite of Rocco Forte's assertive hotel, dominating the Bay, and developments like Scott Harbour (for which CBDC gave a rental guarantee of £1.3 million to Grosvenor Waterside) the most attractive buildings in Cardiff Bay, the ones that adorn PR brochures and posters, remain the Coal Exchange, that imposing red brick Victorian Gothic pile, and the lovingly reconstructed Norwegian Church, in white clapper board; both were familiar landmarks in the area when it was still called Cardiff Docks. Along the Inner Harbour, the Cardiff Bay Arts Trust has commissioned a range of compelling sculptures and friezes which are the district's most attractive features, but per-haps they would look even more appealing against the background of a living waterfront, where tides and rivers ran free.

But, the 2700 derelict acres have been dutifully filled up; it would have been remarkable if massive development had not happened, on a spend of £500 million. However, over the railway line, the terraced council houses of Butetown are left to moulder quietly, isolated from the prosperity around them. The long promised Light Rail Transport system is still on the drawing board; the Corporation were never very enthusiastic about public transport, anyway. The £20 million 'festival shopping' development at Mermaid Quay usually has at least a few empty premises and boarded windows. There are good restaurants and pleasant pubs, to be sure, just as there are in Canton, or Llandaff, or any other prosperous Cardiff suburb.

Did we really need the Barrage for this? It's a waterfront develop-ment certainly, but surely not Europe's most exciting, as the adverts claimed. But then the Bay's promoters were always a little vague about where the other cities competing for that particular title were, and why exactly a barrage was needed to give Cardiff the edge.

In 1986, when the Commons debated the first, relatively innocu-ous Cardiff Barrage, in the South Glamorgan (Taff Crossing) Bill, Alex Carlile the MP for Montgomery opposed it because, he said, it would 'put something which is neat and dull in place of something which is or could be perhaps wild and intriguing.' Cardiff attempts neatness, with varying success; there are flower baskets and well-groomed parks, although we don't do dull very well; wild and intriguing is much more the city's style. But although wild and intriguing may be attractive, they don't necessarily bring the huge increases in land values Nicholas Edwards dreamed of, that July day on Pierhead. The powerful have a strong instinct for order, perhaps it's part of their urge to control their surroundings, and there is noth-ing more orderly than a flat expanse of fresh water. However, the Taff does its subversive best, embellishing the Bay with the occasional dead sheep, or uprooted tree, but mostly these days we have to rely on the midges, the algae and the occasional pungent whiff to break the monotony.

In an article in the *Guardian* in November 2000, Jonathan Jones lamented the closure of Cardiff's Centre for the Visual Arts. He noted the blandness of Cardiff Bay, and pointed out that in the city, as in 'too many other cities in Britain, the bright dream of "cultural regeneration" has been pursued without the courage to believe in culture at all'. In an unconscious echo of Mr Carlile, he suggested, 'if Cardiff wants to be a cultural Mecca, why not create something really wild?'[15]

But the Barrage drowned our wilderness, and has brought nothing to the city, except water pumps and anxiety. The PDR and the rest of the infrastructure, with some inducements from the Treasury and the Welsh Office (which were needed anyway) would still have attracted the property developers and the office blocks, the restaurants and the artwork.

Ironically, the anti-barrage campaign's greatest successes lie outside Cardiff. In the late eighties, a veritable necklace of barrages was planned for the British coast; estuaries from the Solent to the Tyne would be dammed by high concrete walls. The long and costly fight to stop the Cardiff scheme made most of those planners and developers think again. The final straw for many of them was the Transport and Public Works Act of 1992, which meant that such schemes would be subject to local scrutiny and approval, rather than the Parliamentary wheeling and dealing that brought Mr Edwards' dream to Cardiff Bay. The Barrage Bill's lumbering progress through both Houses had been the best possible justification for the new Act.

The great tragedy is not just the destruction of an SSSI, or the threat of rising groundwater, but the loss of possibilities, of what might have been, that lively, prosperous city with an intriguing wilderness at its heart. As Lyndon Davies wrote,

> In Cardiff Bay, they've done away with the mud, and who can blame them?... I am a sucker for such places, it's true, and no doubt I shall idle and promenade with the best of them. But it's difficult to shake off a lingering sense of shame, a feeling that, in some important way, the city's heart has been broken.[16]

References

INTRODUCTION

1. *Western Mail*, 4 November, 1993

CHAPTER 1

1. Crickhowell, Nicholas, *Westminster, Wales and Water* (University of Wales Press, 1999). p. 90.
2. Rammell, Thomas Webster, 'Report to the General Board of Health on a preliminary inquiry into the sewerage, drainage and supply of water and the sanitary condition of the town of Cardiff', (HMSO, 1850 p.35.
3. Finch, Peter: The Peter Finch Archive – *Cardiff, Culture & The City*, <http://www.peterfinch.co.uk/cardiff.htm>
4. County of South Glamorgan, 'County of South Glamorgan structure plan proposed alterations explanatory memorandum' (County of South Glamorgan, 1985) pp.13-14.
5. Crickhowell, *ibid.*, p. 91.
6. *South Wales Echo*, 20 November, 1985.
7. *South Wales Echo*, 31 January, 1986.
8. Private correspondence, 9 February, 1987.
9. Morgan, Rhodri, 'Check against delivery, Institute of Welsh Politics 2000 annual lecture' (Institute of Welsh Politics, 2001) p.4.
10. *Western Mail*, 8th March, 1989
11. *ibid.*
12. Cullingworth, J Barry and Nadin, Vincent (eds.), *Town and Country Planning* 11th edition (Routledge, 1994). p. 207.
13. Lawless, P, 'The economic and physical restructuring of the city: the case of the English Urban Development Corporations.' Sheffield Centre for Regional Economic and Social Research, Sheffield Polytechnic, Working Paper 9. 1990 *quoted in* (eds.) Cullingworth, J Barry and Nadin, Vincent, (1994) *op. cit.* p.206.
14. Cullingworth and Nadin, p. 207.
15. Hannan, Patrick, *The Welsh Illusion* (Seren, 1999) p.103.
16. Crickhowell, *op. cit.*, p.162.
17. *ibid.*, p.93.
18. South Glamorgan County Council, 'The regeneration of South Cardiff, proposals for an Urban Development Corporation' (SGCC, September, 1986) p.4.
19. *ibid.*, p.4.
20. Hambro Company Guide, February Quarter, 1993

CHAPTER 2

1. Ungersma, Mike, *Cardiff – Celebration for a City* (Hackman Printers, 1999), p.121.
2. *ibid.*, p.118.

3. *ibid.*, p.118.
4. Crickhowell, Nicholas, *Westminster, Wales and Water* (University of Wales Press, 1999) pp.48-9.
5. *ibid.*, p.42.
6. Welsh Office, 'South Cardiff Waterfront Barrage preliminary investment report appraisal summary' (Welsh Office, 1986).
7. *ibid.*

CHAPTER 3

1. Rammell, Thomas Webster, 'Report to the General Board of Health on a preliminary inquiry into the sewerage, drainage and supply of water and the sanitary condition of the town of Cardiff' (HMSO, 1850) p.9.
2. Quoted in *Cardiff Times and South Wales Weekly News*, 18 November, 1893.
3. Barbara Jones, *Grangetown* (Archive Photograph Series), (Tempus, 1996) p.25.
4. Quoted in *Cardiff and District News*, 8 December 1960.
5. *South Wales Echo*, 13 January, 1988.
6. *South Wales Echo*, 20 January, 1988.
7. *Renaissance: The Story of Cardiff Bay, 1987-2000* (CBDC, 2000) p.15.
8. Noake, Stuart, *Groundwater report for Cardiff Flood Action Committee*, 1988.
9. *South Wales Echo*, 28 April, 1988.
10. KPMG, 'Cardiff Bay Development Corporation economic evaluation of the Barrage project', August 1988, p.5.
11. KPMG, 'Cardiff Bay Development Corporation updated economic evaluation of the Barrage project', May 1988, p.18.
12. Hansard, House of Commons, vol. 36, Written answers, col. 71-2.
13. Llewellyn Davies Partnership, 'Regeneration Strategy for Cardiff Bay' (LDP, 1988).
14. *South Wales Echo*, 23 May, 1988.
15. *South Wales Echo*, 9 June, 1988.
16. *Western Mail*, 15 September, 1988.
17. *South Wales Echo*, 17 September, 1988.
18. *Western Mail*, 1 November, 1988.

CHAPTER 4

1. Environmental Advisory Unit of Liverpool University Ltd: Cardiff Bay Barrage – Environmental Assessment carried out on behalf of Cardiff Bay Development Corporation and South Glamorgan County Council, February 1989, p.73.
2. *ibid.*, p.74 .
3. Private Bills Office, Notes for petitioners, 1983, p.5.
4. Hansard House of Lords Debates, 23 February, 1989, col. 793-797.
5. *ibid.*
6. *ibid.*, col. 800-801.
7 *ibid.*, col. 813-814.
8. *ibid.*, col. 803-810.
9. House of Lords Minutes of evidence taken before the Committee on the

Cardiff Bay Barrage Bill, Wednesday, 17 April, 1989.
10. *ibid.*, Monday, 24 April, 1989.
11. *ibid.*, Thursday, 20 April, 1989.
12. *ibid.*
13. *ibid.*, Tuesday, 25 April, 1989.
14. *ibid.*
15. *ibid.*
16. *ibid.*
17. *ibid.*
18. *ibid.*
19. *ibid.*
20. *ibid.*
21. *ibid.*
22. *ibid.*, Wednesday, 26 April, 1989.
23. *ibid.*
24. *ibid.*
25. *ibid.*
26. *ibid.*
27. *ibid.*, Thursday, 27 April, 1989.
28. *ibid.*
29. *ibid.*
30. House of Lords, 'Special report from the Select Committee on the Cardiff Bay Barrage Bill.' Session 1988-89, HL Paper 57, 13 June 1989, p.iii.
31. *South Wales Echo*, 14 July, 1989.

CHAPTER 5

1. Ungersma, Mike, *Cardiff: Celebration for a City* (Hackman Printers, 1999) pp.121-2.
2. Hansard, House of Commons Debates, 14th November 1989, col. 243.
3. *ibid.*, col. 248.
4. *ibid.*, col. 247.
5. *ibid.*, col. 251.
6. *ibid.*, col. 255.
7. *ibid.*, col. 256-7.
8. *ibid.*, col. 260.
9. *ibid.*, col. 270.
10. *ibid.*, col. 276.
11. *ibid.*, col. 272.
12. *ibid.*, col. 277.
13. *ibid.*, col. 282.
14. *ibid.*, col. 284.
15. *South Wales Echo*, 21 November, 1989
16. *The Western Mail*, 22 November, 1989
17. Hansard, House of Commons Debates, 19 December, 1989, col. 300.
18. *ibid.*, col. 296.
19. *ibid.*, col. 307-8.
20. *ibid.*, col. 310.
21. *ibid.*, col. 310-1.
22. *ibid.*, col. 290-4.

23. *ibid.*, col. 306.
24. *Cardiff Independent*, 29 June, 1988
25. *The Guardian*, 7 February, 1989
26. *The Western Mail*, 1 February, 1989
27. *Cardiff Independent*, 23 November, 1988
28. Walker, Peter, *Staying Power, an autobiography* (Bloomsbury, 1991), p.29.
29. Hansard, House of Commons Debates, 19 December, 1989, col. 315.

CHAPTER 6

1. Quoted in Llewelyn Davies Planning, 'Cardiff Bay Regeneration Strategy' (CBDC, 1988) p.4.
2. *ibid.*, p. 39.
3. Roger Tym & Partners, Conran Roche, Chesterton and Peat Marwick McLintock, 'Cardiff Bay Barrage planning update and economic appraisal statement' House of Commons' Select Committee – consultants' economic appraisal. Document no. 3.2.11. CBDC 15 January, 1990, pp.8-9.
4. House of Commons Minutes of evidence taken before the Committee on the Cardiff Bay Barrage Bill, 1990 Day 5, p.41.
5. Cardiff Bay Barrage Bill, 5th July, 1989 p.14.
6. House of Commons Minutes of evidence taken before the Committee on the Cardiff Bay Barrage Bill, 1990, Day 21, p.27.
7. *ibid.*, Day 20, p.62.
8. *ibid.*, Day 12, pp.43-4.
9. *ibid.*, Day 13, p.82.
10. *ibid.*, Day 20, p.23.
11. *ibid.*, p.20.
12. *ibid.*
13. *ibid.*, p.21.
14. *ibid.*, p.26.
15. *ibid.*, p.29.
16. *ibid.*, Day 10, pp.36-42.
17. *ibid.*, Day 20, pp.46-56.
18. *ibid.*, p.57.
19. *ibid.*
20. *ibid.*, Day 20, pp.58-9.
21. *ibid.*, Day 21, p.44.
22. *ibid.*, p.59.
23. *ibid.*, p.60.
24. *ibid.*, p.62.
25. *ibid.*
26. *ibid.*, Day 21, p.3.
27. *ibid.*, Day 25, p.9.
28. *ibid.*, Day 25, p.21.
29. *ibid.*, Day 2, p.33.
30. *ibid.*, Day 5, p.3.
31. *ibid.*, Day 17, pp.73-5.
32. *ibid.*, Day 5, p.75.
33. *ibid.*, Day 18, p.6.
34. *ibid.*, Day 22, p.9.

35. *ibid.*, Day 20, pp.7-13.
36. *ibid.*, Day 19, p.50.
37. *ibid.*, Day 18, p. 7.
38. *ibid.*, Day 22, p.12.
39. *ibid.*, Day17, p.28.
40. *ibid.*
41. *ibid.*, Day 22, p.25.
42. *ibid.*, p.26.
43. *ibid.*
44. *ibid.*
45. *ibid.*, p.46.
46. *ibid.*, p.45.
47. South Glamorgan County Council, 'The regeneration of south Cardiff: proposals for an urban development corporation' (County of South Glamorgan, 1986), p.4.
48. *ibid.*, Day 22, p.57.
49. *ibid.*, p.58.
50. *ibid.*, Day 9, pp.29-31.
51. *ibid.*, pp.46-7.
52. *ibid.*, Day 10, p.23.
53. *ibid.*, Day 18, p.48.
54. *ibid.*, p.6
55. *ibid.*, Day 9, p.37.
56. *ibid.*, Day 23, p.33.
57. *ibid.*
58. *ibid.*, Day 23, p.37.
59. *ibid.*, Day 9, p.62.
60. *ibid.*, Day 15, p.9.
61. *ibid.*, p.10.
62. *ibid.*, p.15.
63. *ibid.*, Day 16, p.3.
64. *ibid.*, p.10.
65. *ibid.*, p.12-13.
66. *ibid.*, Day 22, p.63-4.
67. *ibid.*, p.65.
68. *ibid.*, Day 7, p.10.
69. *ibid.* Day 19, p.36.
70. *ibid.*, p. 38.
71. *ibid.*, Day 22, p.61.
72. *ibid.*, Day 1, p.17.
73. *ibid.*, Day 12, p.45-7.
74. *ibid.*, Day 13, pp.22-3.
75. *ibid.*, Day 23, p.55.
76. *ibid.*, Day 11, p.48.
77. *ibid.*, Day 13, p.49.
78. *ibid.*, p.10.
79. *ibid.*, Day 14, p.4.
80. *ibid.*, p.5.
81. *ibid.*, p.12.
82. *ibid.*, p.45.
83. *ibid.*, Day 21, pp.67-71.

84.   *ibid.*, Day 22, pp.13-4.
85.   *ibid.*, Day 11, pp.56-7.
86.   *ibid.*, Day 13(1), pp.6-7.
87.   *ibid.*, p.14.
88.   *ibid.*, Day 13 (2), p.12.
89.   *ibid.*, Day 14, pp. 58-60.
90.   *ibid.*, Day 27, p.5.
91.   *ibid.*, p.12.
92.   *ibid.*, p.8.
93.   *ibid.*, p.14.

CHAPTER 7

1.   Rogert Tym & Partners, Conran Roche, Chesterton and Peat Marwick
      McLintock, 'Cardiff Bay Barrage planning update and economic apprais-
      al statement' (CBDC, 1990), p.28.
2.   Hansard, House of Commons Debates, 19 December, 1989, col. 307-08.
3.   *ibid.*, col. 310.
4.   Hansard, House of Commons Debates, 17 October, 1990, col. 1334.
5.   *ibid.*, col. 1336.
6.   Hansard, House of Commons Debates, 16 April, 1991, col. 212.
7.   *ibid.*, col. 215.
8.   *ibid.*, 16 April, 1991, col. 285.
9.   *ibid.*, 16 April, 1991, col. 359.
10.   *South Wales Echo,* 24 June 1991.
11.   Report of the Joint Committee on Private Bills Procedure, July 1988 – 16
      April, 1991, col. 233 & 238.
12.   Hydrotechnica, 'Cardiff Bay Barrage Final report groundwater modelling.
      Executive summary', August, 1991, p.5.
13.   *South Wales Echo,* 1st October, 1991.
14.   Cardiff Bay Barrage Bill, November, 1991
15.   *Building Design,* 15 November, 1991
16.   Hansard House of Commons Debates, 25 November, 1991, col. 642.
17.   House of Commons Select Committee, 1992, Day 8, p.75.
18.   *ibid.*, Day 1, p.13.
19.   *ibid.*, Day 4, p.12.
20.   *ibid.*, Day 4, p.20-2.
21.   *ibid.*, Day 4, p.65.
22.   *ibid.*, Day 4, p.64.
23.   *ibid.*, Day 5, p.52.
24.   *ibid.*, Day 8, p.102.
25.   *ibid.*, Day 11, p.24.
26.   *ibid.*, Day 11, p.23.
27.   Roy Hattersley in *The Observer,* 17 November, 1996
28.   Hansard, House of Commons Debates, 9 June, 1992, col. 252.
29.   *ibid.*, col. 257.
30.   Hansard, House of Commons Debates, 20 October, 1992, col. 362.
31.   House of Lords Select Committee, 1993, Day 1, p.6.
32.   House of Lords Select Committee, 1993, Day 8, p.72.

33. *ibid.*, Day 5, p.2.
34. *ibid.*, Day 7, p.22.
35. *ibid.*, Day 7, p.41.
36. *ibid.*, Day 7, p.43.
37. *ibid.*, Day 7, p.42.
38. *ibid.*, Day 7 p.44.
39. Hansard, House of Commons, 17 May, 1993, col. 176.
40. Hansard, House of Commons, 3 November 1993, col. 394.
41. *The Western Mail*, 16th November, 1993.
42. *The Western Mail*, 17th November, 1993.

CHAPTER 8

1. *The Western Mail*, 30 June, 1992.
2. *Private Eye*, No. 889, 12 January, 1996.
3. Russell Martin Deacon, *The Governance of Wales: the Welsh Office and the Policy Process* (Welsh Academic Press, 2002), p.30.
4. Ray Hornby of WEP, at a meeting with PRAB, 29 January 1990.
5. Llewellyn-Davies Planning, 'Cardiff Bay regeneration strategy' (CBDC, 1988), p.4.
6. Letter from Building Research Establishment to Norman Robson, 13th May, 1997.
7. *South Wales Echo*, 16 December, 1996.
8. *The Guardian*, 21 April, 1994.
9. Letter from Rhodri Morgan to Peter Boyce of Cardiff FoE, 31 October, 1995, quoted in a letter from Charles Secrett, Director of FoE UK to G. Kremlis, Head of Legal Affairs at the EC's Directorate General, 10 September, 1996.
10. *ibid.*
11. *South Wales Echo*, 13 December, 1995.
12. *The Sunday Telegraph*, 8 June, 1997
13. *ibid.*, 22 June, 1997.
14. CBDC, 'Sustaining Success' (CBDC,1996) p.9.
15. Llewellyn Davies Planning, 'Cardiff Bay Regeneration Strategy' (CBDC, 1988) p.5.
16. KPMG, 'Cardiff Bay Development Corporation updated evaluation of the Barrage project', 4th May 1998, p.5.
17. Hansard, House of Commons, 14 November, 1989, col. 242-3.
18. *Enterprise*, May 1995.
19. South Glamorgan County Council, *South Wales 2000* (SGCC, November 1995), p.33.
20. *South Wales Echo*, 17 September, 1988.
21. *Cardiff Independent*, 24 December, 1994.
22. CBDC, 'Sustaining Success' (CBDC, 1996) p.72.
23. *ibid.*
24. *Western Mail*, 3 December, 1993.
25. *South Wales Echo*, 17 November, 1995.
26. *South Wales Echo*, 12 February, 1996.

CHAPTER 10

1. Crickhowell, Nicholas, *Westminster, Wales and Water* (University of Wales Press, 1999), p.48.
2. Cardiff Bay Barrage Act 1993, Part III, para. 12.8.
3. *South Wales Echo,* 4 September, 1999.
4. *ibid.*
5. *South Wales Echo,* 8 December, 1999.
6. *ibid.*
7. *South Wales Echo,* 21 April, 2000.
8. *Total Flyfishing,* March, 2000.
9. Hannan, Patrick, *Wales Off Message* (Seren, 2000).
10. Llew Smith MP quoted in the *Western Mail,* 8 July, 2000.
11. NAO for the AGW, 'Securing the future of Cardiff Bay', NAW, 19 June, 2001, p.1.
12. AGW report to the NAW, 19 July, 2000.
13. NAW Audit Committee report presented to the NAW on 15 February, 2001.
14. *The Guardian,* 16 October, 2000.
15. *Poetry Wales,* vol. 36 no. 2, 2001.

Appendix 1

CARDIFF BAY BARRAGE STATEMENT BY
THE SECRETARY OF STATE
11th July 1997

1. In 1988 the previous Government decided to support the Barrage project following detailed consideration of comprehensive studies of the financial, economic and environmental implications.

2. The assessments of economic benefits of a barrage scheme, which were subject to detailed Parliamentary scrutiny, were carried out in accordance with detailed Treasury guidelines on the conduct of investment appraisals.

3. The Government of the day took the view that only a barrage related development of Cardiff Bay would provide a sound basis for economic regeneration of that area.

4. An economic appraisal of the Barrage was published in July 1988 which had been agreed by the Treasury. Updated appraisals were produced in April 1989; January 1990; and in October 1992.

5. In 1996, in response to a recommendation in a Financial Management and Policy Report, Parliament was informed that:

   • since 1994 the expected economic outputs of the Barrage-related regeneration had been included in annual revisions of the Cardiff Bay Development Corporation Corporate Plan;

   • economic outputs in the 1996 Corporate Plan compared with those contained in the October 1992 Economic Appraisal Report on a broadly comparable basis were:

Economic Output	October 1992	Corporate Plan
Private Sector Investment	£1,703m	£1,500m
PSI: Public Expenditure Ratio	1 :4	1 :3.8
Residential Units	6,000	5,900
Non-residential development	920,639sqm	1,167,000sqm
Permanent jobs created	30,000	30,000

6. The outputs which had been achieved by the 31 March 1996 and 1997 were:

Economic Output	Achievement by: 31 March 1996	31 March 1997
PSI	£557m	£753m
PSI: Public Expenditure Ratio	1:2.03	1:2.5
Residential Units	2,025	2,231
Non-residential development	272,000sqm	366,000sqm
Permanent jobs created	7,850	9,100

The last full economic appraisal was published in 1992.

7. On assuming office, I sought advice from the Department on the potential financial costs of completing the Barrage project compared with stopping the construction of the Barrage and dismantling it. On 22 July I announced my decision not to intervene and to allow the project to be completed.

8. My conclusion was that, whatever the merits of the original decision, to abandon the Barrage construction would have been difficult to justify.

    • substantial costs would not be recovered – over £140m had already been committed; and there would have been at least a further £30m comprising contract penalties and dismantling the Barrage;

    • there would be criticism for wasting public money;

    • businesses having invested heavily in the area in the expectation that the regeneration of South Cardiff would include the Barrage project, could have considered legal action.

9. The CBDC has estimated the additional economic effect of continuing the Barrage to be:

Private Sector Investment	£265m
Enhanced Land Values	£35m
Jobs	5,700
Home Units	1,000
Tourists in Cardiff	500,000 pa

THE WILD BIRDS DIRECTIVE / THE HABITATS DIRECTIVE

10. From an early stage in the Barrage project it was acknowledged by the UK Government that compensatory measures would be necessary to take account of nature conservation interests which included its obligations to comply with the Wild Birds Directive and subsequently the Habitats Directive.

11. The UK Government gave careful consideration to the question of whether socio-economic factors could be taken into account.

12. The 1991 Leybucht judgement confirmed that Member States had a margin of discretion in choosing the most appropriate areas for SPA classification. The UK Government concluded that this discretion extended to the consideration of socio-economic factors.

13. In the light of that conclusion the UK announced in 1991 its decision not to classify Cardiff Bay.

14. Separate complaints to the Commission were made by the Royal Society for the Protection of Birds and the Friends of the Earth.

15. The 1992 Habitats Directive introduced the concept of projects which affected designated sites being carried out for imperative reasons of overriding public interest, including those of a social or economic nature, provided that compensatory measures are taken as necessary. This concept was extended to SPAs classified under the Birds Directive.

16. The need for compensatory measures in relation to Cardiff Bay was extensively discussed with the Commission.

17. The Commission was satisfied that the UK Government's proposals would meet the requirements laid out in Article 6.4 of the Habitats Directive and, in February 1996, formally closed its examination of the complaint about the failure to classify Cardiff Bay.

18. The July 1996 Lappel Bank judgement clarified the law. From that date it has been clear that in considering the boundaries of an area to be classified as an SPA, a Member State is not entitled to take account of socio-economic factors.

19. While the Lappel Bank judgement has clarified the way the Birds Directive should be applied in the future, the Commission has not suggested that it changes our understanding that the proposals meet the UK Government's obligations under Community Law.

Appendix 2

Rhodri Morgan MP for Cardiff West

12 December 1997

Rt Hon Ron Davies MP
Secretary of State
Welsh Office
Cathays Park
Cardiff CF1 3ND

Dear Ron

Meeting Re Cardiff Bay Barrage. Monday December 1 1997

To follow up the above meeting, I was particularly interested in your view that it was not possible for you to enquire, or therefore for us to enquire via you, into the advice given to previous Ministers.

This is because of the long established convention that files relating to advice given to previous governments are locked away after an election handover. You are not therefore privy to, and may not make enquiries about, what advice was previously given to Ministers at the time of the letting of the Cardiff Bay Barrage contract in 1994/5 when John Redwood was Secretary of State for Wales.

You also said that no government would now be willing to approve the construction contract for the Cardiff Bay Barrage, because the Lappel Bank Judgement before the European Court of Justice would rule it out, because the socio-economic arguments could not now be taken into account in removing the Cardiff Bay SSSI from a proposed special protection area such as the Lower Severn Estuary.

I mentioned at the meeting and I do so now that it was already clear from the leaked letter from the head of English Nature to the Permanent Secretary of the Department of Transport, that the government was being advised long before the Lappel Bank case actually reached a conclusion at the ECJ that they were likely to lose the case. What does seem odd therefore is that a contract of this kind could be let, when Departments had been advised that on the balance of probabilities the Lappel Bank case was going to be lost, given that the then Permanent Secretary of the Welsh Office (but not diminishing Ministerial responsibility in any way) must ensure that expenditure complies with rules relating to financial propriety and regularity as well as value for money.

If you are now of the view and have been advised by your Permanent Secretary, that it is a correct interpretation of European law, that it would not be possible to sign the Cardiff Bay Barrage construction contract now, post-Lappel Bank Judgement, surely it would have been imprudent even before the Lappel Bank Judgement, if the legal advice available to government departments at the time of the letting of the contract was that the Lappel Bank Judgement was going to come out against the government.

That then raises the issue of whether you, as the incoming Secretary of State halfway through the contract have the right to know. As far as I could divine your position as the incoming Secretary of State, you had been advised that you did not have the right to know what legal, value for money, propriety and regularity and more general policy advice was tendered by your Department to the then Secretary of State in the immediate run-up to the letting of the contract. I believe that this is an unnecessarily restrictive interpretation by your Department of the election handover convention.

As you will see from the attached PO from the 24 January, 1980, and which I am told is still the ruling advice to incoming Ministers now, the ban on allowing incoming Ministers to enquire about how departmental policy was formulated between civil servants and Ministers, if there are good public interest reasons for doing so it is by no means absolute. A contract which spans two administrations and about which there may have been some doubt as to its compatibility with European conservation law seems to me to be at least arguably covered by the answer given by Margaret Thatcher to George Cunningham back in 1980. Let us say, for example, that there were in fact two views about how much account should be taken of the expected loss of the Lappel Bank case. Let us say that some civil servants took the view that in the anticipation of the loss of the Lappel Bank case, it was unwise for the contract to proceed until the case was concluded. Other civil servants may have been more gung ho and may have advised the Minister that 'we will be able to get away with it' (or words to that effect).

You were the anticipated incoming Secretary of State. You were known to be much less gung ho on the Barrage than your predecessor Secretaries of State. The civil service 'faction' which I am hypothesising here would have been much more likely to win the day as regards postponing letting the contract until after the Lappel Bank Judgement was finished if you had been the Secretary of State, that would therefore surely justify you having some indication of the totality of the advice given to the then Secretary of State. There must surely have been some discussion of your known position as the Shadow Secretary of State in the advice to the then Secretary of State. As the contract was bound to run over into the post-election period by a year or two, your arrival and its effect on the lawfulness and regularity/propriety must have been thought about. You must surely have the right to know.

My view on this matter is reinforced by the drafting of the Government of Wales Bill. Part V provides for a whole range of powers for the Secretary of State to direct the Assembly to take actions required to comply with EU obligations and to de-bar the Assembly from taking actions which should be incompatible with EU and other international law. If it had been argued pre the letting of the Barrage contract that it would have been far wiser to wait until after the Lappel Bank Judgement, in case it went against the government, that would be very material to any view taken now and in the future about the lawfulness of the Barrage and the inundation of Cardiff Bay.

The Barrage is only lawful if the economic reasons for flooding the Cardiff Bay SSSI are deemed to be stronger than the conservation reasons for conserving the Cardiff Bay SSSI. Were it to become clear over the next couple of years that the economic reasons for the Barrage are far from overwhelming, the inundation of Cardiff Bay ceases to be legal. If the economic case for it does not outweigh the conservation case for keeping Cardiff Bay as a conservation area, you could, in theory, find yourself in future directing the Assembly to take action to cease the inundation of Cardiff Bay in order to comply with European obligations. It would be absurd then to argue that you are unable to do so yourself, simply because you were unable to enquire about the advice given to previous Secretaries of State about the lawfulness of the contract or its compliance with EU conservation law.

It is surely also material for you to establish whether the Treasury did indeed object to the scheme and object to the fiddling of the figures by KPMG on CBDC's instructions in order to show a false figure for leverage as the leaked Treasury documents indicate. If the Treasury objected to the scheme on value for money grounds or on the basis that the leverage figures were obtained more by the time-honoured process of 'do you want the answer to be and I'll do the calculation so as to show that answer?', and that is what we understand the Treasury objections to have been, then the Barrage was clearly unlawful. Parliament was denied the knowledge of the Treasury's objections If it had known of the Treasury's objections, it is clear that the Barrage would not have been approved by both Houses of Parliament, nor by the EU. You therefore seem to me to be under an obligation to discover and see the correspondence between the Treasury and the Welsh Office and CBDC and KPMG. They can't deny you that surely.

Furthermore, it was surely clear to the Welsh Office in 1991 that the Leybucht Judgement, which you refer to in your note, did not confer a right on Member State Governments to permit schemes which destroyed conservation areas under the Wild Birds Directive on socio-economic grounds. It was only reasons of health and safety, such as flood prevention schemes that were conceded by the Leybucht judgement at the ECJ. It was precisely because the Leybucht Judgement did not permit socio-economic factors to be taken into account that the Welsh Office tried to circumnavigate it by removing the Cardiff Bay SSSI from the SPA.

The figures in the note which you produced at the meeting of the job count arising from Cardiff Bay are completely absurd because they take no account of the impact of the Barrage, as distinct from the jobs accommodated on land allocated to Cardiff Bay. To have jobs created on land within the Cardiff Bay area is very far from jobs being created by any linkage with the Barrage. NEG is the most important case in point because that is in fact an 'anti-barrage' investment. It could clearly not go ahead within that part of CBDC's designated area which is near or affected by the Barrage. NEG requires access to the open sea for the importation of sand for the glass furnaces, etc. A manmade lake, blocking access to the sea for ocean going vessels make the NEG factory impossible, as distinct from helping to attract it.

Furthermore, there are the developments within the CBDC area such as the AXA development which moved across town from Westgate Street to Bute Terrace which are likewise clearly not Barrage related in any way whatsoever, because the new AXA site is still north of the mainline railway. The Prudential development on Tyndall Street is clearly not Barrage related either, since it is to the north of the Atlantic Wharf development of the former South Glamorgan County Council, whereas Nicholas Edwards always sold the Barrage idea in that it would help to generate more investment south of Atlantic Wharf.

You could therefore either (a) use the exclusion provided for in Margaret Thatcher's answer to George Cunningham, based on the fact that the contract was clearly going to run over the next General Election by a long way and civil servants advising Ministers would have advised that it was necessary to take that into account, especially in the light of your known views. You therefore have a right to know what account was taken of your views prior to letting the contract of the impact of the General Election coming halfway through the contract, or (b) ask a Barrister to conduct an internal review and look at all the papers including a comment on the Treasury's objections to the cost-benefit analysis and why Parliament was not told and Commission not told, and the advice given on

Cardiff Bay's lawfulness re Leybucht as reinforced by the Santona Marshes and Lappel Bank judgements and their implications on the compatibility of the development with European law. It is for these reasons that I believe that you do have the right to see the papers and to re-examine departmental policy re your rights in this matter.

I also mentioned to you the issue of the fish pass, which I regard as critical because of the conservation loss to Cardiff, and indeed the whole of the Taff Ely Basin, if the fish pass fails to work and denies salmon and sewin access to the Taff and Ely Rivers and the ability to reach upstream spawning grounds, which have only after all recently been re-established in those industrial rivers of South Wales, now that they have ceased to carry coal dust and sewage in them.

Parliament also seems to me to have been denied any knowledge that this fish pass had no parallel anywhere else in the world and that having searched the engineering literature from all countries, the Environment Agency tell me that there is no example of a fish pass at the saline/freshwater interface and that the likelihood of this fish pass working, even though it is going to cost £20m is problematic is the extreme.

I shall be grateful if you could look into that matter as well.

Yours

Copy   All at Meeting

Appendix 3

The Grangetown Gondolier

In dear old Cardiff City
Back in 1993
At a place once known as Tiger Bay
Beloved by you and me
They built a huge barrage
Which left disaster in its wake
When they blocked the Taff and Ely off
To make a yuppie lake.

As the first great rain of winter came
As many people feared
It made Loudon Square an island
And old Grangetown disappeared
And then the sun came out again
We couldn't find the Marl
And where Corporation Road had been
Was a 12 ft deep canal.
So we all had to move upstairs
But we soon got used to that
And a three-bedroomed terraced house
Soon became a two-bedroom flat.

It was just like Little Venice
But no-one could get out
'til later on that night
I thought I heard somebody shout.

"Come to me my darling
I'll transport you far and near
Hop on to my gondola
I'm the Grangetown Gondolier".

Well at first I could not make it out
But coming through the gloom
Was a bloke in a miner's helmet
With an old long handled broom
And the craft that he was sailing on
Was the strangest thing afloat
It was the top of a black and white Lada
On a Roath Park rowing boat.
"Come to me my darling
I'll transport you far and near
Hop on to my gondola
I'm the Grangetown Gondolier".

There was a yuppie maiden
Who from London town did stray
In search of the yuppie's paradise
Now known as Cardiff Bay.
She adored her BMWs
She had a new one every year
But she lost her heart in Cardiff
To Grangetown Gondolier
Who sang
"Come to me my darling
I'll transport you far and near
Hop on to my gondola
I'm the Grangetown Gondolier".

So if you should come to Wales
Then you must visit Cardiff Bay
And see our beautiful city
By our new waterway
But beware the wicked pirates
With gold rings in their ears
Because they moonlight on the Metro fleet
As the Grangetown Gondoliers.

                                        FRANK HENNESSEY

Appendix 4

November 1988	South Glamorgan County Council votes in favour of sponsoring a new Cardiff Bay Barrage Bill
January 1989	First Reading of the new Barrage Bill in the Lords
February 1989	Second Reading of the Barrage Bill in the Lords
April–May 1989	House of Lords Select Committee on the Barrage Bill
July 1989	In the Commons, Ron Davies proposes a blocking motion on the Barrage Bill, delaying both the carry over motion to the next Parliamentary session and the Commons Second Reading
November 1989	Carry over debate on the Barrage Bill in the Commons
December 1989	Second Reading debate on the Barrage Bill in the Commons
February – May 1990	Commons Select Committee on the Barrage Bill
October 1990	Carry over debate on the Barrage Bill in the Commons
February 1991	Report Stage of the Barrage Bill in the Commons
16th April 1991	Third Reading debate on the Barrage Bill in the Commons. The Bill is talked out and falls
17th April 1991	John MacGregor, Leader of the Commons, announces that the Government intends to introduce a new, Hybrid, Barrage Bill
July 1991	The Commons Standing Orders Committee refuse to approve the new Hybrid Bill
November 1991	First and Second Readings of the re-drafted Hybrid Bill in the Commons
January – March 1992	Commons Select Committee on the Hybrid Bill
June 1992	In a Commons debate, Gwilym Jones successfully proposes that the Standing Orders governing the membership of the Welsh Grand Committee on the Hybrid Barrage Bill are amended, so that only a minority of Welsh MPs can take part
October 1992	Report Stage of the Hybrid Barrage Bill in the Commons

February-March1993   Lords Select Committee on the Hybrid Bill

May 1993   Further Lords amendments to the Hybrid Bill
                            mean that it has to return to the Commons for
                            approval

3rd November 1993   The Parliamentary Examiners send the Hybrid Bill
                            back to the Commons again, for agreement to yet
                            more amendments

5th November 1993   The Cardiff Bay Barrage Bill receives the Royal
                            Assent

Acknowledgements

The Parliamentary copyright material quoted is reproduced with the permission of Her Majesty's Stationery Office on behalf of Parliament.

The extract from *Thief of Time* by Terry Pratchett, published by Doubleday, is used by permission of Transworld Publishers, a division of The Random House Group Limited.

Thanks are due to all those CRAB members who gave generously of their time, and their personal archives, to help me complete this record of our campaign. I am particularly grateful for the expert advice of Peter Ferns, John Miles and Dennis Morgan. Any errors that remain are mine.

I am also grateful for the support and encouragement given by my daughters, Catherine and Alison, and my husband, George.

Index